Contesting the Myth of a 'Post Racial' Era

Rochelle Brock and Richard Greggory Johnson III
Executive Editors

Vol. 28

The Black Studies and Critical Thinking series
is part of the Peter Lang Education list.
Every volume is peer reviewed and meets
the highest quality standards for content and production.

PETER LANG
New York • Washington, D.C./Baltimore • Bern
Frankfurt • Berlin • Brussels • Vienna • Oxford

Contesting the Myth of a 'Post Racial' Era

The Continued Significance of Race in U.S. Education

EDITED BY
DORINDA J. CARTER ANDREWS & FRANKLIN TUITT

PETER LANG
New York • Washington, D.C./Baltimore • Bern
Frankfurt • Berlin • Brussels • Vienna • Oxford

Library of Congress Cataloging-in-Publication Data

Contesting the myth of a 'post racial era': the continued significance of race
in U.S. education / Edited by Dorinda J. Carter Andrews, Franklin Tuitt.
pages cm. — (Black studies and critical thinking; v. 28)
Includes bibliographical references.
1. Racism in education—United States. 2. Discrimination in education—United States.
3. Racially mixed people—Education—United States. I. Andrews, Dorinda J. Carter,
editor of compilation. II. Tuitt, Frank (Franklin A.) editor of compilation.
LC212.2.C67   371.829'96073—dc23   2012036415
ISBN 978-1-4331-1518-9 (hardcover)
ISBN 978-1-4331-1517-2 (paperback)
ISBN 978-1-4539-0916-4 (e-book)
ISSN 1947-5985

Bibliographic information published by **Die Deutsche Nationalbibliothek**.
Die Deutsche Nationalbibliothek lists this publication in the "Deutsche
Nationalbibliografie"; detailed bibliographic data is available
on the Internet at http://dnb.d-nb.de/.

The paper in this book meets the guidelines for permanence and durability
of the Committee on Production Guidelines for Book Longevity
of the Council of Library Resources.

© 2013 Peter Lang Publishing, Inc., New York
29 Broadway, 18th floor, New York, NY 10006
www.peterlang.com

All rights reserved.
Reprint or reproduction, even partially, in all forms such as microfilm,
xerography, microfiche, microcard, and offset strictly prohibited.

Printed in the United States of America

CONTENTS

Acknowledgments vii

Foreword: Beyond the Postracial Society ix
    Pedro A. Noguera

Racism as the Environmental Hazard in Educational Spaces:
An Overview and Introduction 1
    Dorinda J. Carter Andrews and Frank Tuitt

PART I: REFRAMING THE DISCOURSE ON RACE IN U.S. EDUCATION

One
"I Am My Brother's Keeper; I Am My Sister's Keeper":
Rejecting Meritocracy and Embracing Relational Pluralism 13
    Judson C. Laughter

Two
Navigating the Space Between: Obama and the Postracial Myth 25
    Bridgette Coble, Floyd Cobb, Kristin Deal, and Frank Tuitt

Three
Learning From Catalina: Reflections on Bridging Communities and
Schools in the Context of a "Postracial" Society 42
    Louie F. Rodriguez

Four
An Introduction to Critical Race Realism:
Theoretical and Methodological Implications for Education Research 50
    Laurence J. Parker and Erin L. Castro

Five
A Critical Race Analysis of the Gaslighting Against African American Teachers:
Considerations for Recruitment and Retention 69
    Tuesda Roberts and Dorinda J. Carter Andrews

PART II: ACCESS, EQUITY, AND CLIMATE CONDITIONS IN THE K–16 CONTEXT

Six
The Resource and Opportunity Gap: The Continued Significance of
Race for African American Student Outcomes 97
    John B. Diamond

Seven
Naming Their Pain: How Everyday Racial Microaggressions
Impact Students and Teachers 112
    María C. Ledesma and Daniel Solórzano

Eight
The Racialization of Threat: Responding to the Punishment and
Purging of Black and Latina/o Youth in School 128
    Tara M. Brown

Nine
Disrupting the Standard Education Storyline for Latin@ Students Across
the P–20 Educational System: Sustaining the *Alma* (Soul) of the Latin@
Community Through a Counterstory of Access to the Culture of Power
and the Power of Culture 143
    María del Carmen Salazar

Ten
African American Politics and Education: An Analysis of Electoral Structures,
African American Representation, and Educational Outcomes 161
    Bettie Ray Butler and Chance W. Lewis

Afterword 176
    Walter R. Allen

List of Contributors 180

Acknowledgments

We wish to thank those who have worked tirelessly for racial justice in the world and in education; those who have struggled to ensure that people can use education as the practice of their freedom. We owe special gratitude to the many scholars, practitioners, and activists who have inspired us to think more deeply about the role of race in education and the importance of bridging theory and practice to effect transformation. Many thanks to Kristen Deal (graduate assistant, University of Denver) for her contributions and support throughout this entire project.

FOREWORD

Beyond the Postracial Society

Pedro A. Noguera

When the African National Congress (ANC) assumed political power after the historic election of 1994, and delivered the world's most famous political prisoner—Nelson Mandela—to the presidency, it was widely expected that the new government would carry out changes that would be far more than merely symbolic. The election brought an abrupt end to the notorious system of apartheid, and with their ascent to power, the ANC was expected to bring justice and deliverance to the Black majority that had suffered for years under White rule. Shortly after taking power, the ANC adopted a new constitution that declared the Republic of South Africa a "non-racial democracy." There was hope and anticipation in South Africa and throughout the world that such a declaration would initiate a process of democratic and social reform that would bring relief, and uplift the millions of Black South Africans who had been systematically disenfranchised by the old regime.

Unfortunately, change has come rather slowly to South Africa. Eighteen years after that historic election, it is clear that for millions of Black people, not much has changed at all from a material standpoint. It is true that they now have the vote, and that they are now led by the former freedom fighters from the ANC who sacrificed their lives fighting the apartheid regime. But in important and profound ways, the basic quality of life—as measured by access to health, housing, food, water, education, and safety—has not improved. In fact, life for the Black majority, who continue to eke out a meager existence in the nation's sprawling townships, continues to be characterized by a high degree of hardship.

In many respects, the election of President Barack Obama in 2008 was nearly as historic and awe-inspiring as the election of Nelson Mandela. Though there are important differences that make the analogy imperfect (e.g., South Africa has a Black majority and America does not), in both cases, the democratic process had given birth to an outpouring of hope and optimism over what could be accomplished by the nation's first Black President, particularly for those who were most marginalized. In the days and weeks following his election, it became fashionable for media pundits to proclaim that we had entered a new stage of race relations, a period of "postracialism" which would bring America freedom from the tremendous burden of its history. Given the ugly legacy of the nation's atrocities—genocide against Native Americans, two hundred years of slavery, a series of colonial occupations, Jim Crow segregation, etc.—it is understandable that Americans would want to find a way to escape from the past. Yet, as is true in South Africa, many of Obama's most ardent supporters—particularly African Americans—are finding that genuine relief from the historic vestiges of racism are as hard to achieve as economic relief during this unrelenting recession.

This does not mean that we should belittle the significance of electing the first Black President (actually, he is half White, but within the American system of racial classification, the White half is trumped by the long-standing "one drop" rule, and therefore he is, for all intents and purposes, Black), anymore than Black South Africans should dismiss the significance of being led by a Black government. Like South Africa, postapartheid America is a society where all legalized racial barriers have been eliminated, and there is a new, heightened awareness against overt forms of racism. Increasingly, racial bias is seen as an outdated and ugly reminder of America's past, and it is no longer acceptable (at least in public). Even among conservatives, blatant racism is regarded as outdated, inhumane, and certainly bad for our image as a nation.

Yet, as the authors of the chapters in this volume show us, undoing the legacy of racism in all its many forms is a long and complex process, and not an event. Particularly in the field of education, it remains abundantly clear that race continues to matter in profound and disturbing ways throughout America society. Fifty-eight years after the Supreme Court's 1954 *Brown v. Board of Education* decision, schools throughout America remain largely segregated on the basis of race and class. To make matters worse, the courts are no longer willing to treat *de facto* educational apartheid as an issue worthy of redress. In nearly every major American city (and many minor cities as well), dropout rates for Black and Latino children are over fifty percent, and on nearly every indicator of academic performance—reading and math scores, SAT scores, college enrollment, etc.—low-income children of color lag conspicuously behind their middle-class White and Asian peers.

Given the enduring reality of race in America and the ways in which racial inequities continue to pervade the social landscape, the real question we should be asking is not whether or not we have entered a new phase of postracialism, but whether or not we are making any progress at all toward the realization of a more just social order. The question is not a straightforward one, for there are others beside President Obama who have managed to transcend the color line. Oprah Winfrey; Jay-Z and his wife, Beyoncé; Ken Chenault, the CEO of American Express; Dick Parsons, the former CEO of Time Warner and former Chairman of Citigroup; Deval Patrick, the Governor of Massachusetts; and legions of well-paid athletes, artists, and professionals remind us that there are more than just a few exceptions. Their status (truthfully, I should say, "our" status, because well-paid professors—the authors in this volume—are clearly among the haves, too) is living proof that while W. E. B. Du Bois may have been right in his ominous prediction that the problem of the 20th century was the "color line," the 21st century is bringing us something different.

In 1978, sociologist William Julius Wilson published his controversial but prophetic book, *The Declining Significance of Race*. In it, he argued that civil rights had made it possible for the Black middle class to prosper while leaving the Black, urban poor even further behind. It was a controversial point, because many within the Black middle class did not perceive their achievements as a sign of genuine progress. They recognized the new forms of racism, and could not help but see the many ways in which the lives of poor and middle-class Black people are completely intertwined.

But clearly, conditions for Black people in 2012 are not the same as conditions in 1912 or even 1962. Hence, the question we should be grappling with is: Are the differences necessarily better, and if so, for whom? Are we truly making progress in overcoming the legacy of racism, or does the emergence of a small Black elite merely demonstrate that America's systems of inequality are elastic enough to include a few darker faces at the top without endangering the hierarchy as a whole?

It would indeed be wonderful if we were entering a period in which a child's race had no bearing at all on their life chances; if opportunity in America were not shaped by circumstances such as the neighborhood one lives in, the school one attends, the food a mother has access to while pregnant, or the air that child will breathe. Perhaps then we could declare a small victory for incremental progress. Yet, we have ample evidence that such circumstances continue to profoundly shape opportunities and trajectories, and that sadly, race continues to play a defining role in determining what a person can achieve over the course of a lifetime.

The great novelist Toni Morrison reminded us that race is paradoxical: "profoundly insignificant and empty as a social category, yet powerfully destructive."

That it can be both simultaneously tells us a great deal about the complexity of the moment.

The election of President Barack Obama is a triumph, for him as a leader with enormous talent and ability, and, more importantly, for the American people who were willing to select him to serve as their leader. It means that the majority of voters (though not the majority of White voters) were willing to embrace a Black man to lead us at a moment of tremendous peril for the nation. It does not mean that there will be a reduction in Black incarceration rates, that fewer Black babies will die during infancy, that graduation rates will rise, or even that Obama will be reelected to a second term. Anyone who expected such accomplishments was, at the minimum, naïve. Yet, Obama's election clearly means something, just as the election of Mandela meant something significant for South Africa.

Perhaps what it means is not that we have entered a postracial period in America, anymore than South Africa has become a nonracial democracy. Rather, what Obama's election may signify is that possibilities for change exist. They exist largely because of generations of struggle by individuals who sacrificed their lives so that others would reap rewards. These struggles have produced cracks in the walls of racism and the racial hierarchy. The question now before us is what are we doing to open those cracks further?

References

Morrison, T. (1992). *Race-ing justice, en-gender-ing power: Essays on Anita Hill, Clarence Thomas, and the construction of social reality*. New York, NY: Pantheon Books.

Wilson, W. J. (1978). *The declining significance of race: Blacks and changing American institutions*. Chicago, IL: University of Chicago Press.

Racism as the Environmental Hazard in Educational Spaces

An Overview and Introduction

Dorinda J. Carter Andrews and Frank Tuitt

For many Americans, the election of Barack Obama as the first African American president of the United States is confirmation that we are a postracial America, and that issues of race and racism have no place in discussions about societal inequalities. Furthermore, the discourse of race and racism is still taboo in relationship to its effect on the academic and life outcomes of people of color and poor people. However, given President Obama's explicit focus on improving educational outcomes for disadvantaged youth (particularly those living in urban communities) in his American Reinvestment and Recovery Act (2009), we know that race—along with other social identity markers, such as social class and gender—still affects students' access to equitable K–12 education, qualified teachers, and equal opportunities for matriculating through college. In fact, Obama himself has acknowledged that one man and one term of office is not enough to "change our history and the stain of race" (Harris, 2009). Thus, in what is now being called a post–civil rights and postracial era, we contend that naming and responding to the ways in which race and racism continue to be significant factors that affect the educational experiences and outcomes of students of color and their learning environments is still a very real and necessary discussion.

The chapters in this volume explore the continuing significance of race, and contest the myth of postracialism in U.S. education by examining racial inequality across the K–16 spectrum, through examination of classroom climate and practices, educational policies and research methods, and equity and access. An additional, unique feature of the volume is its framing of racism as an environmental hazard in educational spaces. As editors of the volume, we ask the question: *under what conditions do the tasks of learning and achieving academically become racialized in harmful ways for Black and Brown youth?* We posed a similar question in earlier work, where we proposed that racism acts as an atmospheric threat to the school success of many African American students (see Tuitt & Carter, 2008). We now answer this question by acknowledging learning conditions where racial hostility is a threat in the air (Steele, 1997), and racism is like smog we breathe. Beverly Daniel Tatum (1997) argued that we are all "smog-breathers"; we contend that the smog has differential effects on our psyche and souls, depending on our racialized experiences in the world. The scholars in this volume provide a variety of ways for readers to consider the racist smog that students of color have been inhaling and suffering the debilitating effects of for hundreds of years.

As Bullard (1999) suggested, in the real world all communities are not created equal, and do not receive equal protection from the toxins that differentially disadvantage. We argue that K–16 learning environments are not all quite the same; all schools are not created equal, and do not receive equal protection from the policies, practices, and directives that differentially affect or disadvantage (whether intended or unintended) individuals, groups, or communities based on race. Thus, educational racism can be likened to environmental racism (Bullard, 1999; Westra & Wenz, 1995). Although the concept of environmental racism is typically used in a geographic context (Bullard, 1999; Chavis, 1994), it is not a far leap from that to considering stereotype threat and racial micro- and macroaggressions as toxins (i.e., poisons and pollutants) that prevent Black and Brown students, at all educational levels, from participating in healthy learning environments. We believe that practitioners, researchers, and policymakers may find it helpful to view stereotype threat and racial micro- and macroaggressions (Solórzano, Ceja, & Yosso, 2000; Sue et al., 2007) in a manner similar to environmental racism. In this regard, identifying immediate remedies or even an overall cure for racist learning environments requires a comprehensive approach.

Conditions of Environmental Racism in Educational Contexts

Bullard (1993, 1994) identified several conditions of environmental racism that we consider helpful in framing racism as an environmental threat in educational contexts. Specifically, we associate the:

1. Unequal enforcement of environmental, civil rights, and public health laws to the unequal enforcement of educational policies and laws;
2. Differential exposure of some populations to harmful chemicals, pesticides, and other toxins in the home, school, neighborhood, and workplace to differential exposure of many students of color to under-resourced schools and community colleges, unqualified and non-inclusive teachers, and ineffective learning environments that fail to graduate minoritized students;

3. Faulty assumptions in calculating, assessing, and managing risks to the inability to design and implement culturally appropriate interventions and pedagogical practices that enhance student success;
4. Discriminatory zoning and land-use practices to the development of K–12 education as a marketplace where school-choice options that are framed to benefit Black and Brown students actually track them out of academic experiences that prepare them for success, and policymakers and school administrators engage in over-reliance on, as well as inappropriate use of, standardized tests to make access-related decisions; and,
5. Exclusionary practices that limit some individuals and groups from participation in decision making to the bureaucratic structures and procedural mazes that prevent members of marginalized communities from participating in the decision-making process (e.g., parents).

In the following paragraphs, we provide a few examples of how Bullard's conditions are illuminated as environmental racism in the educational arena.

Unequal Enforcement of Education as a Civil Right

Language of equality has replaced language of equity, differentially impacting educational access to students of color. State legislatures and the Supreme Court continue to entertain affirmative action arguments, effectively reifying the notion that race no longer matters, and should not be considered as a compelling interest within the public arena. This shifts the call for equality to other socially constructed identities, recentering the normative White experience within the learning environment. Thus, as a color-blind approach, the language of the civil rights era has been co-opted and reframed as abstract liberalism (Bonilla-Silva, 2010), allowing for conversations to change from inequity to achievement gap—where an equal educational starting location is assumed.

Differential Exposure

Structural racism manifests itself as a toxin in the school environment for many students of color. The overrepresentation of Black males and English language learners in special education, the criminalizing effects of zero-tolerance discipline policies on Black and Brown males *and* females, and racial tracking represent (un)intended consequences of "race-neutral" policy development that disproportionately affects students of color. Even school curricula are being attacked so as to culturally inculcate all students with a Eurocentric world view. The ban on K–12 ethnic studies classes in Arizona schools is a prime example of the type of overt racism that gets illuminated through policy implementation. Within higher education, students of color (in particular, Black students) are overrepresented in for-profit institutions. Fourteen of the parent corporations (i.e., The Apollo Group and Corinthian Colleges) of these institutions have accrued well over $26 billion in profit as they are traded on the open market. Yet, as their shareholders become wealthy, students experience higher unemployment rates, lower six-year completion rates, and higher student loan debt and default rates (Deming, Goldin, & Katz, 2012).

Faulty Assumptions

We have become so complacent with referring to certain groups of students as "at risk" that we forget that this framing often perpetuates deficit thinking about students of color; they are broken and need to be fixed. A more nuanced and productive approach to meeting the needs of children of color would require an asset-based approach, in which their cultural backgrounds are seen as funds of knowledge (Moll, 2005) and academic strengths to build upon. Instead of focusing on the at-risk nature of students, schools should focus on the high-risk impact of school culture and climate, curriculum, educational staff, and school board members as implicated in hundreds of Black and Brown youth falling through the cracks. A focus on calculating, assessing, and managing risk at the institutional level is warranted in order to meet the needs of our nation's most struggling students.

Discriminatory Practices

A series of Supreme Court cases[1] in the 1990s have effectively reversed desegregation orders within the public school system, resulting in discriminatory practices that have found new root in the toxic ground of racism and racial bias. The resegregation of schools, as noted in Orfield's (1993) seminal work, and substantiated nearly 10 years later by Frankenberg and Lee (2002), has become all too common in the K–12 system. School districts across the nation are witnessing lower levels of student "inter-racial exposure" (Frankenberg & Lee, 2002, p. 4). In districts where resegregation is not experienced at rates as high as the rest of the nation, there remains an increased "white isolation," suggesting that as the enrollments of students of color increase, White students are insolated, and in turn all students experience a less racially diverse school system (Frankenberg & Lee, 2002). This internal segregation is often a result of tracking students, in essence rezoning schools and curriculum into areas occupied by particular racial groups. Instead of fences, walls, or signs designating which students have particular rights to an academic landscape, standardized tests—including the Advanced Placement exams—aid in funneling students into resegregated education, and, ultimately, resegregated work forces (Solórzano & Ornelas, 2002).

Exclusionary Practices

Though students entering education at all levels are more racially diverse, those who will teach them remain largely White. As 87% of K–12 teachers are White

(National Education Association, 2007), and 75% of postsecondary professors are White (U.S. Department of Education, 2010), it goes without saying that decision making at all levels of education is controlled and sustained by White professionals. From tenure, to curriculum decisions, to promotion, and pedagogy, practices that impact the educational engagement, achievement, and success of students of color are decided upon by individuals who often experienced the benefits of education achieved by the marginalization of others. Further, it is these educators who construct and define the various ways in which student success is measured. For example, in the long-standing educational literature, there is a tendency to center parental involvement in student success at the expense of a more broad definition of family and cultural involvement that engages students from across racial backgrounds (Yosso, 2005). Within higher education, *de facto* racial segregation among faculty continues across the landscape of the academy (i.e., institutional type, faculty rank, and discipline/department), upheld by the "apartheid of knowledge"—the exclusionary practice of epistemological racism that truncates what is considered to be legitimate scholarship, impacting appointment, promotion, and tenure (Bernal & Villalpando, 2002, p. 169).

Environmental racism in education legitimates human exposure to harmful toxins in the learning context, exploits the vulnerability of economically and politically disenfranchised communities of color, creates an industry around risk assessment and risk management, and fails to develop pollution prevention (pollution prevention in education, and pollution intervention as redress) as an overarching and dominant strategy. Environmental justice advocates argue: (a) for fair treatment and meaningful involvement of all people regardless of race with respect to the development, implementation, and enforcement of environmental laws, regulations, and policies; and, (b) that no racial group should bear a disproportionate share of negative consequences resulting from federal, state, and local programs and policies. As advocates for educational justice, the authors represented in this volume argue for racial justice in K–16 learning contexts where racism is an environmental hazard, and demand equitable treatment and meaningful involvement of people of color in the development, implementation, and enforcement of educational laws that affect our schools and communities.

The volume is divided into two parts. We recognize that the way in which educational problems are discussed and framed has the potential to produce, reproduce, sustain, and transform a given discourse (Gee, 1999). Thus, the essays in Part One seek to reframe the discourse on race and racism in educational environments, and offer strategies and solutions that may help educational policymakers, practitioners, and institutions eliminate racism's negative impact on achievement and performance. Judson Laughter uses the metaphor of the Joshua Generation of the 21st-century United States to define a new vision of social justice for the classroom. This vision includes an understanding of both the myth and the fallacy of meritocracy. The myth of meritocracy, already well-defined in the education literature, claims that the United States are in fact a meritocracy. The fallacy of meritocracy questions whether meritocracy is an ideal goal for the classroom at all. Through the introduction of relational pluralism, Laughter hopes to promote a new vision of social justice apt to meet the oppressive master narratives faced by the Joshua Generation in the 21st-century classroom. Bridgette Coble, Floyd Cobb, Kristin Deal, and Frank Tuitt argue that the racial climate surrounding President Obama offers insight into the racial challenges that will continue to impact higher education and its ability to effectively educate a diverse student body. Accordingly, an examination of the 44th President of the United States of America provides us with an avenue to explore what critical race theorists would describe as the embedded nature of race and racism within U.S. society. The authors posit that while the election of Barack Obama was a historic marker of racial progress, it simultaneously increased the discourse of abstract liberalism, further hindering future efforts for social equality.

In a memo to President Obama, Louie Rodriguez dispels the myth that Obama's presidency alone has "fixed" racial inequality. He proposes a radical cultural shift in the way U.S. society conceptualizes the role of social policy in the lives of everyday people. Through the story of Catalina, a young Latina struggling in school, her academic challenges are illuminated as one piece of an entire puzzle. Her family situation, community context, and status in society show that it is necessary to activate other areas of social policy in order to effectively improve Catalina's life. Rodriguez concludes that creating bold social policy solutions is a necessary first step in realizing a true, postracial America. Laurence Parker and Erin Castro introduce Critical Race Realism as an extension of Critical Race Theory (CRT), and explain how it seeks to combine quantitative, qualitative, and interpretive research methodologies from the social sciences to address racial discrimination and provide research critical findings that connect to education policy. The legal challenge to a special affirmative action admissions program for women and underrepresented minorities in graduate education at Southern Illinois University Carbondale is used as an example to illustrate the potential for combining critical race theory with critical race realism in a way that builds a more multidimensional, research-based defense to measure racial disparities and discrimination in educational institutions. Part One concludes with an essay by Tuesda Roberts and Dorinda Carter Andrews, who utilize Sfard and Prusak's (2005a, 2005b) narrative theory of identity and critical race theory to examine how macro-level (i.e., *Brown v. Board of Education of Topeka*) and micro-level (i.e., state- and district-level) laws and policies have historically and contemporarily positioned the Black educator as "outsider," and "on the margins." By using the concept of "gaslighting" metaphorically, they describe how a deficit, normalized master narrative frames Black educators as seemingly "unqualified" in the face of racist practices that perpetuate White supremacy by historically privileging White educators and disenfranchising Black educators. Roberts and Carter Andrews suggest strategies for inserting critical, designated identity narratives of Black educators into educational discourse, and capitalizing on the proven dedication of these educators for enhancing student success.

Part Two of the volume addresses past and current policies and practices related to educational attainment and success, such as access and retention, promotion and advancement, and explores how racism acts as a climate condition that negatively affects the educational environment. In the first essay in this section, John Diamond outlines how race continues to matter for students' educational outcomes, by focusing on race-based structural inequality outside schools, differences in educational resource allocation inside schools, and everyday school practices that help maintain racial inequality. In doing so, Diamond builds on recent sociological, social-psychological, and critical race theory perspectives on contemporary racial inequality. Maria Ledesma and Daniel Solórzano explore the various forms in which racial microaggressions, including both verbal and nonverbal behaviors toward, assumptions about, and lowered expectations for students of color, continue to dampen educational aspirations for marginalized communities. They examine the effects of social and academic microaggressions on communities of color within and beyond higher education, and discuss how the treatment of microaggressions, both institutionally and personally, continues to shape climate. Finally, Ledesma and Solórzano speak about the resiliency and/or resistance that enables marginalized communities to confront microaggressions and challenge White supremacy.

Tara Brown examines how messages about Black and Latina/o youth, as safety and moral or ethical threats, are communicated, manifest, and reinforced in multiple segments of society (including schools), contributing to these students' overrepresentation in school exclusion and, subsequently, school failure. Racialized threat is contextualized within the elusive and structural nature of current-day racism in the United States as a way to frame recommendations for effectively challenging racist school disciplinary practices. Specifically, building political power and capacity, by documenting and exposing disciplinary injustices through participatory action research, is proposed to address the deleterious effects of racialized threat on the lives of Black and Latina/o youth. María del Carmen Salazar uses CRT and LatCrit to contest the dominant narrative of educational achievement about Latin@ students across the P–20 educational system as one of persistent achievement gaps. She asserts that the standard education story about Latin@s is propagated through (a) widespread acceptance and dissemination of the *dominant storyline* about Latin@ students—i.e., the belief that Latin@ "failure" results from students' deficits; and (b) assimilationist policies, programs, and practices—i.e., approaches that strip students of the resources they need to survive and thrive. Subsequently, Salazar asserts that the aforementioned factors deny Latin@ students access to both the *culture of power* (Delpit, 1988)—i.e., the beliefs, skills, and attitudes prized by the mainstream, dominant White culture—and the *power of culture* (Pang & Barba, 1995)—i.e., the "community cultural wealth" (Yosso, 2005) of Latin@s that is inclusive of their linguistic, familial, and immigrant experience.

Part Two concludes with an essay by Bettie Ray Butler and Chance Lewis, who empirically test whether the politics of education—the election and appointment of key education officials—is somehow linked to performance on high-stakes testing. The theory of representative bureaucracy suggests that passive representation oftentimes translates into active representation that takes the form of policy benefits. This representative system has proven particularly advantageous for Black students; critics contend that such advantages come at the expense of Anglo students. However, scholars have found that high levels of representation among Black street-level bureaucrats (teachers) positively influence the educational experiences for both Blacks and Anglos. To further grapple with this issue, Butler and Lewis develop a more interrelated causal story about the effects of a representative bureaucracy on student performance.

Note

1. See *Board of Education v. Dowell* (1991), *Freeman v. Pitts* (1992), and *Missouri v. Jenkins* (1995).

References

Bernal, D. D., & Villalpando, O. (2002). An apartheid of knowledge in academia: The struggle over the 'legitimate' knowledge of faculty of color. *Equity & Excellence in Education*, 35(2), 169–180.
Bonilla-Silva, E. (2010). *Racism without racists: Color-blind racism and the persistence of racial inequality in contemporary America* (3rd ed.). Lanham, MD: Rowman & Littlefield.
Bullard, R. D. (1993). Race and environmental justice in the United States. *Yale Journal of International Law*, 18(1), 319–335.
Bullard, R. D. (1994). *Dumping in Dixie: Race, class, and environmental quality* (2nd ed.). Boulder, CO: Westview Press.
Bullard, R. D. (1999). Dismantling environmental racism in the USA. *Local Environment*, 4(1), 5–19.
Chavis, B. F., Jr. (1994). Preface. In R. D. Bullard (Ed.), *Unequal protection: Environmental justice and communities of color* (pp. xi–xii). San Francisco, CA: Sierra Club Books.
Delpit, L. D. (1988). The silenced dialogue: Power and pedagogy in educating other people's children. *Harvard Educational Review*, 58(3), 280–298.
Deming, D. J., Goldin, C., & Katz, L. F. (2012). The for-profit postsecondary school sector: Nimble critters or agile predators? *Journal of Economic Perspectives*, 26(1), 139–164.
Frankenberg, E., & Lee, C. (2002). *Race in American public schools: Rapidly resegregating school districts*. Cambridge, MA: The Civil Rights Project at Harvard University.
Gee, J. (1999). *An Introduction to Discourse Analysis: Theory and Method*. London: Routledge.
Harris, E. (January 20, 2009). We are not post racial just yet. *The Huffington Post*. Retrieved from http://www.huffingtonpost.com/earnest-harris/we-are-not-post-racial-ju_b_158978.html

Moll, L. C. (2005). Reflections and possibilities. In N. González, L. C. Moll, & C. Amanti (Eds.), *Funds of knowledge: Theorizing practices in households, communities, and classrooms* (pp. 275–288). Mahwah, NJ: Lawrence Erlbaum.

National Education Association. (2007). *Status of the American public school teacher, 2006–2007.* Washington, DC: Author.

Orfield, G. (1993). *The growth of segregation in American schools: Changing patterns of separation and poverty since 1968.* Alexandria, VA: National School Boards Association.

Pang, V. O., & Barba, R. H. (1995). The power of culture: Building culturally affirming instruction. In C. A. Grant (Ed.), *Educating for diversity: An anthology of multicultural voices* (pp. 341–358). Boston, MA: Allyn & Bacon.

Sfard, A., & Prusak, A. (2005a). Identity that makes a difference: Substantial learning as closing the gap between actual and designated identities. *International Group for the Psychology of Mathematics Education, 1,* 37–52.

Sfard, A., & Prusak, A. (2005b). Telling identities: In search of an analytic tool for investigating learning as a culturally shaped activity. *Educational Researcher, 34*(4), 14–22.

Solórzano, D., Ceja, M., & Yosso, T. (2000). Critical race theory, racial microaggressions, and campus racial climate: The experiences of African American college students. *Journal of Negro Education, 69*(1–2), 60–73.

Solórzano, D., & Ornelas A. (2002). A critical race analysis of Advanced Placement classes: A case of educational inequality. *Journal of Latinos and Education, 1*(4), 215–229.

Steele, C. M. (1997). A threat in the air: How stereotypes shape intellectual identity and performance. *American Psychologist, 52*(6), 613–629.

Sue, D. W., Capodilupo, C. M., Torino, G. C., Bucceri, J. M., Holder, A. M. B., Nadal, K. L., & Esquilin, M. (2007). Racial microaggressions in everyday life: Implications for clinical practice. *American Psychologist, 62*(4), 271–286.

Tatum, B. D. (1997). *'Why are all the Black kids sitting together in the cafeteria?': And other conversations about race.* New York, NY: Basic Books.

Tuitt, F. A., & Carter, D. J. (2008). Negotiating atmospheric threats and racial assaults in predominantly White educational institutions. *Journal of Public Management & Social Policy, 14*(2), 51–68.

U.S. Department of Education (2010). National Center for Education Statistics, Integrated Postsecondary Education Data System (IPEDS), Winter 2005–06, Winter 2007–08, and Winter 2009–10, Human Resources component, Fall Staff section. Alexandria, VA: Author.

Westra, L., & Wenz, P. S. (1995). *Faces of environmental racism: Confronting issues of global justice.* Lanham, MD: Rowman & Littlefield.

Yosso, T. J. (2005). Whose culture has capital? A critical race theory discussion of community cultural wealth. *Race, Ethnicity and Education, 8*(1), 69–91.

PART ONE

Reframing the Discourse on Race in U.S. Education

ONE

"I Am My Brother's Keeper; I Am My Sister's Keeper"

Rejecting Meritocracy and Embracing Relational Pluralism

Judson C. Laughter

For many, racism appeared to end with the election of President Barack Obama. The gap between White voters and Black voters disappeared (Roberts, 2009). Race relations improved in general (Stolberg & Connelly, 2009) and on a personal level (Saulny, 2009). The Supreme Court even heard arguments contending that electing a Black President fixed everything the 1965 Voting Rights Act was supposed to fix (Liptak, 2009).

Of course, racism has not ended.

I view the election of President Obama as a call to reevaluate the ways in which racism has evolved to maintain its power, both in society and in the classroom, particularly in the ideal of meritocracy. In this chapter, I argue that the election of President Obama is an opportunity to problematize the idea of meritocracy, which remains an underlying foundation of racism today. I begin by defining meritocracy and two related but distinct issues it comprises: the *myth of meritocracy* and the *fallacy of meritocracy*. I then explore meritocracy in the setting of President Obama's election, particularly through the metaphor of the *Joshua Generation* he employed on the campaign trail. I conclude with implications of this discussion for education through the introduction of a new ideal, the ideal of *relational pluralism*.

American Dream Meritocracy

In the days following President Obama's election, I heard several stories of people personally touched by the rise of a Black man to the nation's highest office. Many of these stories focused on a new conversation happening around the country, a conversation in which a child of any race or ethnicity, stating a desire to grow up and become President of the United States, was met with affirmative possibility ("Yes we can") instead of stunned silence ("Why not think of something more reasonable?"). If Barack Obama can be elected President, so the logic follows, anyone can be elected President, even if he or she is not an upper-class White male. Thusly have the United States achieved meritocracy.

I define meritocracy as a state governed by the fair and equal application of individually earned merit to all its citizens; meritocracy claims that I live in a country (the USA) where anyone can succeed if he or she is willing to work hard. Dorinda Carter (2008) defined meritocracy using its colloquial nickname, the American Dream, a system in which

> One's social and economic mobility are achieved primarily through individual effort and hard work; regardless of race, gender, socio-economic status, or other social identity, individuals can claim a piece of the American Dream by "pulling themselves up by their bootstraps." (p. 466)

The supposed realization of an American Dream in President Obama is not, in my opinion, an unproblematic development, but instead represents an evolution of racism meant to maintain its deep roots by focusing on the success of individuals.

When shifting focus from meritocracy to the *myth of meritocracy*, Carter (2008) described how, "Not only do many individuals think that the system of obtaining upward mobility *should* operate based on individual merit, they also believe that this is how the system actually *does* operate in the United States" (p. 467). The second part of this statement, that people believe that this is how the system *actually does operate*, represents the myth of meritocracy, which I address first. However, I believe that the first part of Carter's definition, that individuals think this is how the system *should operate*, is something different. The concern with *should* represents the *fallacy of meritocracy*, which I address second. I believe that the election of President Obama is a chance to specifically address the fallacy of meritocracy, in society and in education.

The Myth of Meritocracy

The critique of meritocracy as a myth (Carter, 2008; McIntosh, 1989) is well-defined in the literature, for example by Daniel Farber and Suzanna Sherry (2000): "Radical constructivists contend that standards of merit are socially constructed to maintain the power of dominant groups. In other words, 'merit' has no meaning, except as a way for those in power to perpetuate the existing hierarchy" (p. 579).

Understanding the myth of meritocracy is an important step to countering racism, because it is a tool for maintaining the existing racial hierarchy. In my own experiences preparing teachers for diverse[1] classrooms, the myth of meritocracy is one of the most resistant ideals to which preservice teachers cling. The hardest discussion I have with preservice teachers is trying to convince them that there is more than individual effort at play when a student fails to succeed. It is a foundational contention of the United States that if a student works hard, he or she will succeed. To support this contention, a litany of rags-to-riches stories is recited and celebrated during even the earliest years of schooling. President Obama will likely be added to that list, and celebrated as proof that in the United States anyone can succeed through hard work.

However, "American Dream" meritocracy benefits those in power, and maintains racial oppression. I came to understand this myth of meritocracy through my studies in the field of Critical Race Theory (CRT) (Delgado & Stefancic, 2001). The critique of meritocracy is imbedded specifically in CRT's challenge to ideas like neutrality, objectivity, and color blindness (Ladson-Billings & Tate, 1995). For a system of individual merit to exist, all people must begin with equal opportunity and equal possibility. CRT reveals this ideal to be instead methods of camouflage "for the self-interest of powerful entities of society" (Tate, 1997, p. 235).

I now shift my focus from the myth of meritocracy to the fallacy of meritocracy. The former pretends that we do in fact live in a meritocratic system. The latter admits that we do not, but claims that meritocracy represents a worthwhile goal toward which we should work.

The Fallacy of Meritocracy

Perhaps society is moving in the right direction. Maybe the United States, with time and evolution (and the election of a Black President) are becoming more meritocratic and less racist, a place where anyone can succeed. However, this desire for meritocracy can be problematized. Do we really want meritocracy as the ideal toward which we strive? Do we really want to provide everyone an equal opportunity to succeed individually? These questions may appear easily answered in the affirmative, but they require a deeper consideration and critique, lest meritocracy be allowed to continue to define merit and success.

If the myth of meritocracy refers to the belief that the United States are meritocratic when they are not, then the fallacy of meritocracy refers to the belief that we should work to make the United States more meritocratic. I believe this fallacy must be disrupted, lest we fail to address an evolving system of racism; lest I attempt to prepare teachers who equate social advancement with an ideal like meritocracy.

The United States definitely would look different if every citizen had equal opportunity and access. Adequate healthcare would be universal. Education would be free to all who desired it. Human needs for food, clothing, and shelter would be met. But is that all we want? The fallacy of meritocracy equates social betterment with working toward a meritocratic system, and defines success and failure as the results of individual work. In other words, the fallacy of meritocracy tells us that to overcome the myth of meritocracy we need to establish systems of education, politics, and economics that are meritocratic. The establishment of such meritocratic systems, however, would not overcome the problematic nature of meritocracy, or our system of racism. By focusing our attention on the myth of meritocracy, we undermine our attempts to fight it by still believing that individual success is a positive social ideal as long as everyone receives a level chance.

To develop this critique of the fallacy of meritocracy, I return to the election of President Obama, and specifically analyze a metaphor to which he referred often during his campaign. I believe that in exploring the origin of *The Joshua Generation*, the fallacy of meritocracy comes more sharply into focus.

From Moses to Joshua

On November 4, 2008, the people of the United States of America elected Barack Obama to the office of the President. This election was historic for several reasons, primarily because President Obama is Black.[2] While the election of President Obama marked a great leap forward for the national psyche, I believe the tendency to view the 44th President as a validation of an equal chance for all people is problematic, as confirmed by several of President Obama's own speeches. In particular, his references to the *Joshua Generation* (e.g., Obama, 2007) described a different way to read this election than simply the fulfillment of an "American Dream" in which all men are created equal; his election was a challenge to the fallacy of meritocracy, a potential revision of the American Dream.

To understand President Obama's metaphor, I briefly recount here its origin and more recent revival from the 1960s. According to the 34th chapter of Deuteronomy (Green, 1986), Moses climbed Mount Nebo and received a vision of the Promised Land of Canaan. While Moses, the leader of the Israelites, was allowed to see the Promised Land, he was not allowed to enter the Promised Land. The book of Deuteronomy represents Moses's last words to the Israelites before they entered Canaan without him; from these words, a particular view of social justice emerged.

In Chapter 24, Moses described to the Israelites how they should treat the immigrant, the orphan, and the widow. In short, the Israelites may have farms, and orchards, and vineyards in which they worked very hard to produce a crop, but they were not to collect everything they raised. Instead, some was to be left for the immigrant, the orphan, and the widow. Doing this—providing food for someone else who did not work for it—was to remind the Israelites that they once had been enslaved in Egypt. This vision was not based on fairness, or equal pay for equal work, or earned individual merit, but on a communal vision of success. In short, the original Moses Generation rejected the ideal of meritocracy, instead choosing to define success for a whole community, not just for individuals who work hard within a community.

The story of Moses leading the Israelites out of slavery has been adopted throughout history to represent the emotions and desires of enslaved people, including the *de jure* slaves of the 19th-century United States, or the *de facto* slaves of the 20th-century Jim Crow era. In Memphis, Tennessee, in 1968, Martin Luther King, Jr. (1992) made a comparison between himself and Moses on the night before he was assassinated:

> I just want to do God's will. And He's allowed me to go up to the mountain. And I've looked over. And I've seen the Promised Land. I may not get there with you. But I want you to know tonight, that we, as a people, will get to the Promised Land. (p. 203)

Many people have since come to define civil rights leaders like Dr. King as members of the Moses Generation of the Civil Rights Movement. It is to these elders President Obama hearkens when referring to himself as a member of the Joshua Generation.

When Moses died, his aide Joshua began to lead the Israelites on a conquest of the Promised Land that was supposed to be guided by the Deuteronomy vision of communal merit and success. In fact, when Moses wrote the words of Deuteronomy, the Israelites were themselves immigrants. Deuteronomy represented a promise to the Israelites that things would not always be as they had been under Moses.

The election of President Obama signaled for some a similar shift. By standing on the shoulders of the Civil Rights Movement, the current Joshua Generation seeks to continue the legacy of that struggle. However, the struggle of the Joshua Generation does not occur in the same world as the Movement of the 1960s. Racism's power and structure has shifted to take account of and undermine the success of the Moses Generation.

It is to support the myth of meritocracy that I believe many read the election of Barack Obama. The election of a Black man to the presidency, matched by the story of his own lifelong struggles, could empower this American Dream. There is little doubt that President Obama's election marked a new chapter in American history, and his life story should be applauded. However, I do not believe that President Obama ever claimed that he alone earned all that he has attained. From his own words, I do not believe that he insisted on a color-blind, neutral, and objective meritocracy. In order to forestall the sublimation of Obama's story to the

American Dream of Meritocracy, I believe we must view his words through the lens of the fallacy of meritocracy.

The Joshua Generation and the Fallacy of Meritocracy

There was a constant to the speeches President Obama offered on the campaign trail. That constant was a validation of community and an explicit contradiction of individual merit. In his speeches, President Obama explained the sacrifices made by his single mother so that he would be clothed and fed. In his speeches, President Obama described the sacrifices of his grandparents so that he would be well-educated. In his speeches, President Obama (2008a) described the sacrifices of his immediate family so that he might rise to the office of President:

> In the faces of those young veterans who come back from Iraq and Afghanistan, I see my grandfather, who signed up after Pearl Harbor, marched in Patton's Army, and was rewarded by a grateful nation with the chance to go to college on the GI Bill. In the face of that young student who sleeps just three hours before working the night shift, I think about my mom, who raised my sister and me on her own while she worked and earned her degree; who once turned to food stamps but was still able to send us to the best schools in the country with the help of student loans and scholarships.

An American Dream meritocracy would want Obama to claim the meritocratic rights of his hard work and individual success. However, he located his success in the shoulders on which he stood. It was not the meritocracy of his individual labor that made him President, but the communal sacrifices of others.

The fallacy of meritocracy is maintaining a belief in success as something that happens to an individual. The Moses Generation of the 1960s did not believe in individual merit as a defining goal of society. One year before he died, Dr. King (1992) broke his silence on the war in Vietnam with a call to a genuine revolution:

> A genuine revolution of values means in the final analysis that our loyalties must become ecumenical rather than sectional. Every nation must now develop an overriding loyalty to mankind as a whole in order to preserve the best in their individual societies. This call for a world-wide fellowship that lifts neighborly concern beyond one's tribe, race, class, and nation is in reality a call for an all-embracing and unconditional love for all men. (p. 150)

Dr. King's genuine revolution of values was not a call for individual opportunity but for neighborly concern, for a commitment to community.

As spokesman of the Joshua Generation, President Obama continued this call. In his acceptance speech at the Democratic National Convention, then Candidate Obama (2008a) specifically denounced a meritocratic social vision:

> For over two decades, he's [President George W. Bush] subscribed to that old, discredited Republican philosophy—give more and more to those with the most and hope that prosperity trickles down to everyone else. In Washington, they call this the Ownership Society, but what it really means is—you're on your own. Out of work? Tough luck. No health care? The market will fix it. Born into poverty? Pull yourself up by your own bootstraps—even if you don't have boots. You're on your own.

With this last sentence, President Obama directly addressed the myth of meritocracy as an old, discredited idea. He used his election as a podium from which to demonstrate that the American Dream of meritocracy does not really exist. But he did not stop there.

President Obama's speech not only condemned the myth of meritocracy, but also the fallacy of meritocracy:

> It's a promise that says each of us has the freedom to make of our own lives what we will, but that we also have the obligation to treat each other with dignity and respect. . . . That's the promise of America—the idea that we are responsible for ourselves, but that we also rise or fall as one nation; the fundamental belief that I am my brother's keeper; I am my sister's keeper. (Obama, 2008a)

This one statement, that I am my brother's and sister's keeper, ran counter to over two hundred years of an American Dream founded on success and failure as an individual responsibility. President Obama's story was an example of how we must begin to see merit not as the provenance of an individual, but as the struggle of a community. We should not be working to make sure everyone has an equal shot at success, but working to redefine success as something that happens for a whole community, whether that be as small as a classroom or as big as a country. President Obama did not just reject the myth of meritocracy, but also the fallacy that meritocracy is a worthy goal at all.

In reflecting on his inauguration, President Obama (Remnick, 2010) sought to maintain this call to reject meritocracy:

> Never during that week did I somehow feel that this was a celebration of me and my accomplishments. I felt very much that it was a celebration of America and how far we had traveled. And that people were reaffirming our capacity to overcome all the old wounds and old divisions but also new wounds and new divisions. (p. 96)

President Obama continued to reject the idea of his accomplishments being his own, instead injecting "we" and "people" whenever possible. He also recognized that our system of racism continues to evolve, that the old divisions develop into new divisions. In battling these new wounds and divisions of racism, the rejection of meritocracy becomes central.

Having defined, at some length, the myth of meritocracy and the fallacy of meritocracy in the setting of President Obama and the Joshua Generation, I now build on this discussion to provide implications for education, particularly education engaged in the fight against systemic racism.

Fighting Racism with Relational Pluralism

As a prominent member of the Moses Generation, Diane Nash helped found the Student Nonviolent Coordinating Committee, was instrumental in the Nashville Sit-Ins and Freedom Rides, and worked closely with Reverend James Lawson and Dr. King. In recent reflections on the meaning of the Movement today (Remnick, 2010), she pointed out the danger that meritocracy poses to the fight against racism:

> One thing that I think the history books, and the media, have gotten very wrong is portraying the movement as Martin Luther King's movement, when in fact it was a people's movement. If people understood that it was ordinary people who did everything that needed to be done in the movement, instead of thinking, I wish we had a Martin Luther King now, they would ask, "What can I do?" Idolizing just one person undermines the struggle. (p. 97)

The struggle against racism is undermined when we focus on the success of an individual. If we believe that society advances through the success of individuals (that is, in meritocracy), then we will just wait around for Joshua instead of believing in the Joshua Generation. Our system of racism maintains its strength when we believe that only Moses or Joshua can fight it, and a belief in meritocracy inhibits our ability to form communities engaged in such a struggle. Instead of meritocracy, we need an ideal that values individuals in terms of communal success.

It may be easy to concede that every student in the United States does not have an equal opportunity of success. A large portion of education research is dedicated to describing the many ways in which equal opportunity does not exist (e.g., Kozol, 1992, 2006; MacLeod, 1995; Maran, 2000). However, I do not believe that meritocracy is an ideal toward which I should work if I want to make the United States a better place through the preparation of teachers for diverse classrooms. Instead, I must view the success of one as the success of all; likewise, I accept the failure of one as the failure of all. I root out the words, "Yes I Can," and replace them with an American Dream that lays bare the fallacy of meritocracy:

> This is our chance to answer that call. This is our moment. This is our time—to put our people back to work and open doors of opportunity for our kids; to restore prosperity and promote the cause of peace; to reclaim the American Dream and reaffirm that fundamental truth—that out of many, we are one; that while

we breathe, we hope, and where we are met with cynicism, and doubt, and those who tell us that we can't, we will respond with that timeless creed that sums up the spirit of a people: Yes We Can. (Obama, 2008b)

The context of P–20 education is changing, as the social vision espoused by President Obama spreads. From this foundation in the Joshua Generation, I develop a social ideal toward which I believe education might run, an ideal that exposes both the myth and fallacy of meritocracy, the ideal of Relational Pluralism.

What is the purpose of education, of teacher education, and to what end should it be directed? In my mind, the purpose of teacher education is to prepare agents willing to use the classroom as a site for social change; thus, in my mind, the purpose of P–20 education is active social change, like the struggle against racism. But if teachers are to be agents of social change and fight racism, how should they direct their work? If I see teacher education as a site from which to challenge both the myth and fallacy of meritocracy, I must provide an alternative.

I believe that alternative is *relational pluralism*. I define relational pluralism as an ideal in which "we acknowledge, affirm, and find strength in our singularities while at the same time maintaining connections with others in intersecting circles of community" (American Commitments, 1995, p. xxi). Relational pluralism runs counter to American Dream meritocracy by locating the individual as a member of a community, an individual who will succeed or fail as the community succeeds or fails. I believe that a commitment to relational pluralism is important for teachers who want to disrupt notions of meritocracy based on individualism and self-reliance, and thereby engage in the struggle against racism.

In short, the field of education has long fought for the ideal of meritocracy. I believe racism has evolved to such a stage that even if education becomes meritocratic, racism will live on. If I build a classroom around the idea that every student has an equal chance at success, I have still bowed to the racism of meritocracy; I am willing to let one or two or all students fail as individuals. This is unacceptable. The social justice ideal of the Joshua Generation is not equal pay for equal work; it is providing for those who cannot provide for themselves, even at the cost of self-sacrifice. The words of President Obama were not "I will work to provide everyone a fair shot," but "I am my brother's keeper; I am my sister's keeper."

The P–20 classroom adhering to relational pluralism might look very different from the P–20 classrooms of today. The success of one student will be the success of all. Likewise, the failure of one student, the failure of one school, the failure of one system will be the failure of all. The ideal of relational pluralism highlights why the practice of academic tracking is so dangerous. The ideal of relational pluralism highlights why the practice of funding schools with local property taxes is so dangerous. The ideal of relational pluralism highlights why the practice of high-stakes standardized testing is so dangerous. These practices allow the country to believe that the success and failure of individuals are the responsibilities of those individuals, and not the responsibilities of everyone. If we embrace the ideal of meritocracy in tracking, then we tell some students, "You're wasting your time wanting to go to college." If we embrace the ideal of meritocracy when funding schools through property taxes, then we believe that poor neighborhoods deserve poor schools. If we embrace the ideal of meritocracy in standardized testing, then we promote the definition of success for some students as the failure of others. It is not just the myth of meritocracy that is at work here, but the fallacy as well. I do not believe we should try to provide every student with identical skills and dispositions so that we can then push them to individual merit and success. We should challenge the fallacy of individual merit, and instead come to see success as a communal goal.

In my own setting of teacher education, the Joshua Generation holds several implications for the ways in which I prepare teachers for diverse classrooms. First, I must provide my student teachers with a deep theoretical understanding of systemic racism (Laughter, 2010), and give them the tools to begin dismantling that system whenever they encounter it, through the development of relationships. Second, I must engage my students in dialogic pedagogy. It is through dialogue that we come to know the other as a sister or a brother; it is through dialogue that we form community. Third, I must combat notions of individual merit so that my student teachers will come to see the success and failure of students as their own success and failure. Finally, and building on all three of the previous implications, I must prepare my student teachers to be willing to struggle against racist systems that rely on perceived meritocracy, systems like tracking, school funding, and standardized testing. I must let go of my own concerns about whether or not my student teachers can accurately communicate content, and focus most on whether or not they can engage in the struggle against racism and the building of communal relationships. Without the latter, the former really does not matter.

The Relational American Dream

In reflecting on the narratives of the United States, President Obama sees his country as a place that differs from the rest of the world:

> It's fundamentally different from the story that many minority groups go through in other countries. There's no equivalent, if you think about it, in many countries—that sense that, through the deliverance of the least of these, the society as a whole is transformed for the better. (As quoted in Remnick, 2010, p. 97)

The belief that in the United States the betterment of "the least of these" leads to the betterment of all is not a belief centered on the possibility of meritocracy. It is not even a belief that seeks to somehow develop a meritocracy. Instead, it is a belief centered on communal success, a belief that educators and teacher educators must adopt if we want seriously to engage in the struggle against racism.

The election of President Obama is not an example of the success of meritocracy. Instead, he is an example of the possibilities of relational pluralism. Should his call to be the keepers of sisters and brothers be taken seriously, I believe the P–20 classroom will become an effective site for fighting racism, which it cannot be if notions of meritocracy remain. Racism will continue in its many nefarious forms if society continues to believe that meritocracy is the same as social justice. This was not true for Moses or Joshua, and it is not true for their 20th- and 21st-century namesakes. Ending racism through education is not about every person having an equal chance. Ending racism through education is about letting go of the desire to be individually successful, and taking up the call to be the keepers of my sisters and brothers.

Notes

1. I do not intend the word *diverse* to be a synonym for non-White. I believe diversity occurs in infinite ways both among people and within people. A diverse classroom is thus the recognition that each member of a classroom is an individual located in multiple contexts and communities.
2. I use the terms Black and White (with majuscule first letters) to label races and not ethnicities. Thus, I do not use, for example, African American and Black interchangeably.

Bibliography

American Commitments. (1995). *The drama of diversity and democracy: Higher education and American commitments.* Washington, DC: Association of American Colleges and Universities.

Carter, D. J. (2008). Achievement as resistance: The development of a critical race achievement ideology among Black achievers. *Harvard Educational Review, 78*(3), 466–497.

Delgado, R., & Stefancic, J. (2001). *Critical race theory: An introduction.* New York, NY: New York University Press.

Farber, D. A., & Sherry, S. (2000). Is the radical critique of merit anti-Semitic? In R. Delgado & J. Stefancic (Eds.), *Critical race theory: The cutting edge* (2nd ed.; pp. 579–583). Philadelphia, PA: Temple University Press.

Green, J. P. (Ed. & Trans.). (1986). *The interlinear Bible: Hebrew-Greek-English* (2nd ed.). Lafayette, IN: Sovereign Grace.

King, M. L., Jr. (1992). *I have a dream: Writings and speeches that changed the world* (J. M. Washington, Ed.). San Francisco, CA: HarperSanFrancisco.

Kozol, J. (1992). *Savage inequalities: Children in America's schools.* New York, NY: Harper Perennial.

Kozol, J. (2006). *The shame of the nation: The restoration of apartheid schooling in America.* New York, NY: Three Rivers Press.

Ladson-Billings, G. (1998). Just what is critical race theory and what's it doing in a nice field like education? *International Journal of Qualitative Studies in Education, 11*(1), 7–24.

Ladson-Billings, G., & Tate, W. F. (1995). Toward a critical race theory of education. *Teachers College Record, 97*(1), 47–68.

Laughter, J. C. (2010). Talking about race in the 'post-racial' classroom. *English Leadership Quarterly, 32*(3), 15–17.

Liptak, A. (2009, April 28). On voting rights, test of history v. progress. *The New York Times*, p. A16. Retrieved from http://www.nytimes.com/2009/04/28/us/28voting.html?_r=1

MacLeod, J. (1995). *Ain't no makin' it: Aspirations and attainment in a low-income neighborhood.* Boulder, CO: Westview Press.

Maran, M. (2000). *Class dismissed: A year in the life of an American high school, a glimpse into the heart of a nation.* New York, NY: St. Martin's Press.

McIntosh, P. (1989). White privilege: Unpacking the invisible knapsack. *Peace and Freedom, 49*(4), 10–12.

Milner, H. R. (2007). Race, narrative inquiry, and self-study in curriculum and teacher education. *Education and Urban Society, 39*(4), 584–609.

Obama, B. (2007, March 4). Selma voting rights march commemoration. Retrieved from http://www.barackobama.com/2007/03/04/selma_voting_rights_march_ comm.php

Obama, B. (2008a, August 28). Remarks of Senator Obama: The American promise (Democratic convention). Retrieved from http://www.barackobama.com/2008/08/28/ remarks_of_senator_obam_108.php

Obama, B. (2008b, November 4). Remarks of President-Elect Barack Obama: Election night. Retrieved from http://www.barackobama.com/2008/11/04/remarks_of _presidentelect_bara.php

Remnick, D. (2010, February 15 & 20). The promise. *The New Yorker*, 95–115.

Roberts, S. (2009, May 1). Race gap in voter turnout shrank in 2008, study says. *The New York Times*, p. A14.

Saulny, S. (2009, May 3). Voices reflect rising sense of racial optimism. *The New York Times*, p. A1.

Solórzano, D. G., & Yosso, T. J. (2001). From racial stereotyping and deficit discourse toward a critical race theory in teacher education. *Multicultural Education, 9*(1), 2–8.

Stolberg, S. G., & Connelly, M. (2009, April 28). Obama nudging views on race, a survey finds: Blacks more hopeful. *The New York Times*, p. A1.

Tate, W. F. (1997). Critical race theory and education: History, theory, and implications. In M. Apple (Ed.), *Review of research in education* (pp. 195–247). Washington, DC: American Educational Research Association.

TWO

Navigating the Space Between

Obama and the Postracial Myth

Bridgette Coble, Floyd Cobb, Kristin Deal, and Frank Tuitt

Postracialism and the President

When we consider race in the United States, the election of the nation's first Black president is not only a monumental milestone, but a significant data point, providing a unique opportunity to examine the state of race and racial discourse in the US. Arguably, the racial climate that existed before and during Barack Obama's candidacy and eventual presidency exemplifies how the general public regards the president (a Black man) and his policy decisions, and reflects the ways in which race still matters in the United States. In this chapter, we contend that the racial climate surrounding President Obama offers insight into the racial challenges that will continue to impact higher education and its ability to effectively educate a diverse student body. Accordingly, an examination of the 44th President of the United States of America provides us with an avenue to explore what Critical Race Theorists would describe as the embedded nature of race and racism within U.S. society (Delgado & Stefancic, 2001; Dixson & Rousseau, 2005; Russell, Rios, Zamudio, & Bridgeman, 2011).

The Election of a Black President

In the aftermath of this historic election, many discussed how the symbolism elucidated by the majoritarian act of making a Black man the most powerful individual in the world, would impact a future America that would return the favor by ensuring equality for those situated similarly along society's hierarchical rung. Brilliantly encapsulated in the campaign slogans of "hope and change," everywhere conversations highlighted the possibility of an America that could finally live up to the language enshrined in her founding documents, establishing that all of her citizens were truly created equal. Summarized succinctly in the term, *postracial*, citizens were left to imagine whether America had turned the page from her sordid legacy of racial discrimination, and some were even encouraged to adamantly suggest that the problems of the past were behind us (Reed & Louis, 2009).

Although widely criticized by racial scholars (Gates & Steele, 2009; Harris-Perry, 2011; Steele, 2009; Toure, 2011) as being self-congratulatory, the term, *postracial*, quickly became the embodiment of an era that marked the end of a once inconceivable accomplishment in American history. The America about which Martin Luther King, Jr. had fantasized, appeared to be finally within reach. However, as the first few months of the Obama presidency progressed we soon learned that this emotional solidarity would be short-lived. Just as the "I Have a Dream" speech had been co-opted, reducing Martin Luther King, Jr. to a few words out of context, opponents of the President had quickly learned how to utilize the power of the term *postracialism* to ensure that equality-related measures would never succeed.

Postracialism is understood as a new era, where racial discrimination is no longer a societal concern, where racial justice and equality prevail, and where racial differences are ignored through the practice of color blindness (Esposito & Finley, 2009). While some individuals embraced the notion of a postracial America, we contend that this romantic notion is problematic in that it may distract change agents in higher education from the type of attention that is still needed to address the racism present in our institutions, practices, and people. How can anyone assert that America is postracial, when the reality of racial inequity, across all facets of society, tells a different story? How can we ignore continued reports that Blacks are three times more likely than Whites to live in poverty, twenty times more likely to go to prison for illegal drug use, twice as likely to be unemployed, more likely to receive poor or substandard healthcare even when income and health insurance policies are comparable to Whites, less likely to graduate from high school and attend college, six times more likely to be victims of homicide, and more likely to be rejected for prime home loan mortgages and instead directed toward subprime mortgages (Esposito & Finley, 2009)? How can these realities exist while people are still believing that we are a postracial society? Supported largely by the mantra of "no more excuses" (Reed & Louis, 2009), opponents of President Obama have found ways to utilize the notion of postracialism for their benefit, particularly in the field of education. Postracialism serves as a double-edged sword, concurrently empowering and oppressing, through policies and initiatives that reinterpret the purposes of affirmative action, the need for ethnic studies courses, or the educational rights of immigrant students. In these cases, those that have wielded the postracial sword had the power to restructure or simply ban policy, ultimately redefining reality for all.

Critical Race Theory

We use Critical Race Theory (CRT) as our explanatory framework to guide this chapter. A framework founded by Derrick Bell and Alan Freeman in the mid-1970s, stemming from the Critical Legal Studies movement, CRT is designed to challenge contemporary interpretations of Civil Rights language (Delgado & Stefancic, 2001). CRT reminds us that in spite of incremental social progress, racism remains a permanent structure of American society. Therefore, CRT challenges contemporary forms of liberal discourse that overstate minimal racial accomplishments, by foregrounding the broader structural inequalities that continue to marginalize and oppress people of color (Ladson-Billings, 1998). Specifically, CRT challenges us to critique color-blind, objective, and meritocratic discourses that obfuscate the successes of those who have been historically oppressed (Dixson & Rousseau, 2005). The central component of color blindness suggests that to acknowledge a person's race is inappropriate and corrupting to meritocratic practices (Gotanda, 2000). Instead, racial differences are to be ignored. This discourse misjudges race consciousness and race-based strategies as racist, and has created a society that is ripe and ready to embrace a belief in postracialism, no matter how absurd.

The first analytic that we will utilize in this analysis is Bonilla-Silva's (2003) first frame of color blindness, abstract liberalism. When abstract liberalism is employed, individuals find ways to rationalize the disparate impact of historically marginalized groups in the name of equal opportunity by ignoring cumulative effects of past and contemporary discrimination on members of these groups (Bonilla-Silva, 2003). This leads to the challenge of social policy efforts like affirmative action, under the guises of equality, while ignoring the policy's true intent of establishing equitable access. Through this chapter we will argue that while the election of Barack Obama was a historic marker of racial progress, it simultaneously increased the discourse of abstract liberalism, further hindering future efforts for social equality.

Moreover, CRT scholars recognize that even when there are advances in racial progress, these are made only when they benefit the White majority, ensuring that the social hierarchy remains firmly in place (Bell, 1980; Delgado & Stefancic, 2001; Ladson-Billings, 2004; Milner, 2008). Identified specifically as the interest convergence principle, Bell (1995) argued that racial progress is only possible when the interests of Blacks and Whites converge, creating the opportunity for both groups to benefit (Russell, Rios, Zamudio, & Bridgeman, 2011). We use interest convergence as our second analytical tool in examining postracialism in the age of Obama.

The Political Climate of the Obama Presidency

Race has mattered throughout the history of our nation, and is particularly evident in the study of societal climate during President Obama's candidacy, nomination, and presidency. Election of the nation's first Black president is significant, but can it change society? Yes, we have evolved from the practice of legal discrimination based on race, but we have not yet transformed into a society where racism is not practiced (Esposito & Finley, 2009; Lever, 2007; Selmi, 2011). The practice of color blindness impedes our ability as a nation to recover from our ugly past, and instead further embeds racist practices into our environment. CRT reminds us that we have not healed, we have not transformed, and that we must be conscious of the reality that race is a foundational construct that contributes to all manifestations of inequity (Dixson & Rousseau, 2005). Our color-blind ideologies not only render antidiscrimination laws impotent, and contribute to a backlash in previous civil rights efforts, but also reinforce the practice of racism (Esposito & Finley, 2009). As we attempt to ignore race and racism, we actually racialize all aspects of society, and maintain racial inequity. In order to foreground this racialization, we examine Obama's experience, and the degree of racialization that has occurred during his time as president. This can be observed in a multitude of events. Two types are highlighted in this chapter.

The Racialization of Our 44th President

Consider the images created to depict Barack Obama. While many media organizations publicized professional, serious, and complimentary images, Internet images, which "are central to how we represent, make meanings, and communicate in the world around us" (Sturken & Cartwright, 2001, p. 1), reflect a barrage of disconcerting, racist depictions of our 44th president. These images range from overtly racist to inferentially racist, portraying Obama in ways that support the historic and current discourse surrounding race in our nation. The overtly racist images depict Obama as an ape, thug, and terrorist (Joseph, 2011), and align with the fear that has historically been associated with the Black male body. For example, the image of President Obama as a terrorist spread throughout the Internet, and by August 2010, a Pew Research Center poll reported that 18% of Americans believed this Internet-spread rumor (Joseph, 2011). The inferentially racist images are of even greater concern, because while most Americans would acknowledge the ape, thug, and terrorist images as racist, many would struggle to recognize the racism embedded within images of President Obama as messiah, magical creature, and best friend to Whites (Joseph, 2011). While there are positive attributes to these types of characters, they still racialize the president, as they require an abandonment of his Blackness, replaced by the persona of a savior, a nonhuman entity, or a whitewashed, nonthreatening character (Joseph, 2011).

The larger White public's need to consider President Barack Obama as having "overcome" his Blackness is another key marker of the climate of racism that exists in today's society. This may not be considered as overt, racist practice, but much of the commentary and accolades bestowed upon President Obama can be exposed as racial microaggressions. Racial microaggressions can be described as the commonplace, daily slights and indignities directed toward people of color, that are often dismissed as acceptable behavior that does not intend to cause harm. They are extremely problematic because of their subtle nature, and have serious detrimental effects on the target person or group (Sue, Capodilupo, & Holder, 2008). Obama has become the symbol of acceptable Blackness (Esposito & Finley, 2009). This is a form of Blackness that is devoid of observable culture and difference, and does not make some Whites feel threatened or uncomfortable (Esposito & Finley, 2009; Shark-Fu, 2008). According to Ambinder (2009), the writer, Michael Grunwald, described people who are thought to fit this category as "'no-demands' blacks; their acceptance by whites [is] not predicated on whites' having to give up anything fundamental or betray their convictions or untangle a major stereotype" (Ambinder, 2009, p. 65). Recent studies indicate that the perception of Blacks by Whites is that of being unmotivated, dangerous, and drug users (Burston, Jones, & Roberson-Saunders, 1995; Giroux, 2004; Hunt, 2007; Wise, 2009). Barack Obama defies these beliefs by presenting himself as a polished, articulate, attractive, and charismatic Black man whose values align with those of the majority of White Americans. To liberals, he is the safe minority, making it easy to celebrate the illusion of America's postraciality, where racial differences are no longer relevant (Joseph, 2011). To conservatives, his mere presence represents a threat to the current power structure, encouraging an otherization of his very being at every turn. Dominant discourse has produced mass communication that spread racial ideologies supporting heroic, "race-transcending icons" (Brown, 2011, p. 539) such as President Obama. He thus becomes the model of transcendence, navigating the space between being the safe Black man and the dangerous Black man, all by winning the approval of White voters (Esposito & Finley, 2009). At the same time, this racial microaggression ignores the unique experience Barack Obama has faced as a Black man, silences him from all perceived race talk, and ignores and demonizes an entire community of Blacks who are not regarded as safe minorities.

Directly related are the racial macroaggressions that exist in less subtle and even more damaging ways. Macroaggressions are defined as insults or pejorative statements and/or actions by Whites against Blacks. Macroaggressions, unlike microaggressions, are not directed at any particular Black person, but at the whole racial category (Russell, 1996). These macroaggressions are also often minimized and explained away as not racist, but again, their effect is extremely damaging, not only to people of color, but to all Americans who get entangled in a postracial web of lies, political maneuvers, and social confusion that direct us away from real solutions. The magnitude of racial macroaggressions surrounding Barack Obama can be likened to the police practice of racial profiling. Racial profiling occurs when law enforcement officials attribute a person's race (Carter, 2004) to the prediction of criminal behavior. Due to racial profiling, many people of color, particularly Black men, have been subjected to unfair treatment, suspicion, and humiliation.

Consider for a moment that no other United States president has had to face the barrage of demands, investigations, and public outcry regarding his citizenship status. Even after his state of birth repeatedly confirmed his citizenship, his birth certificate was made public, and U.S. courts dismissed all accusations as having no legal grounds, this issue has not gone away. Similarly, the attention on the pastor of President Obama's former church, Reverend Jeremiah Wright, provides an example of a macroaggression, as his sermons were examined and scrutinized for perceived racist comments that were subtly and not so subtly tied to then democratic candidate Obama. The assumption the public was expected to make with this public attention on the pastor, was that if Obama attended that church and expressed positive regard for the pastor, then he, too, must also be racist. No attention was given toward the historical nature of the Black church in America, or even the oppressive, discriminatory legacy that creates a need for distrust of the United States. The public attention was only directed at sensationalizing Reverend Wright's sermons, and inciting fear of Obama in White Americans. The visceral accusations about Barack Obama's citizenship, and the multiple accusations about racist values of the president originate from the same premise that relies on stereotypes about the criminal behavior of people of color regardless of previous behavior. Barack Obama is assumed to be a criminal unworthy of the presidency because of his race.

Perhaps racial profiling is most notably seen on July 22, 2009 during a live, televised press conference in the East Room. Here the President intended to urge Congress to focus on fulfilling his campaign promise of securing universal health care for all Americans. This relatively ordinary event was close to its conclusion when Lynn Sweet of the *Chicago Sun-Times* asked the President to respond to a question that would forever racialize the individual who had been regarded as our first postracial President (Ogletree, 2010). The question was related to the recent arrest of his friend, Harvard Professor Henry Louis Gates Jr., who was arrested on charges of disorderly conduct after growing angry about a mistaken identity case in his own home. As the final question of the night, Sweet asked, "What does that incident say to you? And what does it say about race relations in America?" (Ogletree, 2010, p. 51). In his response, the President acknowledged Dr. Gates as a friend, and openly admitted his difficulty with being impartial in this instance, but nevertheless expressed displeasure with the events he understood led to the arrest by the Cambridge police. He most famously stated that the "Cambridge Police acted stupidly" by arresting someone in their own home. He continued expressing his displeasure by inferring that this incident was the result of racial profiling, and lamenting its very existence by stating,

> As you know, Lynn, when I was in the state legislature in Illinois we worked on a racial profiling bill because there was indisputable evidence that Blacks and Hispanics were being stopped disproportionately. And that is a sign, an example of how, you know, race remains a factor in this society. That doesn't lessen the incredible power of progress that has been made. I am standing here as testimony to the progress that's been made. And yet, the fact of the matter is that you know, this still haunts us. (Ogletree, 2010 p. 52)

The incident was an obvious example of police racial profiling, and President Obama's initial response, which chastised the officer, was met by the medial and general public as presumptive and unfair (Ogletree, 2010). The unwillingness of the media to attest to the president's lived experience as a Black man who has witnessed the harm racial profiling has inflicted upon Black men, or even to consider the reality of racial profiling as a symptom of a racist society, demonstrates the fear of race that is embedded within the current discourse. While we will never truly know the effect of this statement had Obama been White, we do know that this President's decision to weigh in on the topic racialized him as never before. Barack Hussein Obama was postracial no more; on this day he became our first "Black" President (Ogletree, 2010). And with this designation of Blackness, efforts to enact policies that elevated the opportunities of the social underclass would be challenged at every turn.

The Racialization of Presidential Decisions?

Throughout his first few months in office, opponents sought to find ways to highlight his identity, and summarily discredit any modicum of authority the executive branch might grant him. Whether in his appointments to federal roles, policy efforts, or outright authority to make a decision, President Obama fell victim to the skepticism, cynicism, and distrust associated with a Black man not utilizing his newfound authority to disrupt the power structure as it has existed throughout the history of this country. The current racial climate creates an environment where presidential decisions and political strategy are all influenced by race (Brown, 2011).

Consider the critique of President Obama's nomination of Sonia Sotomayor for Supreme Court Justice. Sotomayor embraces her racial identity, and has expressed on several occasions an appreciation for how her race and ethnicity have provided her with a unique set of skills and perspective. She is quoted as saying, "I would hope that a wise Latina woman with the richness of her experiences would more often than not reach a better conclusion than a White male who hasn't lived that life" (Rosen, 2009). Her words of inspiration, reflection, and appropriate challenge of the status quo have been twisted by a fearing public, who challenged her intellectual aptitude, and accused her of being racist, even when a review of her rulings shows her as a moderate and compassionate judge. Her cultural comments were highlighted as evidence of her racism, and became targets that determined how many Whites believe she would perform her Supreme Court duties.

Whether or not one supports the political decisions President Obama has made during his tenure, the case can be made that his approaches, reactions, and decisions have not been made without the influence of how the general public regards race. Barack Obama took on the most difficult job in the world, at possibly the most difficult time in history, under the guise of a dominant racial discourse that will not permit him to accurately tend to the racial inequities that exist in our nation (Joseph, 2011). Interest convergence, theorized by Derrick Bell and included in CRT's critique of liberalism, is a dynamic that suggests that Whites will promote advances for people of color only when these advances also promote their own interests (Bell, 1980). Race neutrality and color blindness support the theory of interest convergence, and disallow any reference to race, prohibiting people of color from naming their own reality (Taylor, 2000). This has proven true in the responses to our first Black president. While Barack Obama holds the most powerful position in the nation, the power to define his own reality is not his. The current racial subcontext ensures that the White majority has the power to define all reality. This climate demands that our first Black president embrace the color-blind ideology, and master interest convergence; his election depended on his ability to deracialize his campaign (Esposito & Finley, 2009). President Obama is quoted as saying, "there is no Black America, there is no White America, there is only the United States of America" (Esposito & Finley, 2009, p. 166). Yet, in his book, *The Audacity of Hope: Thoughts on Reclaiming the American Dream* (Obama, 2006), he also pointed to the experiences he has had as a Black man in America, and to how he has shared in the historical subjugation of Black people.

Higher Education and the Postracial Access Climate

In the decade leading up to Obama's inauguration, four states, utilizing the language of civil rights legislation, ratified constitutional amendments or propositions banning affirmative action within publically funded arenas.[1] During his second year as President, Arizona voters passed a constitutional ban on state-sponsored affirmative action. If the political climate regarding affirmative action was not divisive enough, the judicial arena was the stage for the battle over affirmative action within the education system during the same years. Of the major court cases attending to affirmative action in higher education, *Hopwood v. Texas* (1996), followed by *Gratz v. Bollinger* (2003), forced institutions nationwide to rethink the location of race within admissions policy. The persistent call to repeal affirmative action foregrounds the rationale that race no longer serves as a compelling interest in admission to higher education, and, similar to the continued call for constitutional amendments within state governance, affirmative action education cases continue their meritocratic movement toward the Supreme Court (e.g., *Fisher v. University of Texas* which was heard by the High Court in October of 2012). It is into this racialized higher education climate that President Obama and his administration entered.

As the postracial myth has pervaded the political realm, so, too, can its impact be seen within higher education. With President Obama's election, and throughout the tenure of his first term in office, higher education has continued down the postracial path at an alarming speed. The educational climate established by the belief in and thus defined reality of the postracial myth has shaped, restricted, and complicated the ways that President Obama has been able to engage in creating equitable academic pipelines, policies, and overall access. This climate did not appear the day he entered office, but, rather, had been primed throughout the previous administrations, making it imperative that if President Obama wants to engage U.S. education beyond the postracial myth, he must use the tools of that very myth—abstract liberalism and interest convergence.

During the Bush presidency, Black student enrollment in higher education grew 3 percent, from 11 to 14 percent (Aud et al., 2010). Though this growth might seem slow, in context, Black student enrollment grew at roughly the same pace (2 percent) between 1976 and 2000 (Snyder & Dillow, 2011). The doubling in rate of access over an eight-year period, even as bans on affirmative action admissions policies began to accumulate, signals a beginning of the postracial myth of college access. The quick and unprecedented rise in Black student enrollment, in contrast to the conservative call for equal opportunity regardless of race, is the result of interest convergence, where Black students were granted access only when it served the financial interests of White education investors. This overt, color-blind approach created a higher education access climate where race remains an "absent-presence" (Kuntz, Gildersleeve, & Pasque, 2011, p. 495), as seen in the rise of for-profit higher education, and the decreased nature of federal PELL grants (Cochrane, 2012).

Since the mid-1990s, for-profit colleges and universities have outpaced the nonprofit traditional education sector. By the fall of 2009, approximately 11 percent of all full-time undergraduate students, and 38 percent of full-time students over 35 attended for-profit institutions (Aud & Hannes, 2011). This expansive enrollment created a profitable business, as 14 for-profit parent corporations traded on Wall Street are worth more than $26 billion, and enroll 1.4 million students (Kutz, 2010). However, as concern about affirmative action admissions policies took hold in public nonprofit universities, for-profit institutions capitalized on the anti-affirmative action climate, with the result that Black students were overrepresented in the for-profit educational sector. In the fall of 2008, as President Bush was preparing to leave the Oval Office, 27 percent of for-profit students were Black, a higher percentage than at any other type of institution (Aud et al., 2010). The rise in Black student enrollment between 2000 and 2008 is largely accounted for in the open admissions policies of for-profit higher education, and the aggressive recruiting techniques of such institutions. In an environment where college access is increasingly important, and space at public institutions is at a premium, these colleges and universities rely on the fact that students are in need of postsecondary education, leaving few to question the abysmal retention rates and high student loan debt for those students who attend for-profit institutions.

Along with the decreased access to public postsecondary education, in 2011, Congress made two substantial changes to the federal Pell Grant program. These changes included a reduction in years a student can receive the federal Pell Grant, and a temporary elimination of the six-month repayment grace period. These shifts in policy are cloaked in the language of reining in federal spending to account for the unprecedented national debt. However, one must not turn a blind eye to the demographic makeup of Congress at the time. With a Republican-controlled House of Representatives, and over a third of the 2010 Congressional freshmen class considering themselves members of the Tea Party, these cuts in education funding must not be understood without consideration of these legislators' belief in meritocracy, free-market education, anti-affirmative action, and the dismantling of ethnic studies programs, as seen in the legislative act known as Arizona SB-1070.

According to The Institute for College Access and Success, Black students account for approximately 24 percent of Pell Grant recipients, but comprise 41 percent of those working toward a postsecondary degree after six years (Cochrane, 2012). With the new, 18-semester (or comparable time) Pell Grant funding limit, those most impacted in the completion of their degree are Black students. And as Black college graduates are twice as likely to be unemployed as their White counterparts (*The Hilltop*, 2011), the temporary elimination of the loan repayment grace period has a disproportionate impact on those Black students who have completed their degrees.

Obama Navigating a Postracial Access Reality

We cannot help but wonder if Barack Obama's careful measures to appear race neutral are just a predictable response to the racial climate, and if his plan of attack is infused with Bell's notion of interest convergence in an effort to make change. Overt efforts to dismantle racism will be thwarted by the current racial climate that requires an avoidance of any focus on race. These efforts must then employ the same tools used to further racism (i.e., meritocractic appeal, equal opportunity language, and market-driven outcomes), as a means of engaging the racism embedded within societal structures and institutions.

In his pivotal higher education access speech, at Macomb Community College on July 14, 2009, President Obama made his foray into the higher education access climate. In describing his American Graduation Initiative, President Obama emphasized education, specifically at community colleges, as an "engine of growth" within the American economy, (Obama, 2009). His speech is laden with calls for education to be enhanced at these colleges, in order to outfit new workers with the most up-to-date and needed skills within the job market. Utilizing the language of his postracial adversaries, abstract liberalism—speaking about the individual rather than the collective, and about socioeconomic class rather than race—his focus on community colleges illustrates an awareness of the racial struggles that continue to exist in higher education. This approach was both in distinct contrast to the unfettered regulatory environment that fueled for-profit institutions during the previous administration, and in alignment with the abstract liberal approach to education. President Obama, by using the language of the majority, engaged those who adhere to the postracial myth, in redirecting Black students' access to higher education from for-profits to community colleges, where the decrease in Pell Grant funding will have less of an adverse effect, and where his administration is committed to $8 billion in funding (Obama, 2012).

In the subsequent brief, "The President's Agenda and the African American Community," President Obama more closely explained how his administration's policies "have benefited all Americans, and have direct impacts on the African American community" (Obama, 2011). Though this document continues to navigate the space between individual and collective reasoning, he clearly articulates his understanding of the realities faced by Black communities within the color-blind and meritocratic access system. Those disbelievers in search of more evidence regarding the President's navigation of the space between race-based and race-neutral interventions need only look to the report entitled, "Guidance on the Voluntary Use of Race to Achieve Diversity in Postsecondary Education" (U.S. Department of Justice, 2008).

On December 2, 2011, the U.S. Departments of Justice and Education issued new guidelines proposing how postsecondary institutions could increase diversity at their institutions while remaining in compliance with U.S. Supreme Court decisions. Framed as a resource to assist colleges and universities interested in the voluntary use of race in admissions, this document set forth a series of recommendations postsecondary institutions can consider to enhance the diversity of their student bodies. What is clear in this document is that while diversity can be considered a compelling interest, race in and of itself is not. Specifically, the phrase, "race neutral," appears fourteen times, supported by a list of alternative, race-neutral options for increasing diversity. Understood as a strategy, this approach signals to diversity advocates that in this current and perhaps future racial context the only way we are going to achieve racial equality is by not focusing directly on race.

Implications for Navigating the Space Between in Higher Education

Prior to election night, then Senator Obama utilized his massive campaign contributions to purchase airtime on all of the major networks for his campaign videos titled, "A Mother's Promise: Barack's Biography" and "American Stories, American Solutions." Both focused explicitly on his Midwestern, White heritage, alleviating fears about his otherness. He appealed to a White audience by highlighting his mother and maternal grandparents as exemplars in his life, and his subsequent educational journey toward his presidential campaign. Now, as the nation prepares for another presidential campaign, his Blackness is being exposed in new ways, as conservative news media, using old film footage from his time as Editor of the *Harvard Law Review*, are fixated on President Obama's connection to Derrick Bell. The work of Derrick Bell has propelled many scholars toward passionate engagement in disrupting White supremacy and racism, bringing urgency to the work of addressing racial power and privilege. Thus, the vision of Obama embracing Derrick Bell has been used both to fuel White fears, and to create uncertainty about his location in the movement toward racial equity. President Obama is walking the fine line between White anxiety and non-White urgency (Carlin, 2009). In many ways, this is the same dilemma that awaits those in higher education who seek to increase access and opportunity for students of color.

In closing, we address two implications for promoting racial equity in higher education that result from our analysis of President Obama's navigation of this country's racialized context.

Interest Convergence: Navigating the Space Between Racial Equity for Minoritized Students and the Educational Benefits for Majority Students

The lessons gathered by observing President Barack Obama suggest that a mastery of interest convergence is required in order to achieve success for minoritized individuals who seek to work toward racial equality. The unfortunate reality is that in spite of our better judgments, the proclamation of a postracial America has had a profound impact on the current political landscape in higher education. When thinking about higher education climates, navigating the space between highly racialized contexts and postracialism will be a tedious dance. For those working further up the administrative chain of command, the postracial climate is particularly pervasive. For leaders of color, this dance is more harrowing, as their authority might be enhanced when tokenized, or disrupted if seen as a threat to the meritocratic system. Navigating the space between requires mastery of interest convergence through code switching, to best engage audiences toward the same equity mission through different language. One current example of this strategy has materialized in the American Association of Colleges and Universities' Inclusive Excellence campaign, where several Predominately White Institutions (PWI) have answered the AAC&U's call to move away from a fragmented focus on diversity, and begin to think about how to embed Inclusive Excellence into the educational enterprise. Specifically, the organization challenged leaders to move from rhetoric to action by involving the entire campus community in the work of fusing diversity and excellence (Milem, Chang, & Antonio, 2005).

At face value, the concept of Inclusive Excellence, like its predecessor, diversity, provides change agents concerned with promoting racial equity with a seemingly race-neutral alternative for framing campus initiatives designed to create inclusive educational environments. The attractiveness of the Inclusive Excellence discourse is that it speaks to the interests of campus leaders' desire to be associated with excellence, and aligns with the interests of campus advocates who seek to promote inclusion. In this case, navigating the space between excellence and inclusion is nothing more than a proxy for navigating the space between racial equity and educational benefits for majority students. Moving forward it will be interesting to see if the educational benefits of diversity for majority students, as argued for in both *Gratz v. Bollinger* (2003) and *Grutter v. Bollinger* (2003), remain as a compelling interest for creating increased access for minoritized students.

Navigating the Space Between Restrictive and Expansive Policies

Finally, higher education institutions, in the pursuit of diversity, have relied on the creation of programs, practices, and policies—TRIO, Upward Bound, and Affirmative Action—to supplement the larger admissions system toward reaching racial equity. However, these programs were never meant to change the structures of higher education, but rather sit on the periphery. The space between promoting and building programs and actually changing the entire system toward equity, requires that higher education administrators stop focusing on the objectives of higher education, and instead examine the outcomes for minoritized students. Opening the doors of higher education for students of color through various programs is simply not enough; yet, by evaluating the outcomes for these students once they enter higher education, administrators engage in considering the impacts of an institution on students.

A focus on outcomes requires a shift from a restrictive to an expansive view of racial equality. According to Crenshaw (1988), an expansive view of racial equality would emphasize equality as a result, and measure its effectiveness by evaluating the societal conditions (e.g., outcomes or consequences) of minoritized students. Correspondingly, an expansive view of racial equality aims to eradicate the pervasive conditions that reinforce the subordination of minoritized students, and attempts to enlist the institutional structures to promote racial equity. Often, higher education policies designed to facilitate increased access and opportunity for minoritized students frame equality as a process, and discount the significance of actual conditions (e.g, outcomes or consequences) that contribute to the need for intervening in the first place. A restrictive view of equality, found in existing higher education policies, programs, and practices, seeks to prevent future wrongdoings, as opposed to redressing root causes of racial injustice (Crenshaw, 1988). The danger in restrictive, race-neutral policies, programs, and practices is that they aim to treat students equally, as an approach to ensure equity, viewing equity as being about equality of treatment rather than outcomes. On the surface, this process might seem equitable and fair, but in reality it has and will have negative effects on minoritized students. As suggested earlier, the changes in Pell grant policies are restrictive, in the sense that they focus on numerical equivalency and equality or process, rather than on the actual educational outcomes and experiences of students of color (Dixson & Rousseau, 2005).

In navigating the space between restrictive and expansive views, policies, programs, and practices designed to address racial injustice through race-neutral or color-blind approaches must be balanced against acknowledgement of and attention to the social and historical contexts, and not leave the privileged and oppressive position of Whiteness unchallenged. In closing, we posit that higher education leaders seeking to promote racial equity will need to (a) make sure that their efforts take into consideration the current and historical racial context (internal and external) in which their interventions are situated; (b) identify specific desired outcomes for minoritized students specifically, and all students in general; (c) make informed, data-driven decisions and assess impact; and (d) never forget that advocating for racial equity will require navigating the space between the illusion of a postracial America and the reality that race still matters.

Notes

1. Starting in 1996, California was the first state to ban affirmative action, noting that, "the state shall not discriminate against, or grant preferential treatment to, any individual or group on the basis of race, sex, color, ethnicity, or national origin in the operation of public employment, public education, or public contracting" (Proposition 209). Washington (1998), Michigan (2006),

and Nebraska (2008) followed, while Amendment 46 was narrowly defeated in Colorado in 2008. A federal appeals court later overturned Michigan's ban on affirmative action in 2011.

Bibliography

Alemán, E., Salazar, T., Rorrer, A., & Parker, L. (2011). Introduction to postracialism in U.S. public school and higher education settings: The politics of education in the age of Obama. *Peabody Journal of Education, 86*(5), 479–487. doi:10.1080/0161956X.2011.616129

Ambinder, M. (2009, January/February). Race Over? *The Atlantic, 62*–65. Retrieved from http://www.theatlantic.com/magazine/archive/2009/01/race-over/7215/

Aud, S., & Hannes, G. (Eds.). (2011). *The condition of education 2011 in brief* (NCES 2011-034). U.S. Department of Education, National Center for Education Statistics. Washington, DC: U.S. Government Printing Office.

Aud, S., Hussar, W., Planty, M., Snyder, T., Bianco, K., Fox, . . . Drake, L. (2010). *The condition of education 2010* (NCES 2010-028). National Center for Education Statistics, Institute of Education Sciences, U.S. Department of Education. Washington, DC: U.S. Department of Education.

Bell, D. A. (1980). *Brown v. Board of Education* and the interest convergence dilemma. *Harvard Law Review, 93*, 518-533.

Bell, D. A. (1995). Racial realism. In K. Crenshaw, N. Gotanda, G. Peller, & K. Thomas (Eds.), *Critical Race Theory: The key writings that informed the movement* (pp. 302-312). New York, NY: The New Press.

Bolton, M. J. (2011). Premature exuberance: Police, profiling, and African Americans in a postracial society. *Public Administration Review, 71*(5), 791–795.

Bonilla-Silva, E. (2003). *Racism without racists: Color-blind racism and the persistence of racial inequality in the United States*. Lanham, MD: Rowman & Littlefield.

Brown, C. B. (2011). Barack Obama as the great man: Communicative constructions of racial transcendence in White-male elite discourses. *Communication Monographs, 78*(4), 535–556.

Burston, B. W., Jones. D., & Roberson-Saunders, P. (1995). Drug use and African Americans: Myth versus reality. *Journal of Alcohol and Drug Education, 40*(2), 19–39.

Carter, W. M. (2004). A Thirteenth Amendment framework for combating racial profiling. *Harvard Civil Rights-Civil Liberties Law Review, 39*(1), 17–93.

Cochrane, D. (2012, February 14). Testimony before Assembly Higher Education Committee; Senate Business, Professions and Economic Development Committee; Joint Legislative Oversight Hearing. California's Oversight of Private Postsecondary Education, Sacramento, CA. Retrieved from http://ticas.org/files/pub/Debbie_Cochrane_testimony_2-14-12.pdf

Crenshaw, K. W. (1988). Race, reform, and retrenchment: Transformation and legitimation in antidiscrimination law. *Harvard Law Review, 101*(7), 1331–1387.

Delgado, R., & Stefancic, J. (2001). *Critical race theory: An introduction*. New York, NY: New York University Press.

Dixson, A. D., & Rousseau, C. K. (2005). And we are still not saved: Critical race theory in education ten years later. *Race, Ethnicity and Education, 8*(1), 7–27.

Esposito, L., & Finley, L. (2009). Barack Obama, racial progress, and the future of race relations in the United States. *Western Journal of Black Studies, 33*(3), 164–175.

Gates, H. L., & Steele, C. M. (2009). A conversation with Claude M. Steele: Stereotype threat and Black achievement. *Du Bois Review: Social Science Research on Race, 6*(2), 251–271.

Giroux, H. A. (2004). *The terror of neo-liberalism*. Boulder, CO: Paradigm.

Giroux, H. A. (2009). Judge Sonia Sotomayor and the new racism: Getting beyond the politics of denial. *Policy Futures in Education, 7*(6), 681–684. doi:10.2304/pfie.2009.7.6.681

Givhan, R. (2008, March 16). Edging (at times clumsily) toward a post-racial America. *The Washington Post*. Retrieved from http://www.washingtonpost.com/wp-dyn/content/article/2008/03/14/AR2008031401072.html

Gotanda, N. (2000). A critique of 'our constitution is color-blind.' In R. Delgado & J. Stefancic (Eds.), *Critical race theory: The cutting edge* (2nd ed., pp. 35–38). Philadelphia, PA: Temple University Press.

Gratz v. Bollinger et al., 539 U.S. 244 (2003).

Grutter v. Bollinger et al., 539 U.S. 306 (2003).

Harris-Perry, M. (2011, October 10). Black president, double standard: Why White liberals are abandoning Obama. *The Nation*. Retrieved from http://www.thenation.com/article/163544/black-president-double-standard-why-white-liberals-are-abandoning-obama

The Hilltop. (2011). Unemployment among Black college graduates. Howard University. *Black College Wire*. Retrieved from http://www.blackcollegewire.org/index.php?option=com_ywp_blog&task=view&id=5908&Itemid=36

Hunt, M. O. (2007). African American, Hispanic, and White beliefs about Black/White inequality, 1977–2004. *American Sociological Review, 72*(3), 390–415.

Joseph, R. L. (2011). Imagining Obama: Reading overtly and inferentially racist images of our 44th president, 2007–2008. *Communication Studies, 62*(4), 389–405.

Kuntz, A. M., Gildersleeve, R. E., & Pasque, P. A. (2011). Obama's American Graduation Initiative: Race, conservative modernization, and a logic of abstraction. *Peabody Journal of Education, 86*(5), 488–505.

Kutz, G. D. (2010, August 4). *For-profit colleges: Undercover testing finds colleges encouraged fraud and engaged in deceptive and questionable marketing practices* (GAO-10-948T). Retrieved from http://www.gao.gov/products/GAO-10-948T

Ladson-Billings, G. (1998). Just what is critical race theory and what's it doing in a nice field like education? *International Journal of Qualitative Studies in Education, 11*(1), 7–24.

Ladson-Billings, G. (2004). Landing on the wrong note: The price we paid for *Brown*. *Educational Researcher, 33*(7), 3–13.

Lever, A. (2007). What's wrong with racial profiling? Another look at the problem. *Criminal Justice Ethics, 26*(1), 20–28.

López, G. R. (2003). The (racially neutral) politics of education: A critical race theory perspective. *Educational Administration Quarterly, 39*(1), 68–94.

Loury, G. C. (2009, July 25). Obama, Gates and the American Black man. *The New York Times*. Retrieved from http://www.nytimes.com/2009/07/26/opinion/26loury.html?pagewanted=all

Lum, L. (2009, February 5). Despite the election of President Barack Obama, many longtime scholars whose work intertwines with race disagree that the country has reached a post-racial period. *Diverse: Issues in Higher Education*. Retrieved from http://diverseeducation.worldpress.com

Milem, J. F., Chang, M. J., & Antonio, A. L. (2005). *Making diversity work on campus: A research-based perspective*. Washington, DC: Association of American Colleges and Universities.

Milkis, S. M., & Tichenor, D. J. (2011). Reform's mating dance: Presidents, social movements, and racial realignments. *Journal of Policy History, 23*(4), 451–490.

Milner, H. R. (2008). Critical race theory and interest convergence as analytic tools in teacher education policies and practices. *Journal of Teacher Education, 59*, 332-346.

Norton, H. (2010). The Supreme Court's post-racial turn towards a zero-sum understanding of equality. *William and Mary Law Review, 52*(1), 197–260.

Obama, B. H. (2006). *The audacity of hope: Thoughts on reclaiming the American dream*. New York, NY: Crown.

Obama, B. H. (2009, July 14). *Remarks by the President on the American Graduation Initiative* [Transcript]. Speech at Macomb Community College. Retrieved from the Office of the Press Secretary, White House: http://www.whitehouse.gov/the_press_office/Remarks-by-the-President-on-the-American-Graduation-Initiative-in-Warren-MI/

Obama, B. H. (2011, November). The President's agenda and the African American community. Office of the Press Secretary, The White House. Retrieved from http://www.whitehouse.gov/sites/default/files/af_am_report_final.pdf

Obama, B. H. (2012, February 13). *Remarks by the President on the budget* [Transcript]. Retrieved from the Office of the Press Secretary, White House: http://www.whitehouse.gov/the-press-office/2012/02/13/remarks-president-budget

Ogletree, C. (2010). *The presumption of guilt: The arrest of Henry Louis Gates Jr. and race, class, and crime in America*. New York, NY: Palgrave Macmillan.

Reed, W. L., & Louis, B. M. (2009). 'No more excuses': Problematic responses to Barack Obama's election. *Journal of African American Studies, 13*(2), 97–109. doi:10.1007/s12111-009-9088-3

Rosen, J. (2009, June 11). Where Sonia Sotomayor really stands on race. *Time Magazine*, Retrieved from http://www.time.com/time/magazine/article/0,9171,1904154,00.html

Rossing, J. P. (2011). Comic provocations in racial culture: Barack Obama and the 'politics of fear'. *Communication Studies, 62*(4), 422–438.

Russell, C., Rios, F., Zamudio, M., & Bridgeman, J. (2011). Reinvigorating the teaching of the civil rights movement: The praxis project. *Scholar-Practitioner Quarterly, 5*(1), 5–19.

Russell, K. (1996). Affirmative (re)action: Anything but race. *American University Law Review, 45*(3), 803–810.

Selmi, M. (2011). The Supreme Court's surprising and strategic response to the Civil Rights Act of 1991. *Wake Forest Law Review, 46*(2), 281–306.

Shark-Fu. (2008, April 30). Debunking acceptable Blackness through the second coming of the Rev. Wright drama [Web log post]. Retrieved from http://angryblackbitch.blogspot.com/2008/04/by-request-debunking-acceptable_30.html

Snyder, T. D., & Dillow, S. A. (2011). *Digest of Education Statistics 2010* (NCES 2011-015). National Center for Education Statistics, Institute of Education Sciences, U.S. Department of Education. Washington, DC: U.S. Department of Education.

Steele, S. (2008, November 5). Obama's post-racial promise. *Los Amgeles Times*. Retrieved from http://www.latimes.com/news/opinion/opinionla/la-oe-steele5-2008nov05,0,6049031.story

Steele, S. (2009, December 30). Obama and our post-modern race problem. *The Wall Street Journal*. Retrieved from http://online.wsj.com/article/SB10001424052748704254604574614540488450188.html

Sturken, M., & Cartwright, L. (2001). *Practices of looking: An introduction to visual culture*. Oxford, UK: Oxford University Press.

Sue, D. W., Capodilupo, C. M., & Holder, A. M. B. (2008). Racial microaggressions in the life experience of Black Americans. *Professional Psychology: Research and Practice, 39*(3), 329–336.

Taylor, E. (2000). Critical race theory and interest convergence in the backlash against affirmative action: Washington State and Initiative 200. *Teachers College Record, 102*(3), 539–560.

Touré. (2011). *Who's afraid of post-Blackness?: What it means to be Black now*. New York, NY: Free Press.

United States Department of Justice. (2008). Guidance on the voluntary use of race to achieve diversity in postsecondary education. Washington, DC. Retrieved from http://www.justice.gov/crt/about/edu/documents/guidancepost.pdf

Wingfield, A. H., & Feagin, J. R. (2009). *Yes we can?: White racial framing and the 2008 presidential campaign*. London, UK: Routledge.

Wise, T. (2009). *Between Barack and a hard place: Racism and White denial in the age of Obama*. San Francisco, CA: City Lights Books.

THREE

Learning From Catalina

Reflections on Bridging Communities and Schools in the Context of a "Postracial" Society

Louie F. Rodriguez

I will be the first to admit a feeling of what Cornel West called, "jubilation" after the election of Barack Obama to the U.S. Presidency in 2008. In my view, America will never be the same after this real and symbolic forward in this country's racial, political, and historical struggle for equity and justice for all. Yet, alongside the historic election, the country is facing a faltering economy, various international conflicts, and shortsighted social policy that continue to leave the most vulnerable communities behind. The pervasive mass incarceration of African American males; the cultural assassination of Latinas/os in Arizona, Alabama, and several other places; and the continuous exclusion of immigrant communities from mainstream society all continue to hamper the possibilities for political, economic, and cultural progress for this nation. One obvious and seemingly expanding challenge within American society is the struggle to adequately and equitably serve all children through its public schools, particularly for poor communities of color who continue to be denied fair access to a just and decent quality of life. And, while we know these challenges linger, the election of a Black President to the nation's highest position has triggered a sentiment across the country that racial inequality has been "fixed," creating a so-called postracial America. The realities on the ground, however, demonstrate that the significance of race, racism, and racial inequality remains unresolved, particularly in education and in communities serving historically marginalized groups such as Blacks/African Americans, Latinos, and other racial minorities.

I write this in hopes of shaping the way educators, researchers, and specifically, our government policymakers think and respond to education reform in this country. As of today, the problems facing schools and communities are momentous, and require a momentous response. Only 70% of all high school students graduate from high school, and the number is far more sobering for poor children and children of color, of whom only 50% graduate from high school. Most poor children, children of color, and immigrant children that do finish high school do so with lower reading, writing, and mathematical skill levels compared to those of middle-class White and Asian students. As you know well, this racial achievement gap in our nation has as much to do with poverty as it has to do with race. When one travels through communities throughout the country, one begins to see that struggling school systems are far more likely to serve poor people, whose faces are darker and whose native language is usually one other than English. Chicanos in Southern California, African Americans in Detroit, Haitians in Miami, and Puerto Ricans in New York City are just a few of the communities to which I am referring. Latinos, for instance, are the fastest growing and youngest population in the country, and often find themselves concentrated in schools and communities that are poor, segregated, and that provide education in large, overcrowded high schools that fail to meet the social and academic needs of students. Latinos, Blacks/African Americans, and Native Americans are also more likely to face underprepared or unqualified teachers, attend schools that lack basic resources such as updated curriculum materials (i.e., books), and sometimes are unaware of the name of their school's principal, because of the pervasively high turnover rates among urban school leadership.

In an era of increased accountability, high-stakes standardized testing, largely as a result of the No Child Left Behind Act, has transformed schools into testing mills, creating what I call an era of "Test-Prep Pedagogy." Research in the last five years shows that an overemphasis on test preparation and test scores often marginalizes youth who struggle to achieve on standardized tests, and depresses or altogether eliminates the creativity and will of good teachers, exacerbating the dropout problem in the United States. An even deeper analysis of the factors contributing to dropout shows that Latinas/os, Blacks, and other youth from historically marginalized groups are also least likely to experience high-quality relationships with school adults and access to high-quality intellectual experiences in school. They are also more likely to be suspended and expelled from school for infractions that have historically been dealt with at the school level (i.e., classroom disruptions). Yet, when zero-tolerance policies are used as an easy way to handle difficult challenges with students, expelling students from school becomes the dominant default disciplinary practice and policy in schools serving low-income children of color, contributing to high dropout rates in these schools and communities.

In higher education, Latinos, African Americans, and Native Americans are grossly underrepresented, and make up less than 10% of all recipients of college degrees. The numbers are far worse for graduate and professional school. Less than 1% of all Latinos, for instance, earn a doctorate in any field. Of course this has implications for the future leadership and the social, political, and economic health and mobility of these communities, not to mention the growth and success of U.S. society. My point is that these problems are not merely urban or inner-city problems, but American problems that result from years of public policy neglect.

In addition to focusing on education, it is equally important to take a snapshot of the challenges facing struggling communities beyond public schooling. In these same communities where achievement and graduation is low and failure and dropout is high, children are far less likely to have adequate health care. Many children forgo basic checkups only to find much later that they need eyeglasses, hearing devices, and dental work. Many children are recovering or coping with medical challenges associated with poverty—inhalation of toxic fumes in crowded or unsafe apartment buildings, inconsistent and unhealthy diets, asthma, and childhood diabetes and obesity. In the area of housing, poor communities have been particularly affected by the foreclosure crisis, impacting the wealth and short- and long-term stability of families. In poor communities, violence is all too common, as is unfair criminal justice policies, often targeting young men of color. And as the economy continues to struggle, immigrants are increasingly scapegoated as the root cause, and their social and political marginalization is further exacerbated by continued housing, employment, and education discrimination. Recent reports from the federal government have shown that Latinos are among the fastest growing victims of hate crimes, both immigrant and native-born.

The social and cultural challenges facing society certainly are robust, and span far beyond education. They spill into schools, and educators should be aware of such issues so they can adequately respond in schools and classrooms. However, they cannot solve these problems alone. Thus, the purpose of this reflection is to urge the Obama Administration and our nation's communities to approach school reform not only from a multi-institutional perspective, but also in a spirit of progressive cultural change that has been absent in recent public policy history. For instance, advocates for increasing graduation rates repeatedly point to the significance of quality teachers, adequate student support and counseling, and increased school resources. Yet, policy mandates fall short in ensuring that students experience high expectations, the availability of caring and respectful teachers, and meaningful intellectual engagement, all of which have been shown empirically to boost student engagement and achievement, particularly among low-income children and children of color. Yet, educational policy that aims to curb dropout insinuates the importance of these factors, but continues to focus on class size reduction, curriculum reform, or increased "accountability." The unfortunate fact is that while the presence of good schools matters, many low-income children must return to volatile homes and communities, parents who are unemployed, and an economy that has yet to promise a job after high school or college. Thus, I would like to propose a policy plan that is multi-institutional in recognition of both school and nonschool factors, as well as propose some forms of institutional collaboration and policy creativity that can fundamentally transform the quality of life of all communities in the United States. I do so in the context of my experiences as a teacher with one of my former high school students named Catalina.

Catalina's Story

Before Catalina threw a red brick through my classroom window, I learned, after the fact, that she requested to talk to me in the middle of her scuffle with the school security guard. As a high school algebra teacher in an alternative high school, I had seen students like Catalina before. Catalina is one of tens of thousands of youth who for one reason or another, are removed or remove themselves from the traditional public school system. If one takes the time to find out who Catalina is, her story is one of poverty and the ills associated with it—fractured family, young parents, community violence, and an inner city culture that values street knowledge over book knowledge. The daughter of Puerto Rican migrants, Catalina was a talented artist, had fantastic interpersonal skills, and seemed to have an aura that commanded respect from others. In many ways, she was a natural born leader. However, her obvious duel with the school security guard, and request to talk to me instead of any other school personnel says much about the types of public policy action that is needed to avoid this situation all together—not only the brick-throwing incident, but the need for Catalina to be in alternative education—and to eliminate the conditions in her community that result in social disarray.

Catalina could have benefited from public policy that requires the collaboration of multiple institutions and various stakeholders. Let us take her family situation, for instance. Her parents were completely out of her life—her father was incarcerated, and her mother succumbed to drugs. Living with the scars that only a few can possibly imagine, Catalina lived with her not-so-older sister, her sister's husband, and their children. While Catalina lived with "family," she did not manage to escape the remnants of early childhood trauma and the transfer of poverty from one generation to the next. Catalina and her sister could have benefited from mental health counseling that could have helped address their childhood trauma, as well as their coping resources as young women. Catalina's urge to throw a brick through a classroom window was far more related to anger that emanated from her complicated home and community life than to her frustration with a low standardized test score or run-in with a school security guard.

Part of Catalina's stress was related to the terms of her probation. After several fights with both boys and girls in the school and in her community, Catalina had her share of problems with the law. Her fighting problem was related, in part, to urban culture and the ongoing challenge of posturing for respect, and, to a degree, the formation of a healthy identity. For example, had other young people perceived Catalina as weak, she would have become a target. During the school year, Catalina was involved in an off-campus fight that landed her in jail. One of the conditions of her release was that she wear a GPS-type monitoring device on her ankle. Catalina was anxious to leave school exactly at 2:50 p.m. because it took her nearly two hours to get home on public transportation, which pushed up against her 5:00 p.m. curfew outlined in the conditions of her release.

When Catalina threw a brick through the window that day, her actions presented a threat to school property and physical safety (although she did not aim the brick at another person), according to school policy, and because of the implementation of zero-tolerance policies, Catalina was indefinitely removed from the school, and I never heard from her again.

Policy Solutions That Are Wide-Reaching and On-the-Ground

What I would like to do is construct an alternative story that dramatically transforms Catalina's situation through the implementation of multi-institutional action and progressive cultural change under a structurally and functionally different approach that recognizes the congruence between communities and schools.

Due to the implementation of the new community-school approach, by the time Catalina reached high school she was doing fairly well academically. She had been involved in an afterschool improvement/action research project focused on the beautification of her community, which paid her a modest wage. She was receiving the necessary counseling that was available once a week in this program, had committed to a summer college experience program at a local university, and, subsequently, had an idea that she wanted to major in either pre-law or sociology. Her sister and her husband joined a job-training program, and were able to take advantage of the free childcare provided by the community-school model. In the childcare setting, their children were exposed to healthy food, academic enrichment, and were learning new songs everyday. Catalina was quite optimistic about her future, because her sister and brother-in-law were guaranteed jobs after the training program, and she was promised summer employment during her college years.

But How Is This Scenario Possible?

The community-school model began its work by identifying the most struggling communities around the country in cities like Los Angeles, San Bernardino, Oakland, Atlanta, Detroit, Miami, Boston, Chicago, Paterson, Houston, Dallas, Baltimore, and many others. In collaboration with Administration officials, local surveying teams were assembled in each city. These teams included educators, parents, youth, business leaders (of small and large enterprises), policy makers, legal professionals, religious leaders, community-based organizations, health care providers, employment bureaus, university researchers, law enforcement agencies, and housing and planning stakeholders. The initial charge in each city was to conduct an inventory of the strengths and challenges within the targeted communities, and to examine each stakeholder's role in influencing or hindering school change and reform. Then a list of priorities was created based on each community's unique needs. The principle guiding these efforts was based on the notion that opportunity-rich communities lead to equitable schools, which results in a healthier society and a hopeful future.

In order to understand how this model ensures collaboration among multiple institutions and practices progressive cultural change, I revisit Catalina's new future through the lens of policy action. Consider that when Catalina was in the 7th grade, President Obama was elected the 44th President of the United States. While he worked with his economic team and Congress to revive the economy, his senior administration officials from the Departments of Housing and Urban Development, Health and Human Services, Labor, Commerce, Justice, and Education were meeting with districts, relevant institutional stakeholders, and community members to develop what they dreamed to be a new model for progressive policy and change in America's struggling communities. As the economy began to slowly rebound, stakeholders were assembled to unveil the community-school approach. After a year of planning and development, Catalina returned from holiday break in her eighth-grade year to find a set of opportunities waiting for her at school and in the community. Through the local university and her middle school, she was required to enroll in an afterschool/work-study program focused on youth action research and community development. With the help of a modest stipend, Catalina was able to gain experience, and learn about the history of her community. She was also given the opportunity to undertake various projects dealing with the environment. In this opportunity, the Department of Education made it possible, through their newly created satellite offices in communities across the country, to converge K–12 schools with higher education, in order to create these afterschool opportunities. This initiative also tapped the Department of Commerce to get local government officials to provide opportunities and resources from local experts whose job it was to sustain the city *and* serve as mentors to youth in the community.

Making Catalina's home life just a little brighter, her sister and brother-in-law also enrolled in an intense job-training program operated by local institutions and supported by the Department of Labor. With an arm located directly in struggling communities, a series of policies were created that ensured job training for the persistently unemployed, especially for individuals who had dropped out of school, and those involved in the criminal justice system. Not only was childcare provided as part of an initiative that linked the Department of Health and Human Services with other vital departments, but responsible policies were crafted that provided alternatives to jail for nonviolent repeat drug offenders, especially those who repeatedly failed to pass a simple drug test for gainful employment. Through counseling and rehabilitation, Catalina's brother-in-law was on his way to earning a living wage and supporting his family, the first male in the family to do so. In addition, in the childcare program, Catalina's younger nieces and nephews received strong academic and social skill development, and Catalina's sister and brother-in-law were required to take parenting and health awareness classes. Because her brother-in-law's parole officer had to sign off on his participation in these programs, he was able to take advantage of the Department of Justice's new policies on true rehabilitation and second-chance initiatives for minor offenders by committing to job training, drug rehabilitation, and parent/family development classes. In many ways, this model epitomizes what it means to create cultural change by triggering policies that are equitably responsive to the challenges facing local communities and schools.

As a result of these initiatives, the federal and state governments created thousands of jobs at the local levels, particularly in historically struggling communities. Because of the progressive policy, people began to access health care much earlier. The incidence of low birth weight began to decline, obesity rates were down, and healthy diets were up. Because they earned a living wage, people were able to invest their money, establish good credit, and participate in the growth of their local and state economy by traveling and purchasing various goods and services. Due to the collaborative efforts across job and business development, affordable housing was created, and prime loans were guaranteed for first-time buyers, especially for those who were the first in their families to purchase a home. Parks, walking and biking paths, and free cultural and intellectual opportunities were available in local schools and communities, and were produced by the people from these communities. The creation of green spaces like parks employed thousands, and the intellectual and creative pursuits of youth and community artists were nurtured and displayed across communities, which created collaborative opportunities for students in schools.

For youth disengaged from school and the workforce, there was a much more visible presence of tangible support in schools by community and government agencies, and youth always felt like they had someone to go to when they had questions or needed guidance. Teachers felt supported by the community commitment, and most communities adopted policies that promised teachers respectable salaries for college-educated professionals. Accountability for outcomes were no longer based on teacher performance, test scores, or standards alone; rather responsibility for community excellence, supportive school cultures, and inching towards 100% high school graduation and college-going rates was the goal. And, in this new era of pro-public schools, energy was spent on equitably responding to these schools and communities, rather than focusing on pro-voucher or alternative models that only serve a trivial fraction of the entire public school population.

Looking Forward

If in this new era the issue of dropout was of concern, multiple institutions had a stake in ensuring that dropout was preventable and reversible. Schools promised to care for and engage their students with high expectations through the help of multiple resources. Community groups, with the help of the federal government, ensured that youth had jobs, access to health care and job training, and opportunities to engage with experts and officials that gauged their interest, who would eventually serve as community role models. School dropout was no longer a crisis, but a small crack in the system that could be alleviated by swift, deliberate, and equitable action.

Closing Thoughts

As President Obama enters a second term, it is important to acknowledge that hope and change drive the survival and resilience of struggling communities before and during the Obama Administration's leadership. Through a commitment to bridging communities and schools, policy has the potential to be created through and *with* communities, not merely by working on their behalf. Communities and schools across the United States should be places where everyone gets a chance at a good, decent, and just way of life, not just for those who are already there. With the courage of local communities, and through the will of a government that can choose to equitably respond, students like Catalina will have access to life, liberty, and the pursuit of happiness. Until then, the mirage of a postracial America will linger, void of action, and filled with concentrated struggles that rewind our country's progress rather than fast forwarding us into the 21st century.

FOUR

An Introduction to Critical Race Realism

Theoretical and Methodological Implications for Education Research

Laurence J. Parker and Erin L. Castro

Critical race theory (CRT) has emerged as a central framework of legal perspective on the connection between racial discrimination and the law (Crenshaw, Gotanda, Peller, & Thomas, 1995; Delgado & Stefancic, 2000; Valdes, Culp, & Harris, 2002). CRT has also made inroads into education research and theory discussions around the centrality of race in analyzing the social, cultural, and materialist conditions of racism, and its legal, socioeconomic, and political impact on students of color in K–12 and higher education settings (Chapman, 2007; Dixson & Rousseau, 2006; Ladson-Billings & Tate, 1995; Lynn, 1999; Solórzano, 1998; Tate, 1997; Yosso, Parker, Solórzano, & Lynn, 2004). CRT scholarship is rooted in a number of general themes. One of them is that racism as a normal daily fact of life in society, and the ideology of racism have been so historically ingrained in political and legal structures as to be almost unrecognizable. Legal, racial designations have complex, historical and socially constructed meanings that insure the location of political inferiority of racially marginalized groups. As a form of oppositional scholarship, CRT challenges the experience of White European Americans as the normative standard. Rather, CRT grounds its conceptual framework in the distinctive contextual experiences of people of color and racial oppression, using literary narrative knowledge and counterstories to challenge the existing social construction of race. CRT attacks liberalism and the inherent belief in the law as a means to create an equitable, just society. CRT advocates have pointed to the frustrating legal pace of meaningful reform that has eliminated blatant hateful expressions of racism, but has kept intact exclusionary relations of power, as exemplified by the legal, conservative backlash of the courts, legislative bodies, voters, etc., against special rights for racially marginalized groups. CRT has also evolved from its initial focus on the Black–White racial paradigm, toward a more inclusive analysis of racism, social class, and gender disparities that examines the impact of racism on other groups (e.g., Latinos, Asian American-Pacific Islanders, South Asians, and American Indians) in the U.S. social and legal landscape. CRT's ultimate goal is to participate in the dialogue on eliminating racial oppression as a part of the broader goal of ending all forms of oppression.

Given the tenets of CRT, critical race realism (CRR) has emerged as a complementary methodological and theoretical argument, regarding its utility in law and social science. The purpose of this chapter is to briefly trace the evolution of CRT and how CRR's emphasis on combining quantitative, qualitative, and interpretive methodologies connects the theory to social science research. The controversy surrounding race-based programs to support underrepresented minority groups in graduate school, will serve as an example of the ways in which a CRR analysis can enhance the focus on the continuing centrality of racism in education, with implications for policy change for racial social justice.

Critical Race Theory Connects to Critical Race Realism

Originally developed by legal scholars of color, CRT was rooted in a social reality that was shaped by the collective historical and everyday, lived experiences of persons of color and their legal, political, social, and cultural status in the U.S. and communities of origin. CRT

> focuses on the various ways in which traditions and reasoning in law have an adverse impact on persons of color not as individuals but as a group. CRT examines the law and legal traditions through the history, contemporary experiences and racial sensibilities of racial minorities in the U.S." (Brown, 2003, p. 2)

Evolving from the legal arena, CRT situated the theoretical study of race and racism at the center of legal analysis regarding how the law and policy decisions were adjudicated and operationalized in terms of racism's impact on racial minority groups in the U.S. (Bell, 1979; Crenshaw et al., 1995; Delgado, 1989; Harris, 2002). There are some key defining principles that form the basic assumptions, perspectives, research methods, and pedagogies of CRT (Matsuda, Lawrence, Delgado, & Crenshaw, 1993; Tate, 1997; Delgado Bernal, & Villalpando, 2002). A discussion of these follows.

Race and Racism Are Central to the Analysis
CRT views race and White racism as the defining characteristic of American society. Some CRT scholars such as Bell (1992a) see White racism as endemic to all

legal and social institutions, and as hegemonic and permanent. Lawrence (1994) viewed the centrality of race as structured around the concept of unconscious racism, where it is ingrained in our culture and ideology to such an extent that it can be characterized by tacit understandings of racial inferiority and superiority. Delgado and Stefancic (2000) viewed racism as substantive—in terms of how Whites treat persons of color as legally inferior, which was characteristic of the Jim Crow period of segregation. They also viewed racism as procedural, with regard to how the law and legal discourse can be considered as fair and race neutral, while in reality, "there is a legal insistence that remedies not endanger white well-being" (Brown, 2003, p. 2). This part of CRT reveals how the dominant ideology of color blindness and race neutrality act as a camouflage for the self-interest, power, and privilege of dominant groups in American society (Delgado, 1989; Lopez, 2003).

The Concept of Racial Equality:
An Asymmetrical Commitment to Social Justice and Praxis
CRT has a fundamental commitment to a social justice agenda that struggles to eliminate all forms of racial, gender, language, generation status, and class subordination (Matsuda, 1987). This implies that CRT is committed to asymmetrical equality, so that in order to achieve racial equity, a certain amount of racial imbalance must be tolerated to eventually level the playing field of access and opportunity.

The Epistemology of CRT Is Experiential Knowledge
CRT's epistemological roots lie in the "legal knowledge that includes the perspective of persons of color in their critique and reformulation of legal doctrine" (Brown, 2003, p. 8). Therefore, the experiential knowledge of people of color is legitimate and critical to understanding racial subordination. The CRT framework calls for the experiential knowledge of people of color to be central as a counterstory to official legal analysis that has a built-in bias in favor of Whites. It shifts the source of truth and knowledge from the insider to the outsider's lived experiences. The experiential knowledge can come from storytelling, family history, biographies, scenarios, parables, chronicles, and narratives (Bell, 1979; Delgado, 1989).

An Historical Context and Interdisciplinary Perspective
CRT challenges ahistoricism of the courts and the adjudication process (Harris, 1993). The color-blind ideology that undergirds federal judicial reasoning is to discount historical discrimination as a problem that happened in the past, but which has little relevance for using the law to create a race-neutral society. CRT seeks to analyze race and racism in both historical and contemporary contexts,

using interdisciplinary methods (Delgado, 1989; Solórzano, 1998; Solórzano & Yosso, 2002).

Since its inception as critical race theory, it has taken on many forms in challenging established legal doctrine, including a transition into the educational arena. Situating race and racism at the center of analysis, scholars have examined inequities in K–12 schooling, such as school finance inequities, teacher-student interactions, curriculum issues, and lack of parent involvement in schools (Alemán, 2006; Auerbach, 2002; DeCuir & Dixson, 2004; Ladson-Billings, 1998; Ladson-Billings & Tate, 1995; Lynn & Parker, 2006; Tate, 1997). Critical race theory has also made an impact on evaluating the higher education context in terms of racial climate, and context issues that result in policy decisions that impact racial minority students and faculty on predominantly White campuses (Delgado Bernal, 2002; Duncan, 2002; Harris, 1993; Solórzano & Yosso, 2001; Taylor, 2000; Villalpando, 2003).

Critical Race Realism and Its Connection to the Legal Realist Movement and Racial Realism of Derrick Bell

The origins of critical race realism can be traced to two notable strands of legal theory: the legal realist movement, and the work of Derrick Bell and racial realism. As outlined by Parks (2007) and other legal scholars (see, for example, Ewick, Kagan, & Sarat, 1999), the legal realism movement began in the early to mid 1900s in law schools such as Columbia and Yale, among others at that time. The legal realist movement focused on defining a new direction in legal scholarship and adjudication that focused more on:

1. Exposing the contradictions in classical legal formalism;
2. Using the law to embark on political and social reform; and
3. Using social science empirical methods as tools to understand social problems, and using these methods to assist in formulating legal remedies and solutions.

Notable legal scholars such as U.S. Supreme Court Justices Oliver Wendell Holmes, Jr., Louis Brandeis, and Benjamin Cardozo, as well as Roscoe Pound, former Dean of the Harvard Law School, were some of the most notable names who spearheaded the legal realist movement, in terms of using social science evidence and data as part of litigation strategy to change social policy. Parks (2007) described how this movement in some of the nation's leading law schools influenced attorneys in the emerging movement to end racial segregation in the "separate but equal era" of Jim Crow. One of those attorneys was Charles Hamilton Houston, who was influenced in part by the legal realist movement, in terms of using social science as a tool to change laws around issues of racial equality.

Hamilton Houston and his team were determined to have Black lawyers use the laws as an instrument of direction and change regarding community action. This was to be done by Black lawyers using the law to advance social justice, and change discriminatory racial policies (Parks, 2007, pp. 15–16).

The second part of the critical race realist roots can also be traced to the work of Derrick Bell. In his article entitled, "Racial Realism," Bell (1992b) also pointed to the early theoretical thinking from the legal realist movement to offer a view borrowed from Oliver Wendell Holmes, that posited that judges settled cases not by deductive reasoning and legal formalist thought; rather judges relied on values and personal beliefs and biases within the surrounding social context (Bell, 1992b, p. 365). This background framework gave rise to Bell's perspective that the civil rights movement in the early 1990s should adopt a "racial realist" approach to civil rights litigation for the purpose of social change. The previous direction of civil rights law had been to use the power of the law to shape and change social policy in order to combat discrimination. This, indeed, served as part of the grounding of the legal realist movement in the early civil rights litigation spearheaded in the 1930s and 1940s. But Bell argued that this strategy had run its course, and that we should now embrace a more realistic ideal of the limits of the law, and of what can be done by civil rights legislation to fundamentally change the material conditions and political and social status in which most African Americans find themselves:

> Black people will never gain full equality in this country. Even those herculean efforts we hail as successful will produce no more than temporary peaks of progress, short-lived victories that slide into irrelevance as racial patterns adapt in ways that maintain white dominance. This is a hard-to-accept fact that all history verifies. We must acknowledge it and move on to adopt policies on what I call: Racial Realism. This mind-set or philosophy requires us to acknowledge the permanence of our subordinate status. That acknowledgement enables us to avoid despair, and frees us to imagine and implement racial strategies that can bring fulfillment and even triumph. (Bell, 1992b, pp. 373–374)

Bell goes on to argue that an acceptance of racial realism would enable African Americans to understand and respond to recurring aspects of their subordinate status, and think within the context of reality, rather than idealism. This is because African Americans still suffer high rates of unemployment, poverty, poor health care, housing discrimination, and low achievement in school (Bell, 1992b, p. 377), and still think that racial equality laws can lift them out of this trap; on the contrary, racial realism can offer new ways of thinking and fighting for racial social justice.

Bell's argument for racial realism could be seen as cynical or outdated, now that the United States elected its first African American in 2008 in Barack

Obama. But significant parts of Bell's racial realism theory still hold true when one examines the status of racial minorities in the U.S. For example, Teranishi (2010) reported on the educational gaps among Asian Americans and Pacific Island Americans, indicating that among the subgroups of this category there were major differences among Chinese Americans and Hmong or Cambodian Americans regarding poverty status and educational attainment. In some cases, the educational attainment of Chinese Americans with a BA or greater was at 48.1%, as compared to Hmong Americans at 7.5% or Cambodian Americans at 9.2% (p. 37). Alemán and Alemán (2010) used Bell's racial realism to critique the underrepresentation of Latino and Latina students in K–12 and higher education, racial antagonism around Latinos and immigration issues, and how some education and political leaders view Latinos and Latinas as a threat to American assimilation. Deyhle (1995) and Brayboy (2005) are just a few of the researchers who have documented the everyday racial macro and microaggressions that tribal nation Indian students face in public schools and higher education settings. This has continually resulted in the lowest population (by race) of students completing high school, going on to college, graduating college, and then moving on to graduate work. Gusa (2010) documented the increasing assertion of "white institutional presence" at the expense of racial minorities at some U.S. colleges and universities. Vaught (2011) used a critical race lens to present case study evidence of the everyday, harmful acts of racism by teachers and school officials against African American students, and to describe how the students were held to blame for the problem of African American underachievement. Alexander (2012) presented the argument that the mass incarceration rates of African American males in particular now serves as a *de facto* form of Jim Crow racial disenfranchisement. Brooks (2009) also pointed out that while Obama was elected in 2008, the United States still saw racial and social class disparities between African Americans and Whites, with an example being that "white middle class families have on average 113 times more financial assets than black middle class families (p. xiii)." All of these examples point to the importance of how critical race realism is grounded in viewing the use of social science evidence, both qualitative and quantitative, as an important tool in terms of law and social policy change, but that there are limits to what the law can do to fully remedy the effects of various forms of racial disparity and discrimination.

Critical Race Realism: Its Current Form

Given this history, critical race realism brings a more quantitative approach of research methodologies to legal scholarship, so that the qualitative emphasis on storytelling and counternarratives of CRT are bolstered by an empirical analysis of race and the law (Houh, 2005; Parks, 2007). Given the fact that policy goals and the best methods for pursuing them call for data about the evaluative effects of the policies and underlying assumptions, critical race realism allows for data-driven social science and education studies to provide answers to these important public policy questions (Parks, Jones, & Cardi, 2008, p. 5). Critical race realism acknowledges the importance of the earlier reliance on counterstories and counternarratives in CRT as legitimate social science methods that are grounded in qualitative research. However, critical race realists also call for using this method in combination with quantitative studies to add more convincing evidence to document the discriminatory effects of certain laws and policies, or the need for policy action to provide some type of remedy for past discrimination (Parks, Jones, & Cardi, 2008). One of the main analytic goals of critical race realism is to call for the use of quantitative research to redirect the focus of discrimination analysis away from the intent of the perpetrator, and center the analysis on the material and ideological conditions of those persons of color who are affected by racial discrimination within predominantly White institutions (Houh, 2005).

Critical race realism also adds an additional dimension of social science, data-driven research to document in comprehensive detail a "systematic, race-based evaluation and critique of legal doctrine, institutions, as well as actors" (Parks, 2007, p. 4). Critical race realism seeks to use social science empirical data to: "1) expose racism where it may be found; 2) identify its effects on individuals and institutions, and 3) put forth a concerted attack against it, in part, via public policy arguments" (Parks, 2007, p. 5). Critical race realists argue that since most polls show an overwhelming sentiment of White American skepticism toward claims of continued racism by persons of color, then more race-based methodological tools need to be brought to bear in terms of providing comprehensive proof of discrimination (Brown, 2004). Critical race realism consists of a deconstructive element, in terms of using social science empirical research to critique the law and legal and social institutions (such as schools and colleges and universities). CRR also has a constructive element, which consists of a racially progressive policy agenda, focusing on using the law to litigate, or using CRR research to provide evidence to lobby for change in state capitals and at the federal level to provide equity in terms of education, employment, health care, housing, etc. (Parks, 2007). Critical race realist thought stems from the legal realist movement that has a long history of redefining the use of the law to incorporate empirical sciences as part of litigation strategy, and in defending social policy against constitutional attack. Legal realism is also rooted in the interdisciplinary blending of law, sociology, political science, economics, and other academic disciplinary areas to study how law operates in the real world (Parks, Jones, & Cardi, 2008). Given the documented rise of color-blind thought in everyday beliefs among many White Americans (Lawrence, 1994; Neville, Lilly, Duran, Lee, & Browne, 2000), and the assertion by the more conservative U.S. Supreme Court Justices that the U.S. Constitution is color-blind, we believe that it might be time to consider combining critical race realism with critical race theory to provide more systemic detail on racial disparities related to the law in higher education institutions. Critical race realism brings quantitative research methodologies to legal scholarship, so that the focus on storytelling and counternarratives of CRT is also bolstered by an empirical measurement of racial inequality, discrimination, and the law.

For example, CRT can be used with CRR to comprehensively unlock the notion of unintentional or unconscious racism. Mica Pollock (2008) discussed the general resistance to remedying "everyday" racial justice in schools, particularly in terms of complaints filed through the Office of Civil Rights (OCR). She called for OCR officials, teachers, and administrators to work with parents and students to engage in a more detailed analysis of the subjective, everyday experiences of students of color in schools, to examine specific moments, incidents, practices, and actions by specific actors (i.e., teachers, principals, school security guards, and guidance counselors) that contribute to a cumulative pattern of denial of educational opportunity. Education researchers can frame the inquiry through the specific question of "does this action (or inaction) deny students of color the necessary access to educational opportunity and equity?" (Pollock, 2008, p. 15). A CRT and CRR theoretical methodology can be useful both for gathering qualitative data on the counterstory narrative data of day-to-day experiences in educational settings for students of color, and for providing salient statistical measures of how the effects of unconscious, everyday racism contribute to educational experiences for students of color. For example, an equity audit in a school district can find a racially disparate impact, in terms of comparing dropout and graduation rates, and at what grade; but the counterstories can provide the details as to why students do drop out, which could be rooted in racially problematic relations between students and school teachers and staff (Skrla, Scheurich, Garcia, & Nolly, 2004). Reliance on a "mixed methods" (Johnson & Onwuegbuzie, 2004) research paradigm can provide more comprehensive insights and understandings that can be used to answer questions regarding everyday racial experiences. A mixed-methods approach of this particular type would include a consideration of quantitative research—with its focus on standardized data collection, statistical analysis, and prediction, in terms of measuring racial disparities—and the qualitative research would examine issues related to induction, discovery, and exploration, in order to explain why and how the racial disparities transformed into racial discrimination, and to assess the effect of racial disparities on students of color and their educational opportunities. By combining critical race theory with critical race realism, education researchers can develop a more comprehensive interpretation of racism in educational environments, as well as formulate remedies and recommendations based on qualitative and quantitative data (Parks, 2007). When qualitative and quantitative empirical social science evidence is combined, it provides even more indication on the lived experience of racism in K–12 and postsecondary education. This trend in education research and sociology has been, in fact, an important part of the legal expert witness testimonies in court cases, according to Welner (2006), who discussed the role of education research and the courts regarding information on issues such as the academic effects of segregation on life chances, and classroom learning dynamics. The following example from the higher education arena and race-based affirmative action programs will further illustrate this point.

Southern Illinois University Carbondale and Constitutional Attack

> "We look out for the underdog at Southern. I like underdogs. No where [sic] is the power of higher education more pronounced than when it is afforded to someone who otherwise might have been, by birth or circumstance, denied it." (Chancellor Walter V. Wendler, the annual State of the University Address, March 2005)

Located in the heart of southern Illinois, Southern Illinois University Carbondale (SIUC) is located approximately two hours southeast of St. Louis, Missouri. A school with a long history of serving the underprivileged, SIUC began this commitment in 1869 when it first opened its doors as a teachers college, then named, Southern Illinois Normal College. With its location in the southernmost part of the state, SIUC's unique culture is a result of rural, urban, local, and international presence on campus. Enrollment statistics indicate that SIUC enrolled a total of 20,983 students in the fall of 2007, 16,193 of them as undergraduates (National Center for Education Statistics [NCES], 2009).

In the summer of 2005, the United States Department of Justice requested materials from Southern Illinois University at both the Carbondale and Edwardsville campuses in connection with their hiring and employment practices, under the suspicion that they were engaging in discriminatory behavior under the guise of affirmative action. But as with most current attacks on small-scale affirmative action programs in this country, this attack was preceded by threatening correspondence from the Center for Equal Opportunity, a conservative think tank that boasts as its chairman, a Fox News political analyst and the author of *An Unlikely Conservative*, Linda Chavez.[1]

Part of what makes the affirmative action landscape in a post-*Grutter* era so unique, is that powerful, conservative think tanks, such as the Center for Equal Opportunity (CEO), have a heavy hand in shaping race- and gender-sensitive programs on college and university campuses across this country.[2] Oftentimes, these types of organizations are the first to contact colleges and universities with allegations of bias or unfair treatment. In the case of SIUC, the CEO first contacted the university in the spring of 2004, challenging 10 of its programs, including five graduate programs. Concurrently, the CEO threatened to file a complaint with the U.S. Department of Education Office for Civil Rights if SIUC did not change the language of the fellowships, and open them up to all students regardless of skin color (Blakemore, 2006).

The university responded in disagreement to the letter, and the CEO replied that it would consequently refer SIUC to the federal government, as is customary in these types of endeavors.[3] As a result of this correspondence, approximately a year and a half after this encounter, the United States Department of Justice contacted Southern Illinois University, and requested that they submit materials in relation to five of the graduate fellowship and assistantship programs that they were then implementing.[4] During the investigation process, the Department of Justice reviewed programs such as the McNair Scholars Program, Diversifying Higher Education, the Illinois Consortium for Equal Opportunity, and the Minority Graduate Incentive program, all of which share the common thread of promoting and encouraging minority[5] student recruitment and retention at SIUC.

Three months later, on November 4, 2005, the university received a letter from the U.S. Department of Justice alleging that three of the fellowships that SIUC was then offering were in violation of Title VII of the 1964 Civil Rights Act. Title VII prohibits discrimination on the basis of race, gender, national origin, and religion in *employment* decisions. The three fellowships in question were the Proactive Recruitment of Multicultural Professionals for Tomorrow (PROMPT), which was developed by the SIUC graduate college; the Graduate Deans program, which was also developed by the SIUC graduate college, and; The Bridge to the Doctorate (BRIDGE), which was funded by a grant provided by the National Science Foundation beginning in the fall of 2003 (Jaehnig, 2004). At the time of this confrontation, there were a total of 28 students participating in these programs (Poshard, 2006).

The Department of Justice has rarely taken action against fellowships in higher education (Lewis, 2006). Thus, the use of Title VII and the reasoning of employment discrimination on behalf of the Department of Justice paved a new road for the anti-affirmative action agenda. The case at SIUC (*United States of America v. The Board of Trustees of Southern Illinois University*, 4:06-cv-04037-JPG-DGW, 2006) was perfect for this type of attack, in that the three fellowships in question *did* require a weekly minimum of work hours. Most fellowships in higher education, however, do not involve a work requirement, hence Title VII compliance is irrelevant. It is unclear why SIUC fellowships included this employment condition, but it is certainly worth noting, since it may provide some insight as to how the university understood their relationship with the students, and how they perceived the student's relationship with their own work.

Naming as case precedent, *International Brotherhood of Teamsters v. United States*, 431 U.S. 324 (1977), the letter from the Department of Justice (DOJ) informed the university that based on their investigation process, the university had "engaged in a pattern or practice of intentional discrimination against whites [and] nonpreferred minorities . . . on the basis of race" with respect to three of their fellowships (July 19, 2005 letter from DOJ, p. 3). In an effort to avoid the "burdens of contested litigation," Bradley J. Schlozman, Acting Assistant Attorney General for the Civil Rights Division, invited SIUC to enter into a Consent Decree in order to comply with federal law.[6] SIUC entered into this agreement on February 9, 2008 (*United States of America v. The Board of Trustees of Southern Illinois University*, 4:06-cv-04037-JPG-DGW).

Legal Reasoning and Policy Results

In July of 2006, Vice Chancellor for Research and Graduate Dean, John Koropchak, and General Counsel, Jerry Blakemore, of Southern Illinois University gave a presentation titled, *Recent Challenges to Graduate Diversity Programs at Southern Illinois University* (Blakemore & Koropchak, 2006), at the Council on Research Policy and Graduate Education in South Portland, Maine. During this presentation, they outlined the legal reasoning behind the decision to enter into the Consent Decree with the Department of Justice. The primary issue, according to their presentation and to SIUC Board of Trustee documents, was whether SIUC considered their fellows as employees: "The determining factor is whether the program participants are 'employees' and are therefore within the gambit of Title VII or are students and therefore not within the purview of Title VII" (Blakemore, 2006). With *Czubaj v. Ball State University* (2004) and *Suvannunt v. Thompson* (2003) cited as case precedent, SIUC general legal counsel felt it very likely that the fellows would indeed be categorized as employees by the courts, especially since recipients are subject to work requirements.[7] Thus, amendments were made to the three fellowships deemed in violation by eliminating the exclusive nature of the application criteria.[8]

Applying CRT and CRR to Measure Racial Disparities and Discrimination: Some Examples

From an educational policy perspective, Yosso et al. (2004) and Moses and Saenz (2008) predicted that new attacks against affirmative action would come through the use of color-blind legal rationale. This meant that particular strategies would be deployed, such as the continued use of state-wide ballot measures to ban affirmative action. Outreach programs that seek to increase the numbers of underrepresented students at colleges and universities by offering tutoring, summer courses, information seminars, mentoring, and skill-building workshops would also be challenged.

Given the likelihood of these trends increasing in the future, it is important for education to consider both the use of critical race theory and critical race realism to provide counternarratives and storytelling in conjunction with quantitative and qualitative social science evidence, in order to combat these attacks and provide justification for these types of outreach programs. At its center, critical race theory's central point of analysis is that racism is pervasive and endemic to U.S. society, and that persons of color are subject to subtle discrimination despite the passage of Federal civil rights laws. Critical race theory also argues for the importance of narrative and stories to make the continuing situation of racism real to others, especially Whites (Bell, 1992a; Delgado, 1989; Delgado & Stefancic, 2000).

Furthermore, a critical race theory and methodology under this approach would involve the use of interview and observational data gathered from the research process itself, existing literature on race and racism, and one's own personal and professional experience with race and racism (Solórzano, 1998). From a methodological perspective, the utility of critical race theory and its reliance on counterstories and counternarratives provides a useful qualitative framework for bringing the lived experiences of graduate students of color to the center of discussions around the pros and/or cons of affirmative action at predominantly White universities (Smith, Yosso, & Solórzano, 2007; Solórzano, 1998; Solórzano & Yosso, 2001, 2002; Yosso, 2006). When these qualitative data are combined with quantitative data that focus on measurements of inequality and discrimination, this type of social science provides even more evidence on how race and racism operate in education. It represents a powerful mixed-methods analysis, generating research-based findings to inform the policy debate (Schmukler, Morgan Thompson, & Crosby, 2008).[9]

CRT and CRR can be used in concert with each other to provide more detailed descriptions of racial campus climate issues for students of color on predominantly White campuses. CRR can provide a race-based legal theory and methodological framework for the use of quantitative methods, such as standard regression techniques. The reliance on complete and long-term, descriptive statistical data sets; or audits to analyze discrimination in school acceptance decisions; or performance assessment, would also be useful under a CRR research framework. Finally, some consideration could be given to utilizing natural experiments that could be used to gauge the effects of legislated or court-ordered rulings. This would help to determine the extent to which underlying racial differences actually reflect discrimination (Holzer & Ludwig, 2003). For example, CRR can provide the theoretical and methodological framework for using quantitative studies that document the interactions among variables. These variables may include racial isolation, the structural conditions of concentrated poverty in urban and rural areas, and how these impede low-income, first-generation African American, Latino, Native American, and some Asian American/Pacific Island students' progress.

CRR, in combination with CRT, can also yield analysis and discussion as to how, from a policy perspective, the data collected can serve as a call for overall initiatives to provide better K–12 schooling, economic and financial aid incentives, as well as more campus specific-based affirmative action type programs to address diversity issues once these first-generation college students of color attempt to navigate academic and social life in a predominantly White context. Similarly, critical race realism can be a useful theoretical-methodological tool for conceptualizing studies that look at how concentrated disadvantage in the K–12 system—regarding racial segregation, low teacher expectations, poor curriculum preparation for college, and inequities in school funding—combined with rigid university admissions criteria, create differential opportunities to go to college (Yun & Moreno, 2006). At the graduate level, critical race theory and critical race realism can be mutually joined when we think of the mentoring aspect of graduate school, and how this leads to preparation in the academy or the private sector. The connections between students and faculty are a critical part of this process. Davidson and Foster-Johnson (2001) articulated the importance of racial awareness, understandings, and actions by departments, faculty, and institutions, to foster more cross-racial initiatives in order to enhance the mentoring process with graduate students of color, and move toward more diversity in fields of graduate study.

The use of CRT and CRR, in terms of research methodology, should be considered in terms of informing policy on affirmative action. These methodologies can be helpful, given the long-term importance of enhancing diversity and social justice, and remedying past discrimination in higher education. Given that the future shape of affirmative action and diversity will be partially determined through litigation and state legislative debates or ballot initiatives, a case can be made for using CRR and CRT, as these would provide research evidence for the ongoing effectiveness of race-conscious admissions policies. They would also document the importance of other types of campus diversity projects dealing with the academic and social experiences of students and faculty (Ancheta, 2006). The importance of critical race realism and critical race theory can also provide a useful way to influence the zone of political and judicial constraints discussed by Welner (2012). The combination of both strands of critical race analysis will be even more important now, as the U.S. Supreme Court considers oral arguments in *Fisher v. University of Texas at Austin* (2011). This case will decide the future of using race in admissions decisions, and some commentary has indicated that the U.S. Supreme Court will use this as a way to undermine the *Grutter v. Bollinger* (2003) decision that upheld the use of race as one aspect of diversity, as a compelling state interest with the University of Michigan (Liptak, 2011).

Concluding Thoughts: Can CRT and CRR Coexist?

In this chapter, we posit that critical race theory and critical race realism can be used in concert as powerful methodological evidence to support a research agenda that looks at answering the question posed by Mickelson (2003): when are racial disparities in education the result of discrimination? We do not wish to uphold CRR over CRT or vice versa; on the contrary, we argue that both critical race theory and critical race realism can be used respectively to do research on race in education. We also argue that both, used in concert with each other, have the potential to provide a comprehensive theoretical framework and methodology that is centered on race and the law and their connection to education.

Both qualitative and quantitative research, in a mixed-methods approach, would be potentially useful for answering the aforementioned question. Racism and the power of White supremacy through the law have changed, and are no longer manifested through a single institution, or state agency, or action. Racism is now more evasive, embedded in institutional policies and practices that are unconscious, or that can be interpreted as color-blind. Intentional racism is harder to prove in the courts (Brown, 2004). Furthermore, there is a general public sense that racism is over in U.S. society. We believe it is not, and that CRT, in combination with CRR, can be used by education researchers, in consort with those in the legal profession, to provide data to illustrate everyday racial injustices in the schools and in higher education, and to provide potential remedies for addressing past and current conditions connected to racial disparities that result in discrimination.

Notes

1. According to their website, the CEO is the "nation's only conservative think tank devoted to issues of race and ethnicity," and as such, they work to promote "a colorblind society, one within which race and skin color are no longer an issue." Accordingly they "oppose admission, hiring, and contracting policies that discriminate, sort, or *prefer* [emphasis added] on the basis of race or ethnicity" (www.ceousa.org).
2. Backed with sufficient funding, organizations such as the Center for Individual Rights, the Center for Equal Opportunity, the American Civil Rights Institute, the American Civil Rights Coalition, the Citizens' Initiative on Race and Ethnicity, Diversity.net, and a host of other nonprofit, tax-exempt organizations boast of their successes in the legal arena, as well as their necessary purpose in defending the victims of reverse-discrimination.
3. Most organizational websites of the "color-blind," "civil liberty" nature have an area on their website that encourages patrons to submit their complaints online, so that the organization can look into the allegations. A recent example at the University of Delaware involving the Foundation for Individual Rights in Education (FIRE) resulted in the university abandoning a tolerance-oriented resident life program as the result of the first contact made by FIRE ("University of Delaware Abandons," 2007).
4. Roger Clegg of the Center for Equal Opportunity (CEO) said in 2005 that his organization filed a complaint against SIUC (Quaintance, 2005).

5. For purposes of this chapter, we are defining the term "minority" as those students who identify as women, African American, Native American, Asian American, Latino/a, and/or mixed race and/or ethnicity.
6. The regulations of the Consent Decree required the university to:
    1. Prohibit the recruitment or employment of individuals in paid fellowship positions exclusively on the basis of race, nation, origin, or sex;
    2. Distribute the Consent Decree and equal employment language to various administrators and display it in certain locations on campus and in electronic form;
    3. Discontinue any information that suggests that paid fellowship positions are restricted on the basis of race, national origin or sex;
    4. Provide equal employment training to all academic recruiters and employees engaged in recruiting activities on behalf of the PROMPT, BRIDGE, or Graduate Dean's fellowships, and;
    5. Provide detailed reports on fellowship activities every 6 months for the two-year span of the Consent Decree (Poshard, 2006).
7. In addition, the authors explicitly detail that they entered into the Consent Decree because they wanted to protect other programs from further scrutiny, they did not want the university to be fined or judged, and they did not want the current students in the programs to be harmed or affected (Blakemore, 2006). Of parallel importance, SIUC denied any wrongdoing in the Consent Decree, stating that "The SIU Board admits the allegations of the United States. . . . However, the SIU Board denies that it has engaged in discrimination in violation of Title VII" (Consent Decree, 2006).
8. In addition to changing the language of the fellowships, there is currently an added applicant requirement that calls for students to write an essay indicating how "personal family background, life, cultural, and/or ethnic experiences could contribute to a more reflective responsive environment in the program, the discipline, and in the larger academic community" (Blakemore, 2006).
9. Statistical methods (e.g., multiple regression, HLM) could be used along with descriptive statistical data to demonstrate the short-term and long-term effects of affirmative action type programs on campuses, to improve diversity at the graduate level. For example, data can be collected to document the impact of the Diversifying Faculty Initiative in the state of Illinois higher education system, regarding how graduate students of color are socialized into the professoriate and academic disciplines, their impact in terms of securing faculty positions in the public and private higher education institutions, and how much they also serve as mentors once they finish the program.

Bibliography

Alemán, E. Jr. (2006). Is Robin Hood the 'prince of thieves' or a pathway to equity? Applying critical race theory to school finance political discourse. *Educational Policy, 20*(1), 113–142.

Alemán, E. Jr., & Alemán, S. (2010). "Do Latin@ interest always have to 'converge' with White interest?": (Re)claiming racial realism and interest-convergence in critical race theory praxis. *Race, Ethnicity and Education, 13*(1), 1–21.

Alexander, M. (2012). *The new Jim Crow: Mass incarceration in the age of colorblindness.* New York, NY: New Press.

Ancheta, A. N. (2006). Civil rights, education research, and the courts. *Educational Researcher, 35*(1), 26–29.

Auerbach, S. (2002). 'Why do they give the good classes to some and not to others?' Latino parent narratives of struggle in a college access program. *Teachers College Record, 104*(7), 1369–1392.

Bell, D. A. (1979). Bakke, minority admissions, and the usual price of racial remedies. *California Law Review, 67*(1), 3–19.

Bell, D. A. (1992a). *Faces at the bottom of the well: The permanence of racism.* New York, NY: Basic Books.

Bell, D. A. (1992b). Racial realism. *Connecticut Law Review, 24*(2), 363–379.
Blakemore, J. (2006, February 2). Minutes of the 2005/2006 Graduate Council. Retrieved from http://www.siu.edu/gradschl/council/mn060202.htm (no longer accessible).
Blakemore, J., & Koropchak, J. (2006, April 26–29). *Recent challenges to graduate diversity programs at Southern Illinois University*. Presentation given at the American Association for Affirmative Action 32nd Annual Conference, Tampa, FL.
Brayboy, B. M. J. (2005). Transformational resistance and social justice: American Indians in Ivy League universities. *Anthropology & Education Quarterly, 36*(3), 193–211.
Brown, D. A. (2003). *Critical race theory: Cases, materials, and problems*. St. Paul, MN: Thomson-West.
Brown, D. A. (2004). Fighting racism in the twenty-first century. *Washington and Lee Law Review, 61*(4), 1485–1500.
Brooks, R. L. (2009). *Racial justice in the age of Obama*. Princeton, NJ: Princeton University Press.
Center for Equal Opportunity. About. Retrieved from http://www.ceousa.org
Chapman, T. (2007). Interrogating classroom relationships and events: Using portraiture and critical race theory in education research. *Educational Researcher, 36*(3), 156-162.
Consent decree. (2006, February). *United States of America v. The Board of Trustees of Southern Illinois University*. Retrieved from http://news.siu.edu/news/February06/020906bot6002.jsp
Crenshaw, K. W., Gotanda, N., Peller, G., & Thomas, K. (Eds.). (1995). *Critical race theory: The key writings that formed the movement*. New York, NY: New Press.
Czubaj v. Ball State University, No. 04-1001, 2004 U.S. App. WL 1873213 (7th Cir.Aug. 13, 2004).
Davidson, M. N., & Foster-Johnson, L. (2001). Mentoring in the preparation of graduate researchers of color. *Review of Educational Research, 71*(4), 549–574.
DeCuir, J. T., & Dixson, A. D. (2004). 'So when it comes out, they aren't that surprised that it is there': Using critical race theory as a tool of analysis of race and racism in education. *Educational Researcher, 33*(5), 26–31.
Delgado Bernal, D. (2002). Critical race theory, Latino critical theory, and critical raced-gendered epistemologies: Recognizing students of color as holders and creators of knowledge. *Qualitative Inquiry, 8*(1), 105–126.
Delgado Bernal, D., & Villalpando, O. (2002). An apartheid of knowledge in academia: The struggle over the 'legitimate' knowledge of faculty of color. *Equity & Excellence in Education, 35*(2), 169–180.
Delgado, R. (1989). Storytelling for oppositionists and others: A plea for narrative. *Michigan Law Review, 87*(8), 2411–2441.
Delgado, R., & Stefancic, J. (Eds.). (2000). *Critical race theory: The cutting edge* (2nd ed.). Philadelphia, PA: Temple University Press.
Deyhle, D. (1995). Navajo youth and Anglo racism. Cultural integrity and resistance. *Harvard Educational Review, 65*(3), 403–444.
Dixson, A. D., & Rousseau, C. K. (Eds.). (2006). *Critical race theory in education: All God's children got a song*. New York, NY: Routledge.
Duncan, G. A. (2002). Critical race theory and method: Rendering race in urban ethnographic research. *Qualitative Inquiry, 8*(1), 85–104.
Ewick, P., Kagan, R. A., & Sarat, A. (1999). *Social science, social policy, and the law*. New York, NY: Russell Sage Foundation.
Fisher v. University of Texas at Austin, 631 F.3d 213 (5th Cir. 2011).
Grutter v. Bollinger et al. 539 U.S. 306 (2003).
Gusa, D. L. (2010). White institutional presence: The impact of Whiteness on campus climate. *Harvard Educational Review, 80*(4), 464–489.
Harris, C. I. (1993). Whiteness as property. *Harvard Law Review, 106*(8), 1707–1791.
Harris, C. I. (2002). Critical race studies: An introduction. *UCLA Law Review, 49*(5), 1215–1240.
Holzer, H. J., & Ludwig, J. (2003). Measuring discrimination in education: Are methodologies from labor and markets useful? *Teachers College Record, 105*(6), 1147–1178.

Houh, E. M. S. (2005). Critical race realism: Re-claiming the antidiscrimination principle through the doctrine of good faith in contract law. *University of Pittsburgh Law Review, 66*(3), 455–520.

Jaehnig, K. C. (2004, September 8). NSF funds 'Bridge to the Doctorate' program. Retrieved from http://news.siu.edu/news/September04/090804kj4101.html

Johnson, R. B., & Onwuegbuzie, A. J. (2004). Mixed methods research: A research paradigm whose time has come. *Educational Researcher, 33*(7), 14–26.

Ladson-Billings, G. (1998). Just what is critical race theory and what's it doing in a nice field like education? *International Journal of Qualitative Studies in Education, 11*(1), 7–24.

Ladson-Billings, G., & Tate, W. F. (1995). Toward a critical race theory of education. *Teachers College Record, 97*(1), 47–68.

Lawrence, C. R. (1987). The id, the ego, and equal protection: Reckoning with unconscious racism. *Stanford Law Review, 39*(2), 317–388.

Lewis, T. (2006, February 15). Under pressure from Justice Dept., Southern Illinois University agrees to change minority fellowships. Retrieved from http://www.civilrights.org/equal-opportunity/education/under-pressure-from-justice-dept-southern-illinois-university-agrees-to-change-minority-fellowships.html

Liptak, A. (2011, October 16). College diversity nears its last stand. *The New York Times*, Sec. 4, p. 4.

López, G. R. (2003). The (racially neutral) politics of education: A critical race theory perspective. *Educational Administration Quarterly, 39*(1), 68–94.

Lynn, M., & Parker, L. (2006). Critical race studies in education: Examining a decade of research on U.S. schools. *Urban Review, 38*(4), 257–290.

Lynn, M. (1999). Toward a critical race pedagogy: A research note. *Urban Education, 33*(5), 606–626.

Matsuda, M. (1987). Looking to the bottom: Critical legal studies and reparations. *Harvard Civil-Rights-Civil Liberties Law Review, 22*, 323–399.

Matsuda, M., Lawrence, C., Delgado, R., & Crenshaw, K. (1993). *Words that wound: Critical race theory, assaultive speech, and the first amendment*. Boulder, CO: Westview Press.

Minutes of the Special Meeting of the Board of Trustees. (2006, February 8). Southern Illinois University. Retrieved from www.siu.edu/~botmeet/Feb06/206minutes.pdf (no longer accessible).

Moses, M. S., & Saenz, L. P. (2008). Hijacking education policy decisions: Ballot initiatives and the case of affirmative action. *Harvard Educational Review, 78*(2), 289–310.

National Center for Education Statistics [NCES]. (2009, August). Selected statistics for degree-granting institutions enrolling more than 15,000 students in 2007: Selected years, 1990 through 2007–08. Washington, DC: U.S. Department of Education. Retrieved from http://nces.ed.gov/programs/digest/d09/tables/dt09_236.asp

Neville, H. A., Lilly, R. L., Duran, G., Lee, R. M., & Browne, L. (2000). Construction and initial validation of the color-blind racial attitudes scale (CoBRAS). *Journal of Counseling Psychology, 47*(1), 59–70.

Mickelson, R. A. (2003). When are racial disparities in education the result of racial discrimination? A social science perspective. *Teachers College Record, 105*(6), 1052–1086.

Parks, G. S. (2007). Critical race realism: Towards an integrative model of critical race theory, empirical social science, and public policy. Cornell Law Faculty Working Papers Series. Retrieved from http://lsr.nellco.org/cornell/clsops/papers/23

Parks, G. S., Jones, S., & Cardi, W. J. (Eds.). (2008). *Critical race realism: Intersections of psychology, race, and law*. New York, NY: New Press.

Pollock, M. (2008). *Because of race: How Americans debate harm and opportunity in our schools*. Princeton, NJ: Princeton University Press.

Poshard, G. (2006). Remarks by Dr. Glenn Poshard, President of Southern Illinois University. SIU Board of Trustees Meeting, February 8, 2006. Retrieved from http://news.siu.edu/news/February06/020806bot6001.jsp (no longer accessible).

Quaintance, Z. (2005, November 13). University faces federal lawsuit. Retrieved from http://newshound.de.siu.edu/fall05/stories/storyReader$1332

Schmidt, P. (2006, February 3). Southern Illinois U. and Justice Dept. near accord on minority fellowships. *The Chronicle of Higher Education*, p. A26. Retrieved from http://chronicle.com/article/Southern-Illinois-U-and/12426/

Schmukler, K. R., Thompson, E. M., & Crosby, F. J. (2008). Affirmative action: Images and realities. In G. Parks, S. Jones, & W. J. Cardi (Eds). *Critical race realism: Intersections of psychology, race, and law* (pp. 155–164). New York, NY: New Press.

Skrla, L., Scheurich, J. J., Garcia, J., & Nolly, G. (2004). Equity audits: A practical leadership tool for developing equitable and excellent schools. *Educational Administration Quarterly, 40*(1), 133–161.

Smith, W. A., Yosso, T. J., & Solórzano, D. G. (2007). Racial primes and Black misandry on historically White campuses: Toward critical race accountability in educational administration. *Educational Administration Quarterly, 43*(5), 559–585.

Solórzano, D. G. (1998). Critical race theory, race and gender microaggressions, and the experience of Chicana and Chicano scholars. *International Journal of Qualitative Studies in Education, 11*(1), 121–136.

Solórzano, D. G, & Yosso, T. (2001). Critical race and LatCrit theory and method: Counter-storytelling. *International Journal of Qualitative Studies in Education, 14*(4), 471–495.

Solórzano, D. G., & Yosso, T. J. (2002). Critical race methodology: Counter-storytelling as an analytical framework for education research. *Qualitative Inquiry, 8*(1), 23–44.

Southern Illinois University Board of Trustees. (2006). Minutes of the Special Meeting of the Board of Trustees, February 8, 2006. Carbondale, IL: Author.

Suvannunt v. Thompson, No. 02-2797 58 Fed. Appx. 233; 540 U.S. 910, App. (7th Cir., February 18th, 2003).

Taylor, E. (2000). Critical race theory and interest convergence in the backlash against affirmative action: Washington State and Initiative 200. *Teachers College Record, 102*(3), 539–560.

Tate, W. F. (1997). Critical race theory and education: History, theory, and implications. In M. Apple (Ed.), *Review of research in education* (pp. 195–247). Washington, DC: American Educational Research Association.

Teranishi, R. T. (2010). *Asians in the ivory tower: Dilemmas of racial inequality in American higher education*. New York, NY: Teachers College Press.

United States of America v. The Board of Trustees of Southern Illinois University, 4:06-cv-04037-JPG-DGW (2006).

University of Delaware abandons session on diversity: Effort to teach tolerance in dormitories attacked as 'thought reform.' (2007, November). *The Chronicle of Higher Education, LIV*(12).

Valdes, F., Culp, J. M., & Harris, A. P. (Eds.). (2002). *Crossroads, directions, and a new critical race theory*. Philadelphia, PA: Temple University Press.

Vaught, S. E. (2011). *Racism, public schooling, and the entrenchment of White supremacy: A critical race ethnography*. Albany, NY: State University of New York Press.

Villalpando, O. (2003). Self-segregation or self-preservation? A critical race theory and Latina/o critical theory analysis of a study of Chicana/o college students. *International Journal of Qualitative Studies in Education, 16*(5), 619–646.

Welner, K. G. (2006). K–12 race-conscious student assignment policies: Law, social science, and diversity. *Review of Educational Research, 76*(3), 349–382.

Welner, K. G. (2012). Scholars as policy actors: Research, public discourse, and the zone of judicial constraints. *American Educational Research Journal, 49*(1), 7–29.

Wendler, W. (2005, March 23). State of the University Address. Retrieved from http://www.siuc.edu/chancel/StateOfUniversity2005/index.html (no longer accessible).

Yosso, T. J. (2006). *Critical race counterstories along the Chicana/Chicano educational pipeline*. New York, NY: Routledge.

Yosso, T. J., Parker, L., Solórzano, D. G., & Lynn, M. (2004). From Jim Crow to affirmative action and back again: A critical race discussion of racialized rationales and access to higher education. *Review of Research in Education, 28*(1), 1–25.

Yun, J. T., & Moreno, J. F. (2006). College access, K–12 concentrated disadvantage, and the next 25 years of education research. *Educational Researcher, 35*(1), 12–19.

FIVE

A Critical Race Analysis of the Gaslighting Against African American Teachers

Considerations for Recruitment and Retention

Tuesda Roberts and Dorinda J. Carter Andrews

If and when . . . [the Blacks] are admitted to these [public] schools certain things will inevitably follow. Negro teachers will become rarer and in many cases will disappear. (Du Bois, 1960, p. 163)

In a war there must be some casualties, and perhaps the Black teachers will be the casualties in the fight for equal education of Black students. (Ethridge, 1979, p. 220)

Introduction

In the midst of the celebratory advances of the Civil Rights Movement made during the 1950s and 1960s, these two sobering quotes illuminate the toxic effects of institutional and structural racism on the educational and economic vitality of the Black[1] community pre- and post-*Brown v. Board of Education* (1954). Their sentiments underscore the seemingly systematic removal of Black educators[2] from facilitating the positive and healthy development of Black children, and from the teaching profession altogether. This occurred over an extended period of time, in which Black children were forcibly educated by White teachers either in predominantly White contexts, or in predominantly Black, underresourced contexts. Yet, today we are bombarded with news headlines that bemoan the nation's need for Black teachers. News articles and speeches continuously highlight a "search [for] Black teachers" (Brennan, 2011), and describe Black educators as "a tragically endangered species" (Daniels, 2012; Williams, 2012) and "a missing ingredient" (*Tri-State Defender*, 2009) in public schools. In a speech he delivered at the HBCU[3] Symposium at North Carolina Central University Centennial on June 3, 2010 Arne Duncan stated,

> Less than 15 percent of our teachers are black or Latino. It is especially troubling that less than two percent of our nation's 3.2 million teachers are African-American males. On average, roughly 200,000 new teachers are hired a year in America—and just 4,500 of them are black males. It is not good for any of our country's children that only one in 50 teachers is a black man. (Duncan, 2010).

We argue that it is not good for any of our nation's children that only 7% of K–12 public school teachers are African American (U.S. Department of Education, 2009b). While Duncan's aforementioned words illuminate the dearth of Black male teachers in U.S. schools, his speech lacks attention to the sociohistorical factors that led to the disenfranchisement, marginalization, and overall invisibility of African American teachers writ large in the profession. In this chapter, we demonstrate how the professional isolation, dismissal, and disavowal of African American educators have worked together to create a false, normalized master narrative about their relationship to the profession of teaching. Throughout our nation's history—and even present-day—a continual narrative of the limited presence of Black teachers in teaching has served as an abuse tactic to delude the American public into believing that the Black community is solely at fault for the country's supposed disinterest in successfully recruiting and retaining Black educators into the teaching profession. The lack of realization by those in power that Black teachers' presence in classrooms benefits *all* children is also a failure to realize that the demographic imperative should be vigorously addressed, because the nation's student body has become more ethnically diverse. Our argument is grounded in the use of Critical Race Theory, Narratives-as-Identity, and a concept called *gaslighting*, as frameworks to aid in illuminating this manipulation of the American people.

Gaslighting

Gaslighting is a form of emotional abuse where the abuser intentionally manipulates the physical environment or mental state of the abusee, and then deflects responsibility by provoking the abusee to think that the changes reside in their imagination, thus constituting a weakened perception of reality (Akhtar, 2009; Barton & Whitehead, 1969; Dorpat, 1996; Smith & Sinanan, 1972). By repeatedly and convincingly offering explanations that depict the victim as unstable, the abuser can control the victim's perception of reality while maintaining a position of truth-holder and authority. We propose that a sociohistorical gaslighting against Black educators has yielded a culturally reified designated identity rooted in rhetoric and practices that presume their (much like that of African American students) undesirability, incompetence, and general lack of interest in and/or commitment to education. We argue that this *designated identity narrative* gets constructed and reconstructed historically and contemporarily by broadly positioning Black educators as outsiders and as unqualified.

In the remainder of this chapter, we demonstrate how macro-level (i.e., *Brown*) and micro-level (i.e., state- and district-level) laws and policies have historically and contemporarily positioned the Black educator as "outsider" and as "on the margins." We also describe how the normalized master narrative frames Black educators as seemingly "unqualified" in the face of racist practices that perpetuate White supremacy by historically privileging White educators and disenfranchising Black educators. We view Sfard and Prusak's (2005b) narrative theory of identity through the lens of Critical Race Theory, as a way to argue the deficit master narrative about Black educators' relationship to the teaching profession. Following this historical analysis, we explore critical considerations of Black and White educators, and present factors that contribute both to the maintenance of unstable learning environments for African American youth, and the perpetuation of defamatory narratives about African American educators. In conclusion, we suggest strategies for inserting critical designated identity narratives into educational discourse, and capitalizing on the proven dedication of African American educators.

Narratives as Identity

Before exploring the historical and contemporary treatment of African American educators, it is necessary to first discuss the two theories that inform the positions we argue: Narratives-as-Identities and Critical Race Theory. Sfard and Prusak cosigned with Holland & Lave (2001) in their consideration of identity as being "man-made and . . . constantly created and re-created in interactions between people" (Sfard & Prusak, 2005b, p. 15). Moreover, Sfard and Prusak (2005b) described identity narratives (collections of stories) as being "reifying, endorsable and significant" (p. 16). Specifically, narratives become reified as they are repeated, endorsable if the identity-builder associates the story with the then-current state of affairs, and significant if the story is central to the identity-builder's understanding of reality such that any changes to the story would alter how they feel about the person they are identifying.

Within their narrative theory of identity, Sfard and Prusak differentiated between narratives about the "actual state of affairs" (actual identities), and those that address a state of affairs that is "expected to be the case, if not now, then in the future" (designated identities) (Sfard & Prusak, 2005b, p. 18). For the sake of this analysis, we focus on designated identities, in order to illuminate their normalizing power. Whether designated identities become reified through subtle means, the muting of historical or present realities, or through the deflection of responsibility, we contend that the designated identity which marginalizes African American educators has become so infused in our national discourse that it has become nearly imperceptible in its alteration of reality. Furthermore, we posit that gaslighting against Black educators has allowed for this type of altering to occur. Although educational researchers and school districts could be targeted as (re)enforcers of these "othering" and deficit narratives, our intention is not to place the responsibility for the damaging discourse on any single entity. Rather, what follows is a call for a cross-sectional, critical consideration of the persistent designated identity assigned to African American educators. This call for critical designated identities is reflective of Sfard and Prusak's (2005a) own declaration of designated identities' rather nebulous origins:

> Like any other story, it [the designated identity] is created from narratives that are floating around. One individual cannot count as the sole author even of those stories that sound as if nobody has told them before. To put it differently, identities are products of discursive diffusion—of our tendency to recycle strips of things said by others even if we are unaware of these texts' origins. (p. 46)

It is our intention to not only discuss the dangers of uniformly accepting designated identities, but to (re)introduce "strips" of knowledge about African American educators that, when woven into the fabric of discourse, can lead to a more intricate and complicated tapestry of reality.

Speaking Back to Designated Narratives

In this analysis, we take up the challenge of extending the notion of designated identities by calling their very nature into question. We are not of the opinion that designated identities, as described by Sfard and Prusak, do not exist; rather, that they have the ability to alter the collective understanding of the masses while oppressing a selected few for the purpose of diminishing or altering narratives that could significantly change the way the identified are viewed. Although we recognize the ability and desire of individuals to act on their own behalf as participants in their identifying discourses, the actual ability to "play decisive roles in determining the dynamics of social life and in shaping individual activities" is often curtailed by the stratifying structures, beliefs, and practices of any given society (Sfard & Prusak, 2005b, p. 15). If indeed, then, individuals have great difficulty countering their childhood designated identities, and if "tales of one's repeated success are likely to reincarnate into stories of special 'aptitude,' 'gift,' or 'talent,' whereas those of repeated failure evolve into motifs of 'slowness,' 'incapacity,' or even 'permanent disability'" (Sfard & Prusak, 2005b, p. 18), by extension, collective groups may encounter challenges in refuting uninterrogated and unwarranted third-person identities constructed to portray these groups as weak or as out of touch with the demands of reality.

Likewise, although we agree with the notion that the "difference between identity as a 'thing in the world' and as a discursive construct is subtle," to focus on identifying narratives or "stories as such, accepting them for what they appear to be: words that are taken seriously and that shape one's actions" (Sfard & Prusak, 2005b, p. 21), could encourage a form of historical amnesia where the oppressive actions of yesterday are divorced from the subsequent narratives as they may appear today. In other words, an uninterrogated acceptance of contemporarily designated identities may render the identified persons or collective groups as unstable, while simultaneously removing the burden of responsibility from the narrators who materially and discursively oppressed them. The case of African American educators is an example of sociohistorical gaslighting, in that the disparaging discourse surrounding their qualifications and commitment to the field of education is generally void of critical considerations about the systematic dismantling of the Black teaching force following *Brown I* and *II*, their continued willingness to work in settings others deem undesirable, and the exodus of White educators from predominantly non-White schools.

Critical Race Theory

Critical Race Theory (CRT) serves as a response to power imbalances protected by the unquestioned acceptance of designated identities. CRT has its foundations in Critical Legal Studies, and began to take noticeable shape from the 1980s with works by Bell (1989), Crenshaw, Gotanda, Peller, and Thomas (1995), and Matsuda, Lawrence, Delgado, and Crenshaw (1993). At the forefront of its critiques of *Brown*, the U.S. Civil Rights Movement, and more contemporary social ills, CRT asserts that racism is "normal, not aberrant, in American society," such that its political, economic, and educational practices that structurally advantage Whites are barely perceptible (Delgado, 1995, p. xiv). As such, CRT utilizes historical analyses and the voices of marginalized people of color to provide counterstories to master narratives shrouded in meritocracy, colorblindness, liberalism, and race-neutral policies (Delgado & Stefancic, 2001). Additionally, CRT's focus on counterstories and antiessentialism allows us vehicles by which to argue for the complex personal and professional experiences of Black educators over time as impacted by racism. It also creates an avenue for a move away from a single story that can depict their entrance into and dissipating presence in the teaching profession. Thus, CRT and Narratives-as-Identities both promote narratives as important parts of individual and collective identities. The use of CRT as a part of our call for a more critical, nuanced understanding of Sfard and Prusak's Designated

Identities is appropriate, given CRT's recognition that a common occurrence in discussions about race is a tendency not only to render the complex simple, but to disregard the historic conflict in which it was spawned. This amnesia may not be deliberate, but reflects the ordinary narcissism of each generation, or the worry that dwelling on the past may inhibit our ability to move beyond it (Taylor, Gillborn, & Ladson-Billings, 2009).

Sanctioned Discrimination and Designated Identities

Mainstream U.S. White Americans have, at different times, to varying degrees, and in multiple ways, either been the perpetrators or victims (explained later in the chapter) of gaslighting around the legitimacy and very presence of African American teachers. Through the establishment and enforcement of a dual school system that geographically marginalized African American teachers to all-Black schools, a designated identity was created that positioned African American teachers to be as professionally and socially distant and "othered" as the neighborhoods in which they worked. Professionally, the dual school system situated Black educators as best suited to teach Black youth, in accordance with the country's historical tradition of maintaining a separation between White and non-White races. This specific structuring of the educational system reinforced the "natural order" of segregation by both marking and confirming that Black teachers were singularly qualified to, and thus should, teach students that looked like them. Consequently, the lived possibility that African American teachers were professionals in the same right as White teachers, and that they, too, could effectively educate White children was one that was legally denied. The enforced designated identity of African American teachers as professional "others," then, was a practice in sociohistorical gaslighting, because the effective hiding of African Americans from the schooling of White Americans supported the notion of the educators' social incompatibility and questionable professional status.

With the greatest legal threat to the dual school system on the horizon, the ideological, social, and legal conditions that fostered the gaslighting against African American teachers were also facing a perilous future. A poignant example of how the *Brown* decisions posed a threat to the designated identity of African American teachers can be seen in a 1953 letter written by Wendell Godwin, then the superintendent of Topeka's public schools, to Miss Darla Buchanan, an African American teacher in the same school district. The letter, written just over a year before the Supreme Court ruled on the *Brown* case, in part stated (quoted in Tillman, 2004, p. 280):

> If the Supreme Court should rule that segregation in the elementary grades is unconstitutional our Board will proceed on the assumption that the majority of people in Topeka will not want to employ negro teachers next year for White

children. It is necessary for me to notify you now that your services will not be needed for next year. This is in compliance with the continuing contract law. . . . You will understand that I am sending letters of this kind to only those teachers of negro schools who have been employed during the last year or two. It is presumed that, even though segregation should be declared unconstitutional we would have need for some schools for negro children and we would retain our negro teachers to them. I think I understand that all of you must be under considerable strain, and I sympathize with the uncertainties and inconveniences which you must experience during this period of adjustment. I believe that whatever happens will ultimately turn out to be best for everybody concerned.

A generous reading of the letter would suggest a cognitive dissonance on the superintendent's part concerning the appropriateness of Black teachers being at the helm of a classroom of White students. A closer, more critical reading would render Godwin as an executor of the gaslighting project that restricted African American educators to the margins of proper society. Godwin justified the nonrenewal of Ms. Buchanan's contract, not based on her qualifications or professional outcomes, but rather, because "the majority of the people in Topeka" believed that although the color of her skin made her an undesirable teacher for White children, she remained an ideal teacher for Black children. Ironically, even though Godwin declared that school segregation should be declared unconstitutional, the idea that African American teachers had as much of a legal and moral right to maintain their professional standing in those same, would-be desegregated halls was unconscionable, and was a notion that he, by virtue of the preference of other White Topekans or his own volition, did not support.

While Godwin's letter can be considered a local historical artifact simultaneously representative of White Americans' rhetorical ambivalence concerning desegregation, and of the designated identities used to support the gaslighting project to ideologically and physically maintain the segregation of African American teachers from White students (and by extension White society), the scope of the gaslighting project can also be seen at the federal level. In his policy statement, *School Desegregation: "A Free and Open Society,"* President Richard Nixon (1970) invoked the *United States v. Montgomery County Board of Education* (1969) decision when he stated:

> Pupil assignments involve problems which do not arise in the case of the assignment of teachers. If school administrators were truly color blind and teacher assignments did not reflect the color of the teacher's skin, the law of averages would eventually dictate an approximate racial balance of teachers in each school within a system. (p. 16)

> Segregation of teachers must be eliminated. To this end, each school system in this nation, North and South, East and West, must move immediately, as the Supreme Court has ruled, toward a goal under which 'in each school the ratio

of White to Negro faculty members is substantially the same as it is throughout the system. (p. 21)

Nixon's public stance on the desegregation of the country's teaching force is further evidenced in a *Chicago Tribune* article that announced his administration's $3.2 million funding provision to retrain 1,500 African American teachers that had been demoted or fired ("U.S. to Aid Black Teachers in South," 1970). However, Nixon's sympathetic words and gestures take on a different tone when one attempts to square them with his opinions about African American educators expressed during a private conversation, and the details surrounding the funding. Although Nixon's policy statement on school desegregation officially positioned him as favorable to the desegregation of the nation's teaching force, he claimed in a 1972 Oval Office conversation that,

> Black children are not equal to white children and black teachers are not as good as white teachers. Now goddamn it, that happens to be the truth. So why the hell do you [buck?] against the truth. Isn't that the problem? Now you can't tell them that. That's the problem. (Nixon, 1972)

In the same conversation, the former president went on to say that "racial equality is something that is a figment of the imagination" (Conversation 685-003, 14 March, 1972, Miller Center Transcript). This not only counters his statement on desegregation, but also his 1969 inaugural address, when he stated:

> No man can be fully free while his neighbor is not. To go forward at all is to go forward together. This means black and white together, as one nation, not two. The laws have caught up with our conscience. (*Inaugural Addresses of the Presidents of the United States*, 2001, p. 136)

Nixon's careful crafting of public, political speech to either garner public support or to avoid the condemnation of his fellow Republicans (for a discussion on Nixon's use of the Southern Strategy and school desegregation, see Friedman and Levantrosser, 1991) is not unique to him, but it does speak to a presidentially sanctioned gaslighting project of intentionally manipulating national discourse for political gain, with the result being the (backdoor) continuation of conditions that supported mainstream, White Americans' designated identities of Black teachers as being unqualified and socially and intellectually inferior.

The aid allocated to help displaced Black teachers is an example of the manipulation of speech and action to avoid criticism while still protecting the status quo—a demonstration of interest convergence through color blindness and abstract liberalism. While the disbursement of $3.2 million to retrain Black teachers and principals who had been fired or demoted is in direct alignment with Nixon's public speech and nominal support for the desegregation of the teaching force, the specific channeling of the funds, and the assumptions embedded in the funding goals, are much more closely aligned with his private speech concerning racial equality. Don Davies, Associate Commissioner of the Bureau of Educational Personnel Development, indicated that as part of the aid program "teachers, to be trained at Negro teacher colleges, would get extra or refresher courses in reading, mathematics and English. Many would be trained to teach English as a 'second' language, to supplement Negro or Spanish-American dialects" (Waldron, 1969), and that the program "will insure that children in desegregated schools will not be denied an opportunity to be served by educational personnel of talent and experience" ("Fired Black Educators Offered Retraining Aid: Administration Declines to Challenge Negroes' Ouster in Southern Schools" 1970). Davies's comments offer a glimpse into how Nixon's private ideologies around race found their way into the actions of his administration. The program's assumption that the 1,500 African American teachers chosen to receive the funds were in need of "extra" or "refresher" courses in the core subjects both assumes and suggests that the firings and demotions were the result of the teachers' insufficient/inadequate training or unsatisfactory work. Furthermore, their preparation to teach English as a "second" language, versus Language Arts, would not only work to maintain the order of White teachers remaining in the "upper" or "standard" courses where they would be more likely to teach White students, but also to confirm the notion that African American and Latino students were (a) linguistically deficient, and (b) most appropriately taught by non-White teachers.

Perhaps the greatest indication that the supposedly benevolent retraining of those 1,500 African American teachers was a gaslighting exercise was the fact that the program failed to account for the root cause for the teachers' firing or demotions—the racist actions of White individuals and of school districts. Newspapers across the country noted the contradiction between the retraining program's assumption that African American teachers were losing their jobs based on subpar qualifications, and earlier Senate committee reports by the National Educators Association and reports released by the U.S. Office of Education that the primary cause behind the firings and demotions was in fact racial discrimination (Delaney, 1970; "Fired Black Educators Offered Retraining Aid," 1970; "Ousted Black Teachers," 1970). Ultimately, the aid program allowed the Nixon administration to rhetorically feign concern for racial and professional equality while functionally deepening segregation in the ranks of the nation's teachers and, by virtue of their loss of authority or outright removal, prolonged the delusion that African American teachers were ineffective and undesirable.

The question could be asked: How are mainstream White Americans the targets of gaslighting, when African American teachers were so clearly the ones paying the price of the manipulation (alluded to earlier in this chapter)? Before explaining why African American teachers should be more aptly described as collateral damage in this sociohistorical gaslighting project, a preview of the psychological texts describing the phenomenon of gaslighting (Akhtar, 2009; Barton & Whitehead, 1969; Dorpat, 1996; Lund & Gardiner, 1977; Smith & Sinanan, 1972) may prove instrumental. These texts reveal five basic and recurrent elements of the practice:

> The Gaslighter: The person or group who is not only actively manipulating reality but stands to directly benefit from said manipulation. Examples include spouses, romantic partners, psychoanalysts, administrators of health-care facilities, political figures, etc.
>
> The Gaslightee: The person or group whose perception of reality and/or lived experiences are intentionally and surreptitiously distorted through the manipulation of the gaslighter. By virtue of their possessions, influence, presence or absence, the gaslightee represents a desired reward for the gaslighter. Examples include nursing home patients; spouses; patients undergoing psychological therapy; voters; social, political, and economic strata, etc.
>
> The Object(s) of Manipulation: The physical objects or third parties that are manipulated by the gaslighter to distort the gaslightee's touch with reality and lived experiences. Examples include medication, doctors, historical facts, rhetoric, associates of the gaslightee, colleagues of the gaslighter, etc.
>
> The Consequence(s) Experienced by the Gaslightee: The detrimental effect suffered by the gaslightee as a consequence of the gaslightee's actions. The effects can be physical, financial, psychological, or social. Examples include the loss of property, confinement to psychiatric wards, suicidal thoughts, defamation as an insane individual.
>
> Reward(s) for the Gaslighter: The benefits received or experienced by the gaslighter as a consequence of their manipulative actions, and the resultant advantage gained when the gaslightee is disavowed. Like the consequences experienced by the Gaslightee, the gaslighter's rewards can be physical, financial, psychological, or social. Examples include acquisition of the gaslightee's property, the freedom to marry a secret lover, the advancement of a theory, absolution from the responsibility of being the Gaslightee's caretaker, etc.

The texts reveal gaslighting's primary goal to be the acquisition of a benefit through the intentional distortion of facts, objects, people, etc. The objects of manipulation are inconsequential casualties of the gaslighting project, and only serve the purposes of hiding the gaslighter's guilt and providing them with some form of advancement or gain acquired from the gaslightee. Barton and Whitehead coined the use of the term, *gaslighting*, as a form of psychological manipulation in 1969, and provided the example of a woman who became at odds with an administrator of her nursing home facility (see Table 5.1). The administrator, frustrated by the woman's presence, secretly served the woman a laxative, and used the patient's incontinence to support her request that a local psychiatric hospital admit her on the grounds of her being in a "confusional state" (Barton & Whitehead, 1969, p. 1259). Smith and Sinanan (1972) offered a more complex account of a husband who began an affair with a homeless young woman who had befriended the man's wife. Following the husband's dismissal of his wife's statements to hospital authorities that her children lived abroad (he claimed that the children were deceased), and the discovery that he had written letters to his children that their mother suffered from leukemia and was near death, an investigation by the hospital revealed that the mistress had seduced the man to the point of collusion, and that after being exposed, the woman broke all ties with the husband. In each of these cases, the objects of manipulation (medication, human emotions, perceptions of one's health condition, children, and doctors) are means to an end.

Table 5.1. Corporeal Gaslighting Projects

	Corporeal Gaslighting Projects		
	Barton and Whitehead	Smith and Sinanan—Project #1	Smith and Sinanan—Project #2
Gaslighter	Nursing home administrator	Mistress	Husband
Gaslightee	Nursing home patient	Husband and Wife	Wife
Object of Manipulation	Medication/ Doctor	Husband's affections toward his wife/ Wife's perceptions of her health condition	His children/ Wife's doctors
Reward for the Gaslighter	Absolution of caretaking responsibilities	Stable housing	Freedom to be with the mistress
Consequence for the Gaslightee	Committal to a psychiatric ward	Loss of wife/ Referral to a psychiatric ward	Referral to a psychiatric ward

Barton and Whitehead's nursing home administrator could have opted to alter the patient's food intake, or have given her a water pill in place of a prescribed medication—both of which could have potentially convinced the doctors that the patient was ill. The mistress in Smith and Sinanan's account could have chosen to manipulate the husband's understanding of his health, resulting in his admission to a psychiatric ward. This form of manipulation could have also opened a door for the mistress to find housing. In this instance, too, the specific object or form of manipulation is not nearly as important as the probability that the chosen object would successfully help the gaslighter achieve their selfish goal. In other words, the single greatest value of an object of manipulation lies not in the inherent value, nor in the specificity of the object itself, but rather in its distinct ability, when manipulated, to make the delusion believable, and thus bring the gaslighter closer to their anticipated reward.

Given the need to consolidate schools following the *Brown* decisions, an adjustment in the size and distribution of the nation's overall teaching force seemed plausible. The specific reduction in the number of African American teachers, and the narrative of deficiency advanced through the biased execution of policy protected segregationists' interests and endeared the gaslighters to their support base. Thus, African American teachers were not the targets of the gaslighting project, because in the eyes of the gaslighters, they did not possess the political clout, social advancement, nor professional expertise they sought. For example, John Ehrlichman, Presidential Assistant to Nixon on Domestic Affairs, is credited with urging the segregationist agenda upon then Health, Education, and Welfare Undersecretary, John Veneman, stating, "You know, Jack, the Blacks aren't where our votes are" (Friedman & Levantrosser, 1991, p. 146). Because the Black community did not represent a supportive group of voters, it stands to reason that Black teachers were better suited to be used as a tool to be manipulated in order to gain the favor of other voters. Ultimately, despite the tremendous damage done to the nation's Black teachers, they are not the gaslightees in the sociohistorical project to maintain racial inequities, but a mere object of manipulation, not only because they were aware of the injustices being imposed upon them (Ethridge, 1979; "Ousted Black Teachers," 1970; "U.S. Warned on Firings," 1971; Waldron, 1969), but also because they were considered to be politically expendable.

Consider the clear contrast between Superintendent Godwin's and President Nixon's approaches to gaining the popular support of the individuals whose interests they valued: Godwin used nonhiring to reduce the number of African American teachers, while Nixon used policy statements and funding to purportedly increase the number of African American teachers (see Table 5.2).

In both cases, the employment status of Black teachers functioned as the object of manipulation. Whereas Godwin called upon the collective strength of the designated identities rooted in the presumed objectionable nature of Black teachers to block their employment in desegregated schools, Nixon invoked color blindness to promote the fair entry of Black teachers into all schools, while privately endorsing narratives grounded in justified racial stratification. In both examples, the inherent undesirability of Black teachers was associated not with their qualifications or effectiveness, but with their Blackness. Furthermore, both men were engaging in the practice of gaslighting by concretely and ideologically reinforcing the relegation of African American teachers to all-Black schools, by virtue of popular consent or the supposed natural order of society. In contrast to traditional psychological or emotional gaslighting projects, the sociohistorical gaslighting project, using the marginalization and removal of African American teachers from public schools to retain a visage of the long-standing separation of races, acted as a manipulative form of interest convergence. It thus awarded its perpetrators social and political support, with the resultant consequence being the deceptive appearance of racial equity, when in fact the progress made toward the protection of civil rights was being covertly stalled or attacked. Ultimately, by actively removing African American teachers, opting to not hold authorities responsible for biased hiring practices, and branding African American teachers as professionally substandard and ill-fitted to teach White children, conditions were created that made the absence of African American teachers normal, expected, and a justified part of the identities specifically designated to them.

Table 5.2. Sociohistorical Gaslighting Projects

	Sociohistorical Gaslighting Projects	
Gaslighter	Godwin	Nixon
Gaslightee	White Citizens of Topeka	U.S.A. Citizens
Object of Manipulation	African American Teachers	African American Teachers
Reward for the Gaslighter	Retention of support from segregationists	Political support from segregationists/ Documented support for civil rights legislation
Consequence for the Gaslightee	Subjection to educational and social environments that foster the continued ideological and professional marginalization of African American teachers	Subjection to educational and social environments that foster the continued ideological and professional marginalization of African American teachers

In the mid-1980s, a call for the increased presence of African American teachers began to be sounded, and continues even in more recent times (Goodlad & Soder, 1994; Graham, 1987; Irvine, 1988, 1989; Su, 1993); yet in the 2007–2008 school year, African Americans represented only 6.7% of the nation's (public and private school) teachers (U.S. Department of Education, 2009b). This obvious imbalance in representation is often laced with deficit-laden narratives, hearkening back to a belief that Black people are less qualified to serve as equal contributors to society. Consider in 1987, the assertion made by the Dean of Harvard University's Graduate School of Education, that

> Black teachers can serve that function [role models] only if they are successful (and, for teachers, that means *academically* successful, so that they can, indeed, contribute to the education of the young). If black teachers, as a group, are

substantially and noticeably weaker than White teachers, their effectiveness as role models is dramatically diminished for students—both Black and White. (Graham, 1987, p. 599)

Not only do Dean Patricia Graham's comments indicate a belief that Black teachers conceived of success as something other than academic, that they were not already functioning as role models, they also reflect an apparent belief that Black teachers were not making meaningful contributions to children's education. Furthermore, her comments fail to acknowledge the fact that by 1952, 72% of all Black teachers held a college degree (Fairclough, as cited in Karpinski, 2006, p. 248), and that a national 1964 NEA report indicated that 55% of non-White versus 44% of White teachers had four years of collegiate preparation (as cited in Karpinski, 2006, p. 248). Dean Graham thereby perpetuated the master narrative that Black teachers were academically deficient, in spite of the fact that they have historically earned the necessary credentials at higher levels than their White peers. Ultimately, however, Graham's comments leave gatekeepers such as legislators, university teacher education programs, states, and school districts with "clean hands" in the drastically diminished presence of African American teachers and administrators.

Reintroducing "Strips" of Narratives

Although the underrepresentation of Black teachers is commonly known, it is our contention that what we see today is not an isolated incident to be solely accredited to a lack of competence or interest on the part of Black teachers. Instead, one should also consider historical restrictions to the profession, those imposed upon Black educators, in order to gain a more critical understanding of the state of Black educators.

Keeping this description of Black teachers' qualifications in mind, how was the Black teaching force impacted with the passing of *Brown I* and *II*? Samuel B. Ethridge estimated that between 1954 and 1965 over 38,000 African American educators in southern and border states lost their jobs due directly to the *Brown* decisions (as cited in (Hudson & Holmes, 1994)). Principals received the brunt of the dismissals. Between 1963 and 1970 roughly 50% of Black principals in Georgia were dismissed, and administrators in Kentucky and North Carolina fared worse, as 90% and 95% of their force was eliminated (Karpinski, 2006). Evidence of the resistance to school integration abounds with images of National Guardsmen escorting Black students into schools, and Governor George Wallace standing defiantly in front of a University of Alabama building. Less commonly known are the efforts taken to block Black teachers and administrators from integrating all-White schools. Legislatures and government officials took direct action to prevent this additional form of integration. Civic engagement was targeted by the Georgia State Board of Education in 1955 when they proposed to permanently revoke the teaching licenses of any teacher with membership in the NAACP (Perkins, 1989). The Alabama legislature in that same year entertained a bill which would have permitted local school boards to fire teachers without proof of justification, and would have blocked those dismissed Black teachers from appealing the decision (Haney, 1978). Fultz addressed the intentional isolation of Blacks from the education profession in his reference to an NEA report stating that the systematic elimination of tenure laws and the nonrenewal of contracts inflicted the greatest damage (Fultz, 2004). Outright resistance continued, and by 1957 some Southern states eliminated state requirements for public education, and passed legislation withdrawing financial support from schools that chose to integrate (Fultz, 2004). What these pieces of legislation reflect is a common, immediate, even preemptory and staunch reaction blocking Black educators from finding employment in previously all-White schools. These intentional and overt forms of resistance to retaining and hiring Black educators were characteristic of institutionally endorsed racism against African Americans, and flew in the face not only of the steadily increasing interest of African Americans in becoming educators, but in their higher levels of qualifications over their White peers.

In spite of the *Brown II* decision of 1955, and, according to Fultz and Haney, in great part due to the Civil Rights Act of 1964 and especially the Elementary and Secondary Education Act of 1965, integration dissenters gained a stronger foothold in their attempts to dismantle the Black teaching force. On the heels of these landmark acts, the Race Relations Information Center produced a 1970 report exposing the persistent disenfranchisement of Black educators due to three dominant trends:

1. The practice of districts hiring White teachers in significantly higher proportions than Black teachers,

2. The use of the National Teachers Examination as a gatekeeping instrument to disqualify prospective Black educators, and

3. The liquidation of Black principals (Fultz, 2004).

Haney makes a more direct connection between the Education Act of 1965 and Black teachers in his reference to Coahoma County, Mississippi. In this instance, the jobs of Black teachers and aides in Coahoma were reclassified, so as to place their positions under a category funded by Title I monies. The school board then failed to comply with federal regulations governing those newly reclassified teachers, which resulted in the cessation of funding. Even after these teachers were dismissed, they voluntarily taught for the remainder of the year while pursuing litigation against the Board. Ultimately, the Federal court found the Board's actions to be unconstitutional, and ordered that the educators' jobs be reinstated (Haney,

1978). Other successful cases contested teacher dismissal for civil rights activities, and those executed without reasonable "good faith." The 1970 *Singleton v. Jackson Municipal Separate School District* ruling was extremely direct in its order for "objective and reasonably nondiscriminatory standards" to prevent displaced teachers' positions from being filled by teachers of another race until all qualified applicants of the displaced teachers' race had been duly considered (*Singleton v. Jackson Municipal Separate School District*, as cited in Fultz, 2004, p. 32). These victories did not fully abate the tidal wave of Black educators dismissed from their positions; however, the dismissal of Black educators was garnering greater recognition.

The disproportionate dismissal of Black teachers and principals denied these men and women their right to practice their profession and thus make a living. As educators formed a significant percentage of the Black middle class, collectively losing nearly $250,000 a year (Tillman, 2004) inflicted unspeakable damage on the economic stability of the Black community. Their disenfranchisement also affected Black children, as it was the Black educators who were systematically removed from the decision-making processes governing the "tracking, placement, suspension and expulsion of Black students" (Karpinski, 2006, p. 257). Holmes further explicated the impact on the Black community by attributing a decline in self-esteem and aspirations, and remedial tracking of Black children to the drastic loss of Black teachers after *Brown* (cited in Hawkins, 1994). Although the current state of Black students and educators cannot be completely explained by the aftermath of *Brown v. Board of Education of Topeka* decisions, the loss of Black educators cannot be denied. Intentional, covert, and systematic efforts against these honored figures in the Black community are indeed shameful, and have had undeniable effects. These statistics and tactical methods indicate that the narrative Graham (1987) used to describe African American teachers in the late 1980s was not grounded within the context of their long-standing legacy of dedication to the profession of teaching, nor did it acknowledge the decimation of the Black teaching force due to White fear and discrimination following the mandates of *Brown I* and *II* to desegregate public schools.

As described by Sfard and Prusak (2005b), designated identities are narratives that represent an anticipated or "expected" state of affairs (p. 18). We propose, however, that expectations (for good or bad) are reached based on individuals' responses to identifying narratives they have heard, borne, or themselves designated in the past. Therefore, to accept these narratives "for what they appear to be"—without holding the identifying person accountable for critical self-reflection, for investigating their narratives' origins, and for possibly inflicting harm on the person they seek to identify—will yield damaging repercussions, especially in matters of race (p. 21). Wellman's (1977) description of racism, in fact, reads like an eerie byproduct of Sfard and Prusak's defense of narratives as identity. Wellman defined racism as, "culturally sanctioned beliefs which, regardless of the intentions involved, defend the advantages Whites have because of the subordinated positions of racial minorities" (p. xviii). Again, Sfard and Prusak asserted that identities are the products "of our tendency to recycle strips of things said by others even if we are unaware of these texts' origins," and that they should be accepted "for what they appear to be" (Sfard & Prusak, 2005b, p. 21; 2005a, p. 46). This is not to say that designated identities are by definition racist, but that when exercised in racialized contexts with power imbalances, they can become master-sanctioned, uninterrogated narratives that lead to oppression.

The natural consequences for accepting designated identities as they are, include:

1. Stalling the advancement of equity and social justice agendas due to the power of repeated narratives to move from designated to actual identities,
2. Minimizing or ignoring the perpetrators of past injustices, and
3. Silencing those who have been victimized by earlier discriminatory narratives, leaving them less able to call oppressors into question.

In the case of African American teachers, their lack of representation in the field must be narrated in a way that honors their long-standing pursuit of education—even when banned from doing so, prevented from entering institutions of higher learning, or systematically barred from their profession. Failing to do so would allow the gaslighting against African American teachers and their commitment to education to continue, by blaming them alone for the current state of affairs, and failing to take into consideration the fact that they officially and effectively had severe restrictions placed upon them as students and as educators.

African American Educators of Today

Focusing on the sociohistorical marginalization of African Americans from the collective identity of the United States could lead to a more accurate narrative about African American educators but, arguably, may also distract from the urgencies they may be experiencing today. As such, our attention will now turn to more contemporary considerations. The proposed goal of equitable distribution of resources, as represented by the mandated desegregation of U.S. public schools, was premised on the elimination of racially identifiable schools. Table 5.3 reveals that in many ways, the classroom remains a site of racial separation, with Black and Latino students attending school in urbanized, principle cities, and the majority of White students in schools at least 10 miles away from urbanized areas. These urban schools are typically located in residential areas with low tax bases, and primarily educate students of color and those with limited English proficiency. Teachers working at majority Black and Latino schools, and/or large numbers

Table 5.3. Public Elementary and Secondary Students and School Locales: 2007–2008, 2008–2009

	Total	City, large	City, mid-size	City, small	Suburban, large	Suburban, mid-size	Suburban, small	Town, fringe	Town, distant	Town, remote	Rural, fringe	Rural, distant	Rural, remote
Black	16.9	30.0	29.3	19.0	15.6	10.8	10.7	8.6	13.7	10.9	12.3	8.4	7.6
Hispanic/ Latino	21.5	39.6	28.2	22.9	22.0	17.7	16.4	15.5	14.6	17.3	13.9	6.9	7.7
White	54.9	21.2	35.0	50.3	54.7	65.6	67.6	72.8	68.4	64.8	68.8	81.7	76.1

\1\ Located inside an urbanized area and inside a principal city with a population of at least 250,000.
\2\ Located inside an urbanized area and inside a principal city with a population of at least 100,000, but less than 250,000.
\3\ Located inside an urbanized area and inside a principal city with a population less than 100,000.
\4\ Located inside an urbanized area and outside a principal city with a population of 250,000 or more.
\5\ Located inside an urbanized area and outside a principal city with a population of at least 100,000, but less than 250,000.
\6\ Located inside an urbanized area and outside a principal city with a population less than 100,000.
\7\ Located inside an urban cluster that is 10 miles or less from an urbanized area.
\8\ Located inside an urban cluster that is more than 10 but less than or equal to 35 miles from an urbanized area.
\9\ Located inside an urban cluster that is more than 35 miles from an urbanized area.
\10\ Located outside any urbanized area or urban cluster, but 5 miles or less from an urbanized area, or 2.5 miles or less from an urban cluster.
\11\ Located outside any urbanized area or urban cluster, and more than 5 miles but less than or equal to 25 miles from an urbanized area, or more than 2.5 miles but less than or equal to 10 miles from an urban cluster.
\12\ Located outside any urbanized area or urban cluster, more than 25 miles from an urbanized area, and more than 10 miles from an urban cluster.
NOTE: Detail may not sum to totals because of rounding. Race categories exclude persons of Hispanic ethnicity.
SOURCE: U.S. Department of Education, National Center for Education Statistics, Common Core of Data (CCD), "Public Elementary/Secondary School Universe Survey," 2008–09, and "Local Education Agency Universe Survey," 2007–08 and 2008–09; and "School District Finance Survey (Form F-33)," 2007–08. (This table was prepared November 2010.)

of English language learners, report challenges in filling vacant teacher positions, and poor facility conditions (Loeb, Darling-Hammond, & Luczak, 2005).

Table 5.4. Percentage Distribution of Public School Teachers by Race/Ethnicity and Select School Characteristics: 2007–2008

	Black, non-Hispanic	Hispanic, regardless of race	White, non-Hispanic
All public schools	7.0	7.1	83.1
Community type			
City	12.0	13.1	71.0
Suburban	6.3	6.2	84.6
Town	4.1	4.7	89.0
Rural	4.6	3.3	90.3
Student enrollment			
Less than 100	7.8	5.4!	84.0
100–199	6.2	2.3!	88.4
200–499	6.9	5.4	85.2
500–749	6.0	6.0	85.5
750–999	7.8	8.9	80.7
1,000 or more	7.9	9.8	78.9
% of K–12 students who were approved for free or reduced lunch			
0–34	2.9	3.0	91.9
35–49	6.4	5.9	85.4
50–74	9.2	8.9	78.6
75 or more	16.2	17.0	62.6

SOURCE: U.S. Department of Education, National Center for Education Statistics, Schools and Staffing Survey (SASS), "Public School Teacher, BIE School Teacher, and Private School Teacher Data Files," 2007–08.

What, then, can be said about the choices teachers make when looking for employment? In short, the pattern revealed in Table 5.3 of Whites concentrating residentially where people of color are not (White flight) is similarly reflected in

African American and White teachers' employment distribution patterns. Table 5.4 describes a similar employment profile among Black and Latino teachers; they tend to work in large urban schools with percentages of students on free and reduced lunch. Conversely, White teachers are more likely to work in small schools located in towns or rural areas with very low rates of students receiving free or reduced lunch (U.S. Department of Education, 2009b).

Although this data is only a snapshot of where teachers are currently working, and does not account for potential district-lead channeling of particular candidates to specific schools, Hanushek, Kain, and Rivkin (2004) suggested a possible link between teachers' residency and work site preferences: "if there is extensive residential segregation and teachers prefer to work closer to where they live, Blacks may rank predominantly Black schools much more highly than Hispanic or White" (p. 340). Furthermore, a study on New York City teachers' mobility within and outside of the district estimated that teachers who lived in New York City, three miles or less from their place of employment immediately prior to starting their position, were twice as likely to stay at that school. Whereas those living outside of New York City before starting their duties had a 20% chance of staying at the school for a minimum of five years, and a likelihood over 30% of leaving the district altogether (Boyd, Lankford, Loeb, & Wyckoff, 2005). These findings suggest that a promising way to fill those seemingly perpetually empty teacher positions could be to recruit and cultivate a school's teaching block from within the building, or by conducting direct recruitment in the areas in close proximity to the school. Careful and innovative recruitment efforts are essential to urban schools, not only because during any given school year White teachers (who constitute 83% of all public U.S. schools) demonstrate a preference to work away from areas most in need of teachers, but because over time, and even through school and district transfers, race remains a factor in the tendency of urban teachers to walk away (Boyd et al., 2005; Hanushek et al., 2004; Jacob, 2007; Scafidi, Sjoquist, & Stinebrickner, 2007). Thus, recruitment alone is not the answer. Districts must also determine ways to retain the teachers they acquire. It is our belief that the persistence of residential and professional segregation is a critical point for future investigations about African American teachers' continued marginalization. Together, the two patterns are potentially indicative of lingering racially divisive hiring practices and/or employment preferences, and could be instrumental in not only filling the many teacher vacancies in urban schools, but also in ensuring that all students will learn from teachers that reflect the brilliant mosaic of our nation's diversity.

So how do race, achievement, and retention intersect? First, we consider the impact of the students' race on the retention of teachers. Knowing the factors that lead to greater rates of retention can help individual schools identify their teachers' and students' priorities, and can help retain the qualified and effective teachers working with students who are acutely vulnerable to the long-term effects of poor academic skills. Boyd et al. (2005) found that it is highly qualified teachers who are most likely to quit teaching in New York City Schools, especially if they work in low-achieving areas. It was also observed that teachers who worked at low-performing schools with students of color, and who were male or lived outside of New York City before beginning employment were the most likely to either leave the district or to transfer within the district. The work of Hanushek et al. (2004) in Texas schools led to their observation that whether a teacher was moving from an urban to a suburban district or moving within an urban district, the tendency is for teachers to move to schools with better student achievement scores and fewer students of color. More specifically, for teachers transferring from large urban schools to suburban schools, there was not only a substantial increase in average test scores, but also a 14–20% fewer African American and Latino presence in the teachers' new schools. This trend, though to a lesser extent, was also noticeable among moves from one suburban school to another. A key finding was that the trend to seek out schools with fewer students of color only held true for White teachers, whereas "for Black teachers, the reactions to varying concentrations of Black students are almost exactly the opposite than for White in both sign and magnitude," although a far more modest level of test score increase was still evident (Hanushek et al., 2004, p. 347). Perhaps most striking was Hanushek's estimation that in order to negate the influence of student race on White educators' decision to leave, they would require a 25–40% increase in salary.

Statistics about the constant traffic of incoming and outgoing teachers should be supplemented with teachers' indications of why they enter the profession. This would have ramifications for those who recruit students into teacher education programs, and for those hiring teachers in our schools. Su's (1997) conclusions revealed a consistent social justice motivation among preservice teachers of color, especially among the African American participants. Some of their responses included:

> "I love working with kids. A lot of problems that exist in poor areas can be greatly reduced by intervening when the kids are young."

> "I will go where the poor minority populations dwell. Because there is a lot of negativity in textbooks. I will make it a point to supplement with my own knowledge to make the students feel validated. . . . Teachers have to take it upon themselves to solve the problem. You can't wait for the state to change texts or the district to change learning material. I will take it upon myself in one classroom." (Su, 1997, pp. 332, 333)

Overall, Su found that the preservice teachers of color were driven to favor working in urban settings by their critical awareness of social inequities, and by envisioning themselves as change agents in the transformation of schools and society at large. In contrast, "none of the White candidates expressed concerns for the conditions of education for the poor and minority children and what they could do for them as teachers" (Su, 1997, p. 331). Su's participants indicated that the study's interviews were the first or only time during their program of study that they were given an opportunity to speak about their self-perceptions of being change agents in schools. This is indicative of the continuing need for teacher educators and educational researchers to see the value of narratives, not only as data, but as tools necessary in the proper preparation of educators that are critically self-aware and socially conscious.

These studies and statistics about the present state of African American preservice and in-service educators reflect a more nuanced and accurate actual identity of African American educators. In sum, they acknowledge that although African American educators are grossly underrepresented in the U.S. teaching force, they:

1. Choose to work and remain in schools others prefer to leave, namely those with students of color, lower-achieving students (the commas separating these characteristics is intentional as none should function as a proxy for the other), and students from impoverished backgrounds who come from segregated urban areas,

2. Are motivated by the desire to be change agents against forms of social oppression, and

3. Are electing to do so while sacrificing the salary increases their colleagues often pursue by moving away from urban schools.

Challenging the Narratives

Returning to our call for a rejection of carelessly derived designated identities, we return to the words of Sfard and Prusak (2005b):

> In addition, although narrative osmosis goes mainly from designated to actual identities, one cannot exclude the possibility of influence that travels in the opposite direction. As implied by the common wisdom that "success begets success and failure begets failure," stories of victories and losses have a particular tendency for self-perpetuation. On their way into designated identities, tales of one's repeated success are likely to reincarnate into stories of this person's special "aptitude", "gift" or "talent", whereas the motifs of repeated failure would take the form of narratives on anything from "slowness" to "permanent disability". (p. 18)

There is much to say, then, about the actual and designated identities of African American teachers, but what is more important than sharing the narratives is that they be crafted responsibly and critically. A mere "responsible" designated narrative could very well only tell of their absence, supposed lack of qualification, and apparent disinterest in teaching. A critical view, on the other hand, would acknowledge that although White people in the United States have and continue to have limited exposure to African American teachers, due to long-standing *de jure* and *de facto* segregation in our communities and schools (and thus are less likely to experience the osmosis Sfard and Prusak speak of), African American educators are qualified, resilient, and committed to educating the youth of our nation. The reclamation of African American educators' actual identities, and the reconstruction of their designated identities are needed in order to end the more general practice of gaslighting against African Americans, where the ever-mutating construction of otherness and deficiency is rendered invisible, while African Americans are regarded as suffering from pathologies of anti-intellectualism, laziness, and poverty.

Next Steps

Ladson-Billings and Tate (1995) highlighted CRT's tradition of naming one's own reality (consider Sfard and Prusak's $_A A_A$ form of identity where the story originates and is told to one's self) by noting that by creating our own narratives, we can heal and preserve our moral selves against oppression, and can disrupt master narratives by creating social dissonance, bringing awareness to oppressors. To work toward this end, it is imperative that all educators, regardless of race, become familiar with the history of Black educators in the United States. This type of education will likely be new to many teacher education students, and should be presented by faculty members who are intellectually and socially well-acquainted with African American history, and can apply the critical lens needed to address the ingrained issue of power struggles in contemporary sites. In order to meet this goal, it will be just as important that schools and colleges of education recruit and retain knowledgeable African American faculty members with sound backgrounds in social criticism, so as to train future K–12 teachers. School district officials and principals should be held accountable for the active recruitment and retention of a diverse body of teachers that is fairly and equitably distributed across the district, as well as professional development and student-centered initiatives that acknowledge and support Black communities' desire to be involved in the education of their youth. These interventions at the K–12 and higher education levels will be bolstered significantly by forming true, reciprocal collaborations with Black community institutions, including neighborhood associations, civic organizations, churches, Greek letter sororities and fraternities, professional organizations, and historically Black colleges and universities (HBCUs). Finally, educational researchers' historically and socially critical contributions that illuminate the experiences and professional and academic contributions of African American teachers, successful practices in the recruitment and retention of African American teachers, and push-out factors at various stages along the professional trajectory should not be underestimated. While the historical and contemporary considerations presented in this chapter have been discussed according to a conceptual framework, careful examinations of the effects of the privatization of teacher preparation and schools, traditional university-based teacher education programs, various teacher incentive and evaluation programs, district and state-level employment policies and practices, and the effects of school and district consolidations on the diversity of the corps of teachers and administrators could yield key information about the marginalization and siphoning off African American teachers.

Sociohistorical gaslighting projects, such as the one being carried out against African American teachers and administrators, can be deflated when the acts of manipulation are brought to light in ways that

1. Remove or significantly diminish the benefits gained by the gaslighter,
2. Convince the gaslightees of their own victimhood, and motivate them to disrupt the acts of manipulation, or
3. Position the objects of manipulation in ways that increase their agency and empower them to prevent or to circumvent gaslighters' manipulation.

We believe that various stakeholders (including preservice and in-service African American educators, parents, and educational researchers, among others) can, in effect, short-circuit this gaslighting project by not only naming their own reality, but by using the tools they have mastered to engage in their own brand of praxis against individual and systemic gaslighters, in order to name the real consequences of policies and practices that have been used to disenfranchise African American teachers, and by extension, the families and communities they represent.

Notes

1. This quotation is taken from Du Bois's essay, "Whither Now and Why," originally delivered in 1960 as a speech given at Johnson C. Smith University. The essay was later published in the book, *The Education of Black People* (Du Bois, 1973; H. Aptheker, Ed.).
2. We acknowledge the common use of *African American* to refer to Africans enslaved in the United States of America and their descendants, as well as the use of *Black* to refer to the members of the African Diaspora, including those from the U.S. context. In this chapter, we have used both terms, not because they are interchangeable in all discussions, but rather, in recognition that a historical and contemporary consideration of educators affected by gaslighting would include individuals who could be described by either or both terms.
3. In this paper, we use the term, *Black educators*, to refer to Black teachers and administrators in U.S. schools. We use the term, *Black teachers*, to refer to Black individuals who teach students in the classroom.
4. Historically Black Colleges and Universities (HBCU).

References

Akhtar, S. (2009). *Comprehensive dictionary of psychoanalysis*. London: Karnac Books.

Barton, R., & Whitehead, J. A. (1969). The Gas-Light Phenomenon. *The Lancet, 293*(7608), 1258–1260.

Boyd, D., Hamilton Lankford, Loeb, S., & Wyckoff, J. (2005). Explaining the Short Careers of High-Achieving Teachers in Schools with Low-Performing Students. *The American Economic Review, 95*(2), 166–171.

Delaney, P. (1970, June 17). Negro Jobs Loss Found in Schools. *New York Times*, p. 1.

Dorpat, T. L. (1996). *Gaslighting, the double whammy, interrogation, and other methods of covert control in psychotherapy and psychoanalysis*. Seattle: J. Aronson.

Du Bois, W. E. B. (1960). Whither Now and Why. *Quarterly Review of Higher Education Among Negroes, 28*(3), 135–141.

Ethridge, S. B. (1979). Impact of the 1954 *Brown vs. Topeka Board of Education* Decision on Black Educators. *Negro Educational Review, 30*(4), 217–32.

Fired Black Educators Offered Retraining Aid: Administration Declines to Challenge Negroes' Ouster in Southern Schools. (1970, December 12). *Los Angeles Times (1923-Current File)*, p. a27. Los Angeles, Calif.

Friedman, L., & Levantrosser, W. F. (1991). *Richard M. Nixon: politician, president, administrator*. Westport, CT: Greenwood Press.

Fultz, M. (2004). The Displacement of Black Educators Post-*Brown*: An Overview and Analysis. *History of Education Quarterly, 44*(1), 11–45.

Goodlad, J. I., & Soder, R. (1994). *Teachers for Our Nation's Schools*. San Francisco: Jossey-Bass.

Graham, P. A. (1987). Black Teachers: A Drastically Scarce Resource. *The Phi Delta Kappan, 68*(8), 598–605.

Haney, J. E. (1978). The Effects of the *Brown* Decision on Black Educators. *The Journal of Negro Education, 47*(1), 88–95. doi:10.2307/2967104

Hanushek, E. A., Kain, J. F., & Rivkin, S. G. (2004). Why Public Schools Lose Teachers. *Journal of Human Resources, XXXIX*(2), 326–354.

Hawkins, B. D. (1994). Casualties: Losses among Black educators were high after *Brown*. *Black Issues in Higher Education, 10*(23), 26–31.

Hudson, M. J., & Holmes, B. J. (1994). Missing Teachers, Impaired Communities: The Unanticipated Consequences of *Brown v. Board of Education* on the African American Teaching Force at the Precollegiate Level. *The Journal of Negro Education, 63*(3), 388–393. doi:10.2307/2967189

Irvine, J. J. (1988). An Analysis of the Problem of Disappearing Black Educators. *The Elementary School Journal, 88*(5), 503–513.

Jacob, B. A. (2007). The Challenges of Staffing Urban Schools with Effective Teachers. *The Future of Children, 17*(1), 129–153.

Loeb, S., Darling-Hammond, L., & Luczak, J. (2005). How Teaching Conditions Predict Teacher Turnover in California Schools. *Peabody Journal of Education, 80*, 44–70.

Lund, C. A., & Gardiner, A. Q. (1977). The Gaslight Phenomenon—An Institutional Variant. *The British Journal of Psychiatry, 131*(5), 533–534. doi:10.1192/bjp.131.5.533

Nixon, R. (1970, March 24). School Desegregation: "A Free and Open Society"; Policy Statement by Richard Nixon, President of the United States. U.S. Department of Health, Education and Welfare. Retrieved from http://www.eric.ed.gov/ERICWebPortal/contentdelivery/servlet/ERICServlet?accno=ED039311

Ousted Black Teachers. (1970, December 22). *Chicago Daily Defender (Daily Edition) (1960-1973)*, p. 13.

Perkins, L. M. (1989). The History of Blacks in Teaching: Growth and Decline Within the Profession. In D. R. Warren (Ed.), *American teachers: histories of a profession at work*. New York: Macmillan.

Scafidi, B., Sjoquist, D. L., & Stinebrickner, T. R. (2007). Race, Poverty, and Teacher Mobility. *Economics of Education Review, 26*(2), 145–159.

Sfard, A., & Prusak, A. (2005a). Telling Identities: In Search of an Analytic Tool for Investigating Learning as a Culturally Shaped Activity. *Educational Researcher, 34*(4), 14 –22.

Sfard, A., & Prusak, A. (2005b). Identity That Makes a Difference: Substantial Learning as Closing the Gap between Actual and Designated Identities. *International Group for the Psychology of Mathematics Education* (Vol. 1, pp. 37–52). Cape Town, South Africa: International Group for the Psychology of Mathematics Education.

Smith, C. G., & Sinanan, K. (1972). The 'Gaslight Phenomenon' Reappears. *The British Journal of Psychiatry, 120*(559), 685 –686.

Su, J. Z. X. (1993). The Study of the Education of Educators: A Profile of Teacher Education Students. *Journal of Research and Development in Education, 26*(3), 125–132.

Su, Z. (1997). Teaching as a Profession and as a Career: Minority Candidates' Perspectives. *Teaching and Teacher Education, 13*(3), 325–340. doi:10.1016/S0742-051X(96)00021-2

Taylor, E., Gillborn, D., & Ladson-Billings, G. (2009). *Foundations of Critical Race Theory in Education*. New York: Routledge.

Tillman, L. C. (2004). (Un)Intended Consequences? *Education and Urban Society, 36*(3), 280–303. doi:10.1177/0013124504264360

U. S. to Aid Black Teachers in South. (1970, December 12).*Chicago Tribune (1963-Current file)*, p. 6. Chicago, Ill.

U. S. Warned on Firings. (1971, January 30).*New Pittsburgh Courier (1966-1981)*. Pittsburgh, Pa.

Waldron, M. (1969, July 16). Negro Educators Counseled on Aid: Urged to Apply for Grants to Better Teacher Training. *New York Times*.

Wellman, D. T. (1977). *Portraits of White racism*. Cambridge, UK: Cambridge University Press.

Williams, R. C. Jr. (2012). We Need More Black Teachers. *The Kansas City Star*. Retrieved from http://voices.kansascity.com/entries/we-need-more-black-teachers/

PART TWO

Access, Equity, and Climate Conditions in the K–16 Context

SIX

The Resource and Opportunity Gap

The Continued Significance of Race for African American Student Outcomes

John B. Diamond

The election of President Barack Obama in 2008 was hailed as a milestone in the march toward racial justice and equality. Some commentators suggested that his candidacy and election signaled a transition to a postracial politics in the United States (Schorr, 2008). The self-congratulatory tone of many commentators glossed over the stark racial inequality that continues to exist between African Americans[1] and Whites in income, wealth, incarceration rates, health outcomes, and educational opportunity (Alexander, 2010; Bonilla-Silva, 2001, 2003; Blank, Dabady, & Citro, 2004; Oliver & Shapiro, 1995; Shapiro, 2004).[2]

In education, the Black/White "achievement gap" has been a central focus in educational research, policy, and practice in recent decades (Ferguson, 2007; Jencks & Phillips, 1998).[3] This work has focused on Black/White disparities in grades, test scores, college enrollment, and high school and college graduation rates, all of which show White advantages over Blacks. However, much of this work fails to carefully unpack how race matters for education, and how differences in educational opportunity drive differences in school outcomes. Instead, race often remains under-theorized in work on the racial "achievement gap" (Ladson-Billings & Tate, 1995)—treated as an all-encompassing set of cultural characteristics, or as a variable in statistical analyses (O'Connor, Lewis, & Mueller, 2007; Zuberi, 2001). To understand how race matters for school outcomes, "we need to have an understanding of what the nature of the task of achievement is for African Americans as African Americans" (Perry, 2003, p. 4). That means carefully examining the relationship between race and educational opportunity.[4]

In what follows, I outline just a few of the myriad ways that race continues to matter for students' educational outcomes, by focusing on how historic and contemporary patterns of inequality contribute to structural inequality outside schools, differences in educational resource allocation inside schools, and everyday school processes that help maintain racial inequality (Diamond, 2006). These inequalities often go unrecognized. For instance, in a recent nationally representative survey, nearly eighty percent of Whites believed that "minority children" and "white children" in their communities have equal educational opportunities (Rose & Gallup, 2004), even though Black students (and their families) must navigate a demonstrably unequal landscape as they pursue education.[5]

Contemporary racial inequality has transformed from overt racial policies and practices to covert patterns that are more difficult to identify (Bonilla-Silva, 2001, 2003; Coates, 2011; Payne, 1984). Scholars have discussed this contemporary racial context as the post-civil rights era (Bonilla-Silva, 2001), or the new civil rights era (Pollock, 2008), which is characterized by a dominant ideology of color-blind racism (Bonilla-Silva, 2001, 2003; Collins, 2009; Forman & Lewis, 2006; Lewis, 2001). These scholars emphasize the shifting nature of the racial landscape, and highlight the ways in which racial stratification is reproduced through the normal functioning of ostensibly racially neutral institutions. As Bonilla-Silva (2001) wrote about this contemporary context, "whereas white privilege was achieved through overt and usually explicit racial practices, today . . . it is accomplished through institutional, subtle, and apparently nonracial means" (p. 12). Historically, for example, racial inequality was reinforced through legally sanctioned practices that helped maintain White supremacy. In education this meant *de jure* segregation of schools, and the allocation of vastly different resources across them. It also meant wholesale exclusion of African Americans from certain occupational categories, and even the most basic legal protections. In the contemporary context, racial inequality is maintained through more subtle processes, including *de facto* segregation and the normal functioning of educational institutions that maintain the unequal allocation of educational resources under the guise of an open, meritocratic system. In what follows, I build on this framing of contemporary racial inequality to discuss the resource and opportunity gap in education, and outline some of the ways that race continues to shape the educational outcomes of Black students.

Racial History, Contemporary Discrimination, and Structural Inequality

One cannot understand contemporary racial stratification without an appreciation for how racial privileges and penalties shape the contemporary racial landscape.⁶ For example, in the contemporary United States, a racial income gap exists between African Americans and Whites. African American families earn about sixty-seven cents for every dollar earned by Whites (Shapiro, 2004). This actually represents an improvement of historic patterns of income inequality. However, when compared to White families, Black families have substantially less wealth. African Americans possess about 14% of White wealth (Shapiro, 2004).⁷ Moreover, the racial wealth gap has been increasing. Between 1984 and 2007, the Black/White wealth gap increased from $20,000 to $95,000 (Shapiro, Meschede, & Sullivan, 2010). To understand this wealth disparity, one needs to look to the historic and contemporary processes that helped to create this pattern. Melvin Oliver and Thomas Shapiro (1995) referred to the cumulative impact of this history as the "sedimentation of racial inequality" (p. 5). They wrote that:

> To argue that blacks form the sediment of the American stratification order is to recognize the extent to which they began at the bottom of the hierarchy during slavery, and the cumulative and reinforcing effects of Jim Crow and de facto segregation through the mid-twentieth century. Generation after generation of blacks remained anchored to the lowest economic status in American society. The effect of this inherited poverty and economic scarcity for the accumulation of wealth has been to sediment inequality into the social structure. (p. 5)⁸

Suburbanization provides an example of one mechanism through which racial stratification was reinforced during the twentieth century. Between 1940 and 2000 the percentage of the United States population living in suburbs grew from 13.4% to 50% (Nicolaides & Wiese, 2006). Purchasing suburban homes was a major driving force behind wealth accumulation for those who moved to suburbs (Oliver & Shapiro, 1995). As a result of discriminatory state policies (Katznelson, 2005), racial discrimination in the real estate industry, and restrictive covenants among White, suburban residents, African Americans were largely excluded from this suburban population growth.⁹ In contrast to many Whites, who benefited from government-subsidized suburbanization (through low-interest-rate Federal Housing Authority (FHA) loans, for example), many African American communities suffered because of redlining—the decision not to make home loans in communities where African Americans lived. These practices meant that home values appreciated much less rapidly in cities (or declined in value), directly impacting Black city residents (Anyon, 1997; Oliver & Shapiro, 1995; Shapiro, 2004). This is particularly important, because a large percentage of wealth—what a family owns minus its debts—in most U.S. families comes from home ownership and the value of homes.

These differences in wealth have real implications for Black versus White educational opportunities. Stark differences in wealth mean that Whites are better positioned to use their assets to purchase homes in school districts that demonstrate better outcomes for their children. They do this by parlaying assets into advantages across domains such that additional residential options (rooted in historic discrimination and White racial privilege) lead to advantages in the educational domain (Johnson, 2006; Shapiro, 2004). Shapiro (2004) discussed these as transformative assets that allow Whites to gain important advantages in terms of the amount of inheritances, strategic infusions of money, the ability to pay for supplemental educational services, and the ability to buy educational materials for the home (e.g., books, computers, educational games, etc.). In other words, Whites are able to use transformative assets to accrue *unearned* educational advantages for their children (Shapiro, 2004).

These wealth disparities also mean that social class comparisons between African Americans and Whites must be made cautiously (Diamond, 2006; Gosa & Alexander, 2007; Pattillo, 2005; Pattillo-McCoy, 1999). Work that compares African Americans and Whites of the same social class, focusing on traditional measures such as income, college graduation, and employment status, overlook a critical component of racial inequality. As Shapiro wrote, "Black and White professionals in the same occupation earning the same salary typically move through life with significantly unequal housing, residential, and educational prospects, which means that their children are not really on the same playing field" (Shapiro, 2004, p. x).

Race continues to matter in the contemporary context across many other domains as well. For example, while a simplistic link between education and employment outcomes is often assumed, Blacks continue to face striking patterns of labor market discrimination (Pager, Bonikowski, & Western, 2009). In field tests conducted in New York, Black and Latino/a applicants were only half as likely to be called back for follow-up interviews or hired as White applicants with the same qualifications. Moreover, Black applicants with no criminal records were less likely to be hired than Whites who reported just being released from prison (Pager et al., 2009). While African Americans hold more pro-school attitudes than their White peers (Downey, 2008), even when they recognize discrimination in the labor market (Harris, 2008), such discrimination may lead *some* young African Americans to question the extent to which their educational credentials will be valued once they leave school. At the very least, it highlights some of the "extra social, emotional, cognitive, and political competencies required of African American youth, precisely because they are African American" (Perry, 2003, p. 4). Black students must commit to education while often recognizing that racial discrimination may impact the returns they receive for their commitment (Perry, 2003).

Institutional Inequality Inside Schools

Racial inequality outside schools is often compounded by unequal allocation of educational resources inside them. One example of this educational inequality is access to quality teachers. The quality of teachers that students are exposed to is a critical driver of students' educational outcomes (Konstantopoulos & Chung, 2011). Unfortunately, in comparison to White students, Black students attend schools with teachers who are less well-qualified on a number of dimensions (Darling-Hammond, Wei, & Johnson, 2009; Uhlenberg & Brown, 2004). Presley, White, & Gong (2005) combined several measures of teacher quality into a composite index called the teacher quality index (TQI).[10] They found that in Illinois, increases in percent low income and percent minority students led to decreases in teacher quality. In schools with 0–9% low-income students, only 5% of teachers were in the lowest teacher quality quartile. In schools with between 90 and 100% low-income students, 84% of teachers were in the lowest quartile. Likewise, when the percentage of minority students was below 50%, only 11% of teachers were in the lowest TQI quartile. In schools with 90–98% minority students 70% of teachers were in the lowest TQI quartile, and in schools between 99 and 100% minority, 88% of teachers were in the lowest quartile. This means that low-income students and students of color in Illinois are more likely to be taught by the least experienced and well-trained teachers. The pattern in Illinois is reflective of broader patterns. As Darling-Hammond et al. (2009) wrote,

> On any measure of qualification—extent of preparation, level of experience, certification, content background in the field taught, advanced degrees, selectivity of educational institution, or test scores on college admissions and teacher licensure tests—studies show that students of color . . . are disproportionately taught by less qualified teachers. (p. 614)

Access to quality teachers is associated with two other troubling contemporary patterns—the resegregation of schools (Orfield, 1996; Orfield & Lee, 2005), and secondary generation segregation through tracking (Mickelson, 2001). Even as the percentage of Asian, Black, and Latino/a students in U.S. schools has increased over the past several decades, White students still tend to be isolated in mostly White schools, with greater educational resources and higher-income students. For example, in schools that are predominantly Black, the percentage of low-income students is much higher than in predominantly White schools. Fifty percent of Black students in city schools in the U.S. attend schools where 75% or more of their classmates are from low-income families (Planty et al., 2009). As we have seen, as the percentage of racial minority and low-income students increases, the quality of teachers decreases.

Access to high-quality learning opportunities remains a problem when Black and White students attend the same schools, because of educational tracking and the distribution of teachers across tracks. Black students are concentrated in lower educational tracks in integrated schools, even when prior school achievement is taken into account (Clotfelter, 2004; Kelly, 2009; Lucas & Berends, 2007; Mickelson, 2001). Students in lower educational tracks experience a range of negative outcomes, from slower academic growth (Gamoran, 1987) to lower rates of college attendance (Lucas, 2001). Racialized tracking can also contribute to status hierarchies among students. This can further contribute to race-based conceptions of achievement, and the development of animosity between high- and low-performing students (Tyson, 2011).

These disadvantages in track placement are linked to the structural inequalities documented above. Affluent (and often White) parents use their social class backgrounds, social networks, and knowledge of educational contexts to secure these privileged positions for their children (Baker & Stevenson, 1986; Lucas, 2001; Lucas and Berends, 2002; Mickelson, 2003; Useem, 1991). Exacerbating this problem, particularly in racially mixed schools, is the pattern of teacher tracking—the matching of the most experienced teachers with the highest performing students (Kelly, 2004). In this way, educational resources are concentrated on students who arguably need them the least.

In addition to these issues of teacher quality, teachers hold lower expectations for African American students than they do for White students, even when controlling for indicators of prior performance (Downey & Pribesh, 2004; Ferguson 2007; Roscigno, 2000). These lower expectations may lead teachers to engage in instructional practices that lower students' academic performance by bringing it in line with teachers' expectations. These expectations are tied to teachers' social class and racial backgrounds. Teachers from middle-class backgrounds have lower expectations for low-income students than do teachers from working-class backgrounds (Alexander, Entwisle, & Thompson, 1987). The racial background of the teacher may also matter. One study using nationally representative data examined teachers' perceptions of kindergarten and eighth-grade students' academic engagement and behavior.[11] They found that,

> black students are consistently rated as poorer classroom citizens than are white students, but . . . this pattern does not persist when teacher's race is taken into account . . . once black students and white students are both placed with same race teachers . . . black students' behavior is rated more favorably than is white students. (Downey & Pribesh, 2004, p. 277)

Black students are often in classrooms with White teachers, making this finding particularly troubling. In the data set used by Downey and Pribesh (2004), Black students are paired with White teachers 64% of the time.

Moving beyond the individual level, the socioeconomic status (SES) of students is associated with teachers' expectations of them, such that students in classrooms with a lower average SES have their cognitive abilities underestimated by teachers (Ready & Wright, 2011). This suggests important contextual influences on teachers' expectations. Other work has also attended to these context-specific issues through examining teachers' individual and collective efficacy beliefs, and their sense of responsibility for student learning (Diamond, Randolph, & Spillane, 2004; Lee & Smith, 2001). Research suggests that when teachers believe in their own capacity to improve students' outcomes, and the capacity of their colleagues to do the same, students' educational outcomes are more likely to improve (Lee & Smith, 2001). Higher teacher efficacy beliefs contribute to higher academic outcomes for students, more persistence in the face of challenges among teachers, and more positive teacher attitudes (Adams & Forsyth, 2006; Takahashi, 2011). Schools serving Black students (as well as low-income students) are characterized by lower individual and collective efficacy beliefs among teachers (Adams & Forsyth, 2006; Takahashi, 2011).

Likewise, work suggests that the related construct of teachers' sense of responsibility for student learning is also influenced by the race and social class composition of schools (Diamond et al., 2004; Lee & Smith, 2001). In schools where teachers possess a high sense of responsibility, teachers feel personally responsible for their students' academic success or failure. In contrast, in schools with low levels of collective responsibility, "most teachers see potential impediments between their own teaching and students' learning, namely, students' ability (or lack of it), students' family background, or their motivation" (Lee & Loeb, 2000, p. 8). Teachers' sense of responsibility seems to be lower in schools serving low-income students. Since Black students are more likely to attend schools that are predominantly low-income, this pattern of lower expectations and reduced sense of responsibility for student learning likely contributes to racial differences in school outcomes.

Finally, Black students experience inequality in terms of school discipline. Black students are more likely to be referred to the office by teachers, suspended from school, and expelled (Gregory, Skiba, & Noguera, 2010). These higher rates of disciplinary action reflect school practices, and cannot be explained by differences in students' behavior alone. As Gregory et al. (2010) wrote, "there appears to be a notable paucity of evidence that could support a hypothesis that the racial discipline gap can be explained through differential rates of misbehavior" (p. 62).[12] Rather than differences in behavior, research suggests that Black students' behavior is interpreted as more problematic even when it is objectively similar to White students' behavior (Ferguson, 2000; Skiba, Michael, Nardo, & Peterson, 2002). Some work suggests that this may result from Black students' cultural styles being interpreted as defiant, threatening, or antischool.[13] Such disparities in disciplinary experiences are very likely associated with racial differences in educational outcomes, leading some to suggest that discipline and achievement gaps are really "two sides of the same coin" (Gregory et al., 2010, p. 59).

Everyday Racial Processes

Differences in educational resources, opportunities, and outcomes at the structural and institutional levels are relatively well-documented. Everyday processes of discrimination are less well-documented, and in some ways, more elusive. They are elusive in part because they often function on the symbolic level of taken-for-granted meaning and unconscious perceptions that often go unnoticed in daily interactions. They are no less important to examine, however, particularly because of their potentially powerful cumulative effects (Blank et al., 2004; Pollock, 2008). For example, there is a long history in the U.S. of equating Whiteness with intellectual superiority, and Blackness with intellectual inferiority (Gould, 1981; Perry, 2003, Zuberi, 2001), and recent research suggests that these ideas still shape Whites' perceptions of intelligence (Bobo, 2004; Bobo & Charles, 2009). Such ideas have ripple effects in daily interactions, particularly in the education domain where issues of race and intelligence collide. We know from research on gender and status beliefs that broader stereotypes shape interpersonal interactions (Ridgeway & Correll, 2006). For instance, those with higher status (for our purposes here, Whites) are given more opportunities to participate in group interactions and have their contributions valued at higher levels than other group members (Ridgeway & Correll, 2006). Research has also demonstrated some key ways that ideas about race and intelligence shape students' academic performance (Aronson & Steele, 2005; Steele, 2010).

One everyday process that impacts students' academic performance is stereotype threat (Steele, 2010). Research on stereotype threat originally arose in response to racial differences in students' outcomes in higher education. Steele and colleagues were attempting to understand why equally capable Black college students were outperformed by their White colleagues in terms of grades. What he found was that Black students' performance was depressed by stereotype threat—the fear of confirming negative stereotypes about one's group. In repeated experimental studies, Steele and colleagues have found that when race is made salient, Black students perform less well on cognitive tasks. Research has also demonstrated that under stereotype threat conditions, students experience increases in blood pressure, heart rate variability, and other physiological symptoms, all of which can inhibit academic performance (Aronson & Steele, 2005). While most of this research has been conducted in experimental as opposed to naturalistic settings, and in higher education contexts, there is good reason to believe that stereotype threat impacts K–12 students as well.

A second, everyday racial process connects to students' cultural expressions, and how they are interpreted and rewarded by school officials. Dominant cultural expectations are embedded in schools, and students who abide by them receive rewards, while those who do not receive sanctions (Bourdieu & Passeron, 1990;

Carter, 2005). The cultural styles that are rewarded in schools are often those associated with the White middle and upper classes. Thus, Black students often must navigate schools that devalue their cultural styles. For example, Carter (2005) showed that low-income Black and Latino/a students who are invested in education and see it as a route to social mobility, still must grapple with a balancing act between the behaviors and expressions that provide them with peer status, and those that are rewarded by the school. In the contemporary context, educators have come to associate popular cultural forms like hip-hop culture and rap music with African American youth culture and the perception of anti-intellectualism (Warikoo, 2011). Those students who embrace these cultural styles often pay a price in the school setting, even though students who embrace rap music are just as invested in education as other students (Warikoo, 2011).

A final everyday process that disadvantages Black students is what critical race theorists call racial microaggressions.[14] Solórzano, Ceja, and Yosso (2000) defined racial microaggressions as "subtle insults (verbal, nonverbal, and/or visual) directed toward people of color, often automatically and unconsciously" (p. 60). Tuitt and Carter (2008) wrote that these are "subtle but stunning verbal, nonverbal, and/or visual assaults" (p. 53) that, as Davis (1989) wrote, "stem from unconscious attitudes of White superiority and constitute a verification of Black inferiority." (Davis, 1989, as cited in Tuitt & Carter, 2008, p. 53). Because schools reward middle-class, White cultural dispositions and devalue cultural styles identified with African American urban youth culture (P. Carter, 2005), and because race and intelligence are often perceived to be linked, Black students can experience school learning environments (particularly in integrated and predominantly White schools) as hostile (D. Carter, 2007). For example, Black students experience low performance expectations on the part of their teachers and peers in racially mixed schools (Diamond, Lewis, & Gordon, 2007), are forced to become spokespersons for all African Americans in class discussions (Carter, 2005; hooks, 1994; Tuitt & Carter, 2008), are overpraised for what they perceive as average displays of intelligence (Diamond et al., 2007), have their race spotlighted or ignored in the classroom (Carter, 2005, 2008), and are subject to hyper-surveillance on university campuses (Smith, Allen, & Danley, 2007).

Conclusion

Racial differences in school outcomes are often discussed as differences in achievement, rather than as differences in educational resources and opportunities. In this chapter, I have argued that in order to understand racial differences in student outcomes, issues of race, resources, and educational opportunities need to be taken seriously. The historic and contemporary realities of racial inequality exist in the structural, institutional, and interpersonal domains, and have important implications for students' educational outcomes. Discussions of the so-called racial "achievement gap" that do not attend to these issues run the risk of misrepresenting the problem, and failing to reach adequate solutions. This chapter represents an effort to highlight how educational resources and opportunities shape the terrain that students navigate, even in an era that has mistakenly been identified as postracial.

Acknowledgments

Some passages in this chapter also appear in Diamond & Huguley (2011) and in Diamond (2012).

Notes

1. I use the terms, *African American* and *Black* interchangeably throughout this chapter. I view them as having essentially the same meaning in contemporary usage.
2. In this chapter, I focus on Black/White disparities in educational opportunities and outcomes. Other work focuses on racial and ethnic disparities that exist among other groups. For instance, for a discussion of the educational outcomes of Latino/a students in the U.S., see Gándara & Contreras (2009), and Schneider, Martinez, & Owens (2006).
3. The discussion of the "achievement gap" has been wide and varied. Many, however, have suggested that the focus on the achievement gap should shift to a focus on an opportunity gap (Milner, 2010; da Silva, Huguley, Kakli, & Rao, 2007) or the accumulated education debt (Ladson-Billings, 2006) that is owed to students who have never received equal educational opportunities.
4. Given that there is more genetic diversity within racial groups than between them, social scientists generally agree that race is a socially constructed category. Therefore, race is meaningful not because of any biological reality, but because people attach meaning to these categories and allocated, valued resources (including educational resources) differently across racial categories (Massey, 2007; Zuberi, 2001).
5. The flip side of this, of course, is that White students navigate contexts in which their racial category is privileged in comparison to other groups. Clearly, racial groups are not monolithic. There are social class and gender differences, for example, within racial groups. Here, I highlight race while recognizing that class and gender are also important categories around which stratification is organized, and that these categories interact with and reinforce each other in important ways.
6. In discussing racial privileges and penalties I borrow from the work of Antonia Randolph (2006).
7. This is one reason why comparisons across racial groups based solely on income or employment status fail to capture the full implications of race. Comparing African American and White social class groups based on conventional measures of employment, education, and income misses the complex ways in which social classes across racial groups are not equivalent (Pattillo-McCoy, 1999; Pattillo, 2005). While some work suggests that race-based educational disparities persist even when controlling for social class, other work suggests that once wealth is controlled, Black/White differences in educational outcomes disappear.
8. For a further discussion of social mobility that compares African Americans and Whites, please see Hertz (2005).
9. In recent decades, suburban population growth has been fueled by African Americans, Latinos/as and Asians. For example, Reardon and Yun (2001) showed that in the 1980s the White suburban population grew by 8% while the Asian, African American, Latino/a populations

combined to grow 60% during the same period. Therefore, historic trends in suburban population growth have shifted over the past 30 years.
10. "The TQI is composed of six different school-level measures that have been shown in previous research to make a difference for students' performance . . . teachers' average ACT composite score, teachers' average ACT English score, percent of teachers failing the Basic Skills Test on their first attempt, percent of teachers with emergency or provisional certification, teachers' average undergraduate college competitiveness ranking, and percent of teachers with three or fewer years of experience" (Presley et al., 2005, p. 5).
11. The authors used data from the Early Childhood Longitudinal Study and the National Educational Longitudinal Study. For more on these sources, see the National Center for Education Statistics' website, http://nces.ed.gov/
12. In fact, Black students report pro-school attitudes across a wide range of indicators on nationally representative surveys with the exception of their perceptions of the fairness of discipline practices in schools (Downey, 2008).
13. Such misinterpretations can lead teachers to assume that investment in hip-hop culture or rap music reflects antischool orientations. However, research shows that students who embrace such cultural styles are just as invested in education as other students (Warikoo, 2011).
14. Much of the work on microaggressions has focused on African American college-level students. For example, Smith and his colleagues conducted focus groups with African American male college students across five universities. These students reported experiencing racial microaggression across campus academic, social, and public spaces. Several authors have discussed racial microaggressions as critical to understanding contemporary racism. While expressions of overt racial antipathy have traditionally dominated the discussion of racial discrimination historically, in what has been referred to as the post-civil rights era, much of the work on contemporary racism has focused on more subtle and implicit manifestations of racism (Pierce, 1974; Smith et al., 2007; Solórzano et al., 2000).

References

Adams, C. M., & Forsyth, P. B. (2006). Proximate sources of collective teacher efficacy. *Journal of Educational Administration, 44*(6), 625–642.

Alexander, K. L., Entwisle, D. R., & Thompson, M. S. (1987). School performance, status relations, and the structure of sentiment: Bringing the teacher back in. *American Sociological Review, 52*(5), 665–682.

Alexander, M. (2010). *The new Jim Crow: Mass incarceration in the age of colorblindness*. New York, NY: New Press.

Anyon, J. (1997). *Ghetto schooling: A political economy of urban educational reform*. New York, NY: Teachers College Press.

Aronson, J., & Steele, C. M. (2005). Stereotypes and the fragility of academic competence, motivation, and self concept. In A. J. Elliot & C. S. Dweck (Eds.), *Handbook of competence and motivation* (pp. 436–456). New York, NY: Guilford Press.

Baker, D. P., & Stevenson, D. L. (1986). Mother's strategies for children's school achievement: Managing the transition to high school. *Sociology of Education, 59*(3), 156–166.

Blank, R. M., Dabady, M., & Citro, C. F. (Eds.). (2004). *Measuring racial discrimination*. Washington, DC: National Academies Press.

Bobo, L. D. (2004). Inequalities that endure?: Racial ideology, American politics, and the peculiar role of the social sciences. In M. Krysan & A. Lewis *(Eds.), The changing terrain of race and ethnicity* (pp. 13–42). New York, NY: Russell Sage Foundation.

Bobo, L. D., & Charles, C. Z. (2009). Race in the American mind: From the Moynihan report to the Obama candidacy. *Annals of the American Academy of Political and Social Science, 621*(1), 243–259.

Bonilla-Silva, E. (2001). *White supremacy and racism in the post-civil rights era*. Boulder, CO: Lynne Rienner.

Bonilla-Silva, E. (2003). *Racism without racists: Color-blind racism and the persistence of racial inequality in the United States*. Lanham, MD: Rowman & Littlefield.

Bourdieu, P., & Passeron, J.-C. (1990). *Reproduction in education, society, and culture*. Thousand Oaks, CA: Sage.

Carter, D. J. (2005) *In a sea of White people: An analysis of the experiences and behaviors of high achieving Black students in a predominantly White high school* (Unpublished doctoral dissertation). Harvard University, Cambridge, MA.

Carter, D. J. (2007). Why the Black kids sit together at the stairs: The role of identity-affirming counter-spaces in a predominantly White high school. *The Journal of Negro Education, 76*(4), 542–554.

Carter, D. J. (2008). On spotlighting and ignoring racial group members in the classroom. In M. Pollock (Ed.), *Everyday antiracism: Getting real about race in school* (pp. 230–234). New York, NY: New Press.

Carter, P. L. (2005). *Keepin' it real: School success beyond Black & White*. New York, NY: Oxford University Press.

Clotfelter, C. T. (2004). *After Brown: The rise and retreat of school desegregation*. Princeton, NJ: Princeton University Press.

Coates, R. (Ed.). (2011). *Covert racism: Theories, institutions, and experiences*. Leiden, the Netherlands: Brill.

Collins, P. H. (2009). *Another kind of public education: Race, schools, the media, and democratic possibilities*. Boston, MA: Beacon Press.

Darling-Hammond, L., Wei, R. C., & Johnson, C. M. (2009). Teacher preparation and teacher learning: A changing policy landscape. In G. Sykes, B. Schneider, & D. Plank (Eds.), *Handbook of education policy research* (pp. 613–636). New York, NY: Routledge.

da Silva, C. D., Huguley, J. P., Kakli, Z., & Rao, R. (Eds.). (2007). *The opportunity gap: Achievement and inequality in education*. Cambridge, MA: Harvard Educational Review.

Diamond, J. B. (2006). Still separate and unequal: Examining race, opportunity, and school achievement in 'integrated' suburbs. *Journal of Negro Education, 75*(3), 495–505.

Diamond, J. B. (2012). Accountability policy, school organization, and classroom practice: Partial recoupling and educational opportunity. *Education and Urban Society, 44*(2), 151–182.

Diamond, J. B., & Huguley, J. P. (2011). Black/White disparities in educational outcomes: Rethinking issues of race, culture, and context. In N. E. Hill, T. L. Mann, & H. E. Fitzgerald (Eds.), *African American children and mental health: Vol.1, Development and context* (pp. 63–94). New York, NY: Praeger.

Diamond, J. B., Lewis, A. E., & Gordon, L. (2007). Race and school achievement in a desegregated suburb: Reconsidering the oppositional culture explanation. *International Journal of Qualitative Studies in Education, 20*(6), 655–679.

Diamond, J. B., Randolph, A., & Spillane, J. P. (2004). Teachers' expectations and sense of responsibility for student learning: The importance of race, class, and organizational habitus [Special issue on race, power, and the ethnography of urban schools]. *Anthropology and Education Quarterly, 35*(1), 75–98.

Downey, D. B. (2008). A funny thing happened on the way to confirming oppositional culture theory. In J. Ogbu (Ed.), *Minority status, oppositional culture, and schooling* (pp. 298–311). New York, NY: Routledge.

Downey, D. B., & Pribesh, S. (2004). When race matters: Teachers' evaluations of students' classroom behavior. *Sociology of Education, 77*(4), 267–282.

Ferguson, A. A. (2000). *Bad boys: Public schools in the making of Black masculinity*. Ann Arbor, MI: University of Michigan Press.

Ferguson, R. F. (2007). *Toward excellence with equity: An emerging vision for closing the achievement gap*. Cambridge, MA: Harvard Education Press.

Forman, T. A., & Lewis, A. E. (2006). Racial apathy and hurricane Katrina: The social anatomy of prejudice in the post-civil rights era. *Du Bois Review, 3*(1), 175–202.

Gamoran, A. (1987). The stratification of high school learning opportunities. *Sociology of Education, 60*(3), 135–155.

Gosa, T. L., & Alexander, K. (2007). Family (dis)advantage and the educational prospects of better-off African American youth: How race still matters. *Teachers College Record, 109*(2), 285–321.

Gould, S. J. (1981). *The mismeasure of man*. New York, NY: W. W. Norton.

Gregory, A., Skiba, R. J., & Noguera, P. A. (2010). The achievement gap and the discipline gap: Two sides of the same coin? *Educational Researcher, 39*(1), 59–68.

Harris, A. L. (2008). Optimism in the face of despair: Black-White differences in beliefs about school as a means for upward social mobility. *Social Science Quarterly, 89*(3), 608–630.

Hertz, T. (2005). Rags, riches, and race: The intergenerational economic mobility of Black and White families in the United States. In S. Bowles, H. Gintis, & M. O. Groves (Eds.), *Unequal chances: Family background and economic success* (pp. 165–191). Princeton, NJ: Princeton University Press.

hooks, b. (1994). *Teaching to transgress: Education as the practice of freedom*. London, UK: Routledge.

Jencks, C., & Phillips, M. (1998). *The Black-White test score gap*. Washington, DC: Brookings Institution Press.

Johnson, H. B. (2006). *The American dream and the power of wealth: Choosing schools and inheriting inequality in the land of opportunity*. New York, NY: Routledge.

Katznelson, I. (2005). *When affirmative action was White: An untold history of racial inequality in twentieth-century America*. New York, NY: W.W. Norton.

Kelly, S. (2004). Are teachers tracked? On what basis and with what consequences? *Social Psychology of Education, 7*(1), 55–72.

Kelly, S. (2009). The Black-White gap in mathematics course taking. *Sociology of Education, 82*(1), 47–69.

Konstantopoulos, S., & Chung, V. (2011). The persistence of teacher effects in elementary grades. *American Educational Research Journal, 48*(2), 361–386.

Ladson-Billings, G. (2006). From the achievement gap to the education debt: Understanding achievement in U.S. schools. *Educational Researcher, 35*(7), 3–12.

Ladson-Billings, G., & Tate, W. F. (1995). Toward a critical race theory of education. *Teachers College Record, 97*(1), 47–68.

Lee, V. E., & Loeb, S. (2000). School size in Chicago elementary schools: Effects on teachers' attitudes and students' achievement. *American Educational Research Journal, 37*(1), 3–31.

Lee, V. E., & Smith, J. B. (2001). *Restructuring high schools for equity and excellence: What works*. New York, NY: Teachers College Press.

Lewis, A. E. (2001). There is no 'race' in the schoolyard: Color-blind ideology in an (almost) all-White school. *American Educational Research Journal, 38*(4), 781–811.

Lucas, S. R. (2001). Effectively maintained inequality: Education transitions, track mobility, and social background effects. *American Journal of Sociology, 106*(6), 1642–1690.

Lucas, S. R., & Berends. M. (2002). Sociodemographic diversity, correlated achievement, and de facto tracking. *Sociology of Education, 75*(4), 328–348.

Lucas, S. R., & Berends, M. (2007). Race and track location in U.S. public schools. *Research in Social Stratification and Mobility, 25*(3), 169–187.

Massey, D. S. (2007). *Categorically unequal: The American stratification system*. New York: Russell Sage Foundation.

Mickelson, R. A. (2001). Subverting Swann: First- and second-generation segregation in the Charlotte-Mecklenburg schools. *American Educational Research Journal, 38*(2), 215–252.

Mickelson, R. A. (2003). When are racial disparities in education the result of racial discrimination? A social science perspective. *Teachers College Record, 105*(6), 1052–1086.

Milner, H. R. (2010). *Start where you are, but don't stay there: Understanding diversity, opportunity gaps, and teaching in today's classrooms*. Cambridge, MA: Harvard Education Press.

Nicolaides, B., & Wiese, A. (2006). *The suburb reader*. New York, NY: Routledge.

O'Connor, C., Lewis, A., & Mueller, J. (2007). Researching 'Black' educational experiences and outcomes: Theoretical and methodological considerations. *Educational Researcher*, *36*(9), 541–552.

Oliver, M. L., & Shapiro, T. M. (1995). *Black wealth/White wealth: A new perspective on racial inequality*. New York, NY: Routledge.

Orfield, G. (1996). The growth of segregation: African Americans, Latinos, and unequal education. In G. Orfield & S. E. Eaton (Eds.), *Dismantling desegregation: The quiet reversal of* Brown v. Board of Education (pp. 53–72). New York, NY: New Press.

Orfield, G., & Lee, C. (2005). *Why segregation matters: Poverty and educational inequality*. The Civil Rights Project at Harvard University. Retrieved from http://civilrightsproject.ucla.edu/research/k-12-education/integration-and-diversity/why-segregation-matters-poverty-and-educational-inequality/?searchterm=%22why%20segregation%20matters%22

Pager, D., Bonikowski, B., & Western, B. (2009). Discrimination in a low-wage labor market: A field experiment. *American Sociological Review*, *74*(5), 777–799.

Pattillo, M. (2005). Black middle-class neighborhoods. *Annual Review of Sociology*, *31*(1), 305–329.

Pattillo-McCoy, M. (1999). *Black picket fences: Privilege and peril among the Black middle class*. Chicago, IL: University of Chicago Press.

Payne, C. M. (1984). *Getting what we ask for: The ambiguity of success and failure in urban education*. Westport, CT: Greenwood Press.

Perry, T. (2003). Up from the parched earth: Toward a theory of African-American achievement. In T. Perry, C. Steele, & A. Hilliard III (Eds.), *Young, gifted, and Black: Promoting high achievement among African American students* (pp. 1–10). Boston, MA: Beacon Press.

Pierce, C. M. (1974). Psychiatric problems of the Black minority. In S. Arieti (Ed.), *American handbook of psychiatry* (pp. 512–523). New York, NY: Basic Books.

Planty, M., Hussar, W., Snyder, T., Kena, G., KewalRamani, A., Kemp, J., Bianco, K., & Dinkes, R. (2009). *The condition of education 2009* (NCES 2009-081). National Center for Education Statistics, Institute of Education Sciences. Washington, DC: U.S. Department of Education.

Pollock, M. (2008). *Because of race: How Americans debate harm and opportunity in our schools*. Princeton, NJ: Princeton University Press.

Presley, J., White, B., & Gong, Y. (2005). *Examining the distribution and impact of teacher quality in Illinois*. Edwardsville: Illinois Education Research Council. Retrieved from http://ierc.siue.edu/documents/Teacher%20Quality%20IERC%202005-2.pdf

Randolph, A. (2006). *The worth of a student: Teacher perceptions and the social value of racial and ethnic difference* (Unpublished doctoral dissertation). Northwestern University, Evanston, IL.

Ready, D. D., & Wright, D. L. (2011). Accuracy and inaccuracy in teachers' perceptions of young children's cognitive abilities: The role of child background and classroom context. *American Educational Research Journal*, *48*(2), 335–360.

Reardon, S. F., & Yun, J. T. (2001). Suburban racial change and suburban school segregation, 1987–95. *Sociology of Education*, *74*(2), 79–101.

Ridgeway, C. L., & Correll, S. J. (2006). Consensus and the creation of status beliefs. *Social Forces*, *85*(1), 431–453.

Roscigno, V. J. (2000). Family/school inequality and African-American/Hispanic achievement. *Social Problems*, *47*(2), 266–290.

Rose, L. C., & Gallup, A. M. (2004). The 36th annual Phi Delta Kappa/Gallup Poll of the public's attitude toward the public schools. *Phi Delta Kappan*, *86*(1), 41–56. Retrieved from http://www.kappanmagazine.org/content/86/1/41.abstract

Schneider, B., Martinez, S. & Owens, A. (2006). Barriers to educational opportunities for Hispanics in the United States. In M. Tienda & F. Mitchell (Eds.), *Hispanics and the future of America* (pp. 179–227). Washington, DC: National Academies Press.

Schorr, D. (2008, January 28). A new, post racial politics in the United States [Radio broadcast]. All Things Considered. *National Public Radio (NPR)*.

Shapiro, T. M. (2004). *The hidden cost of being African American: How wealth perpetuates inequality*. New York, NY: Oxford University Press.

Shapiro, T. M., Meschede, T., & Sullivan, L. (2010). The racial wealth gap increases fourfold. Brandeis University Institute on Assets and Social Policy Research and Policy Brief. Retrieved from http://iasp.brandeis.edu/pdfs/Racial-Wealth-Gap-Brief.pdf

Skiba, R. J., Michael, R. S., Nardo, A. C., & Peterson, R. L. (2002). The color of discipline: Sources of racial and gender disproportionality in school punishment. *Urban Review, 34*(4), 317–342.

Smith, W. A., Allen, W. R., & Danley, L. L. (2007). 'Assume the position . . . you fit the description': Psychosocial experiences and racial battle fatigue among African American male college students. *American Behavioral Scientist, 51*(4), 551–578.

Solórzano, D., Ceja, M., & Yosso, T. (2000). Critical race theory, racial microaggressions, and campus racial climate: The experiences of African American college students. *Journal of Negro Education, 69*(1–2), 60–73.

Steele, C. (2010). *Whistling Vivaldi: And other clues to how stereotypes affect us*. New York, NY: W. W. Norton.

Takahashi, S. (2011). Co-constructing efficacy: A 'communities of practice' perspective on teachers' efficacy beliefs. *Teaching and Teacher Education, 27*(4), 732–741.

Tuitt, F. A., & Carter, D. J. (2008). Negotiating atmospheric threats and racial assaults in predominantly White educational institutions. *Journal of Public Management & Social Policy, 14*(2), 51–68.

Tyson, K. (2011). *Integration interrupted: Tracking, Black students, and acting White after Brown*. New York, NY: Oxford University Press.

Uhlenberg, J., & Brown, K. M. (2004). Racial gap in teachers' perceptions of the achievement gap. *Education and Urban Society, 34*(4), 493–530.

Useem, E. L. (1991). Student selection into course sequences in mathematics: The impact of parental involvement and school policies. *Journal of Research on Adolescence, 1*(3), 231–250.

Warikoo, N. K. (2011). *Balancing acts: Youth culture in the global city*. Berkeley, CA: University of California Press.

Zuberi, T. (2001). *Thicker than blood: How racial statistics lie*. Minneapolis, MN: University of Minnesota Press.

SEVEN

Naming Their Pain

How Everyday Racial Microaggressions Impact Students and Teachers

María C. Ledesma and Daniel Solórzano

I remember the day vividly. I was sitting in my eighth-grade English class in my middle school. My school, located in the heart of the inner city, enrolled 99.9% students of color. On this warm spring day, the classroom was quiet and still, my classmates and I were absorbed reading Les Misérables, *waiting to learn Jean Valjean's fate. Over the quiet it was easy to hear the substitute teacher call my name. "The English department head would like to see you," I was told. I shrugged, and headed to the door, but not before looking over my shoulder to acknowledge that I would fall behind my friends, who kept on reading. I arrived at Ms. Brewer's door. She was seated towards the back of the library, under a panel of sunny windows. She sat with four boys I did not know or recognize. All four were Latino and Spanish-speaking, and had recently arrived at our middle school. She met me in the doorway, where we stood as she looked over the clipboard in her hand. Looking down at her notes, she asked if I felt I needed any help in my English class. "No," I replied. "That's what I thought," she said. "But your name was on this list ... I don't know why they have you here," she mumbled to herself. After a brief pause, she jotted down some notes and waved me away, "You can go back to class." I nodded and turned back, catching a glimpse of the boys who remained at the table waiting for Ms. Brewer. It was not until later that it dawned on me what had happened. Because of my Spanish surname I had been taken out of my gifted English class and sent to the library, where Ms. Brewer was busy placing the four new students into remedial English classes. I was angry that I would be considered a candidate for remediation classes, especially since I had already spent a year and a half in my school's gifted education program. As an eighth grader my anger was displaced and directed against the boys in the library. It was not until later that I realized that this was not their fault. The fact was that we had all been profiled. The assumption was that because they lacked English fluency, they needed remediation, and by extension, because of my Spanish last name, I, too, needed to be transferred out of my gifted English class. It was only later that I recognized that we had just experienced a racial microaggression.*

Dr. Chester Pierce, Emeritus Professor of Education and Psychiatry, pioneered the work of "microaggressions," or "offensive actions." Pierce's (1970) early work on extreme environments recognized that "Most offensive actions are not gross and crippling. They are subtle and stunning." Pierce noted that the enormity, and the problem, of racial microaggressions can only be appreciated when one considers that these "blows are delivered incessantly" (1970, pp. 265–266). Furthermore, Pierce added that the condition intensifies when race is factored into the equation. Reflecting on history and race relations in the United States in 1970, Pierce concluded that racism in the US is a "public health and mental health illness" (1970, p. 266). As his work evolved, Pierce (1974) adopted the term, *micro-aggressions*, to explain the chronic toll that extreme environments take upon their subjects, especially African Americans, and other marginalized people. He affirmed,

> What the reader must bear in mind is that these [*racial*] *assaults* to black dignity and black hope are incessant and cumulative. Any single one may be gross. In fact, the major vehicle for racism in this country is *offenses* done to blacks by whites in this sort of gratuitous never-ending way. These *offenses* are *microaggressions* [emphasis added]. Almost all black-white racial interactions are characterized by white put-downs, done in automatic, preconscious, or unconscious fashion. These minidisasters accumulate. It is the sum total of multiple microaggressions by whites to blacks that has pervasive effect to the stability and peace of this world. (Pierce, 1974, p. 515)

Although Pierce's (1970, 1974, 1975) research has been exclusively anchored in the field of public health, we posit that his work, and diagnosis, on the permanence of race and the impact of microaggressions, is also applicable within the realm and field of education. We are not the first to so opine. The work of Gloria Ladson-Billings (1994), Beverly Daniel Tatum (1997), and Angela Valenzuela (1999), just to name a few, also speaks to the enduring power of race in framing and shaping learning opportunities for historically marginalized students. Likewise, we argue that historically disenfranchised students, such as first-generation students, low-income students, and students of color, among others, encounter microaggressions on a daily basis, which often impacts their progress towards attaining their educational aspirations. As such, continuing and aspiring educators would do well to understand how, and why, microaggressions permeate their classrooms. This means acknowledging, and talking, about race and racism in the classroom in a candid and constructive manner.

In many ways, Pierce's (1974) prescription of talking about and acknowledging the power of race goes against the grain. The mention of "race," let alone "racism," makes many people cringe. They either do not know how to talk about it, or do not want to talk about it. Still others might argue that we have arrived at a time and place where race and racism no longer matter, so there is no need to talk about it (D'Souza, 1995). As proof, they may point to the White House, which for the first time in history houses an African American president. However, the election of Barack H. Obama as the 44th President of the United States has not made the country, or for that matter, any of its segments, postracial. Race still matters because racism matters, and the field of education is no exception.

The emergence of the concept of "postracialism," defined as the belief that we have arrived at a time and place where we are beyond race, where racism no longer matters, suggests otherwise. In the shadow of this new postracial rhetoric, chances are that if you ask people to reflect upon "race" and "racism" within the context of education, these words may conjure up black and white images of the hard-fought struggles for racial justice waged during the civil rights era. Images like Arkansas' "Little Rock Nine"—nine African American high schoolers—who in 1957, against the wishes of then Governor, Orval Faubus, faced mobs and death threats to integrate Central High School. Or the image of six-year-old Ruby Bridges, in late 1960, flanked by federal marshals, as she ascended the steps of the all-White William Frantz Elementary School in New Orleans, Louisiana. More than five decades later, manifestations around race and racism in education may tend to be less blatant, but to be sure, they still linger.[1] Instead of facing mobs and federal marshals, today's struggles to secure quality opportunities to learn (Oakes, 2005) and to challenge race and racism are subtler and more covert (Coates, 2008). Adding to the confusion, these challenges are often cloaked under veils of color-blind rhetoric and ideology (Lakoff, 2002, 2006). Struggles remain, in terms of determining who or what defines "meritocracy," deciding how to evaluate a student's "performance gap" without taking into account her or his "opportunity gap," or debating whether or not race-conscious affirmative action policies in higher education have run their course. Ironically, a rise in claims of "reverse racism" from White students, also stirs up controversy and confusion.[2] Nonetheless, bound up within each of these issues are the stories of hundreds of thousands of students of color, for whom issues of race and racism, however mundane they may appear to others, are real, everyday stressors (Carroll, 1998).

Critical Race Theory

The introduction of Critical Race Theory (CRT) as an outgrowth of the field of critical legal studies in the 1980s provided a groundbreaking and revolutionary framework for scholars dedicated to the pursuit of social justice within and outside the law (Crenshaw, 2011; Tate, 1997). What CRT did was acknowledge in unequivocal terms that race and racism remain an indelible part of daily life for most people of color. The result of the work of progressive legal scholars of color (Bell, 1989, 1992, 2004, 2005a, 2005b; Crenshaw, Gotanda, Peller, & Thomas, 1995; Delgado & Stefancic, 2001; Lawrence, 1995), CRT introduced five tenets for understanding and deconstructing power and racial relations in the law. To begin with, CRT acknowledges the permanence of race by recognizing that race and racism remain a central and endemic part of the human experience. Second, CRT challenges the maintenance of White supremacy by exposing how dominant ideologies, even those thought to be race-neutral, such as "colorblindness," are nonetheless shaped and framed around normative conceptions of Whiteness. Third, CRT embraces the notion that there is value in the experiences of historically underrepresented groups, by positing that there is knowledge to be gained from the experiences of historically marginalized peoples. Borrowing from the tradition of "legal storytelling," tenet three also argues that counternarratives or counterstories are important and necessary tools to challenge "majoritarian" narratives, which work to reproduce the status quo. Fourth, CRT is multidisciplinary, it is shaped and informed by a rich array of disciplines including history, ethnic studies, gender studies, and sociology, to name a few. Likewise, tenet four also recognizes that although race is a dominant social construction, personal identity is complex and shaped by intersecting experiences with domains beyond race, such as class and gender. Finally, CRT's fifth tenet expresses an unapologetic commitment to social justice, and towards the elimination of all forms of oppression and subordination.

The development of a critical race theory in education (Ladson-Billings & Tate, 1995; Solórzano, 1997) introduced CRT as an "analytic tool for understanding school inequity" (Ladson-Billings & Tate, 1995, p. 48). While Ladson-Billings and Tate (1995) pioneered the application of CRT toward the analysis of K–12 schooling and educational opportunities, Solórzano (1997) extended the concept and application of CRT in education toward the analysis of students of color in higher education. Drawing from the works of Chester Pierce (1970, 1974) and founding CRT scholars (Bell, 1989, 1992, 2004, 2005a, 2005b; Crenshaw et al., 1995; Delgado & Stefancic, 2001; Lawrence, 1995), Solórzano (1998) adapted the concept of "racial microaggressions" to educational discourse. Just as Pierce (1974) spoke to the toll of microaggressions, or "minidisasters" on the physical and psychological well-being and dignity and hope of people of color, especially, African Americans, so, too, did Solórzano (1998) address the cumulative impact of racial microaggressions on students of color in higher education. What Solórzano uncovered was that for even those students of color resilient enough to gain entry into the nation's most competitive institutions of higher education, the daily task of confronting racial microaggressions took its toll.

With the steady demographic growth of historically underrepresented students in higher education (Fry & Gonzales, 2008; Gándara & Contreras, 2009), the relevance and application of CRT and CRT in education as analytic tools to examine educational inequity and opportunity remain as timely as ever. Indeed, despite proclamations that we have arrived at a new era of "postracialism," we believe that race will continue to matter, and that all educators would do well to understand how these issues are confronted and addressed. We call for aspiring educators to wrestle with their (mis)understandings of the concepts associated with, and complexities of, racial microaggressions and critical race theory more broadly. We have found these frameworks very useful in addressing contemporary issues of race and racism in education, and while some might balk at or question the need for a CRT framework when addressing K–12 educational issues, the unfortunate reality is that the educational playing field is not yet level. Race continues to be an indelible reality for nondominant students and their families. This chapter will offer recommendations for aspiring and continuing K–12 educators on the importance of managing difficult dialogues in the classroom, especially those dealing with race and racism. For teachers committed to social justice, we recommend critical race theory as a useful classroom tool for fostering a healthy classroom climate.

Giving Voice

As the University of Michigan's affirmative action cases, *Grutter v. Bollinger* (2003) and *Gratz v. Bollinger* (2003), worked their way through the Circuit Court System on their path towards the Supreme Court, researchers and scholars throughout the country were busy producing a body of research on the value and merits of race-conscious affirmative action in higher education. One study, undertaken by one of the authors of this paper (Solórzano, Ceja, & Yosso, 2000; Solórzano, Allen, & Carroll, 2002), sought to analyze how the "campus climate" encountered by students of color upon their arrival into predominantly White institutions, like the University of Michigan's Law School, impacted their educational aspirations and attainment. Through the use of student focus group data, the authors uncovered how racial microaggressions manifested on predominately White campuses. What the study uncovered suggested that for even the most highly accomplished and academically gifted students of color, the cumulative impact of racial microaggressions influences, and at times compromises, their college achievement.

In anticipation of the Supreme Court's rulings, in January of 2001 the study findings were shared with students from local universities and Detroit-area high schools at the University of Michigan (see Allen & Solórzano, 2001; Solórzano et al., 2002; Solórzano, Ceja, & Yosso, 2000; Yosso, Smith, Ceja, & Solórzano, 2009). The research was based on our work as expert witnesses for the student intervenors in the University of Michigan affirmative action case (*Grutter v. Bollinger* 539 U.S. 306, 2003). Based on data we had gathered among undergraduate and law students at Michigan (as well as from four main feeder undergraduate campuses to the Michigan Law School), we argued that "critical mass" is especially important for historically marginalized students attending predominantly White institutions of higher education.[3] On this particular day, our presentation focused on explaining Pierce's concept of "racial microaggressions."

We defined racial microaggressions as one form of systemic, *everyday* racism used to keep those at the racial margins in their place, and explained that those who are racially marginalized often experience various forms of racial microaggressions, such as:

- *Subtle verbal and non-verbal insults/assaults* directed toward people of color, often carried out automatically or unconsciously;
- *Layered insults/assaults*, based on one's race, gender, class, sexuality, language, immigration status, phenotype, accent, or surname;
- *Cumulative insults/assaults* that take their toll on people of color.

We also highlighted examples of everyday forms of racism that undergraduate and law students of color had shared with us as part of our research. For instance, some of the students shared scenarios recounting the incessant nature of racial microaggressions. In many instances students also acknowledged, just as Pierce (1974) had diagnosed, that those making the offensive remarks often did so in automatic, preconscious, or unconscious fashion. Remarks such as,

- "When I talk about *those Blacks*, I really wasn't talking about you."
- "You're not like the rest of *them*. You're different."
- "If only there were more of *them* like you."

In addition, we shared examples collected from our student participants of racial micro-aggressions in the classroom, such as:

- Making a comment in class (or meeting) and being ignored, only to find your idea described as "profound" coming from a White student (or colleague).
- Assuming that students of color are spokespersons for the race.

- Seeing students when it is convenient, but rendering them invisible most of the other times ("Today we're talking about slavery. James, how do you feel about slavery?").
- Not hearing students who have an accent.

As we ended the presentation and opened the floor for discussion, a young African American woman identified herself as a high school student from Detroit, and started crying. Through her tears, this young teen described how, for the first time in her life, she was able to see her own life experience reflected in research. She explained how our research on racial microaggressions resonated with her own lived experience, and how, until this point, she had struggled to share, or explain, her experiences with others. She described experiences such as being the only person of color in a classroom, and being expected to speak on behalf of her race, or being interrogated by teachers about whether she deserved to be enrolled in her advanced or honors classes. On this day, however, after hearing us talk about the concept of racial microaggressions, she stated simply, "you've given me a name for my pain."

For this young woman, learning about the concept of racial microaggressions provided a new language and framework for her to reflect upon, and speak about, her own experiences. For educators committed to social justice, helping students *name their pain* is an important first step in acknowledging and addressing the persistence of race and racism in our society at large, and within our classrooms and educational system. However, in order for this to happen, educators must first ensure that they acknowledge and understand that race and racism continue to matter in the 21st century (West, 1993). Educators must understand that although some would have us believe otherwise, racism is not a thing of the past;[4] we are nowhere near postracial as a society. Despite the election of our first African American President—which does nothing to alleviate the structural and institutional racism that exists in systems of employment, housing, health care, and education—racism still permeates throughout, albeit more covertly. Ironically, more than half a century after the iconic *Brown v. Board of Education* (1954) Supreme Court decision striking down *de jure* segregation, students of color live in and attend schools in more highly segregated neighborhoods than pre-*Brown* (Orfield, 2001). *De facto* segregation is alive and well in the new century. Prematurely embracing the rhetoric and ideology of color blindness, while ignoring the permanence of race and racism in contemporary America, not only ignores and invalidates the daily reality of millions of nondominant students, in most cases it also aggravates existing problems. Furthermore, the reality is that schools do not exist or operate in isolation. Schools are an extension and reflection of the sociopolitical world around them, and in 21st century America, race still matters. In light of this fact, we recommend that educators be wary and mindful of the historical and contextual underpinnings that inform and frame their students' experiences. And for those educators committed to championing equity and social justice, we recommend critical race theory as a useful theoretical framework and tool.

Critical Race Theory in Education

We have found that critical race theory is an especially useful framework when addressing issues of race and racism. As aforementioned, critical race theory (CRT), rooted in part in the scholarship of progressive legal scholars of color, works to account for the role of race and racism in American law, and toward "the elimination of all forms of subordination in society" (Matsuda, 1991, p. 1331). Despite the fact that CRT's origins are rooted in jurisprudence, the theory has gained popularity in usage beyond legal studies. For example, scholars in the sociology of race and ethnic studies in education employ a CRT lens as they seek to explain how inequitable learning conditions produce disparate learning opportunities and outcomes for students of color.

For those concerned with analyzing the permanence of race and racism within the P–20 educational pipeline, critical race theory in education (CRT in Ed) is imperative. Tate (1997) and Solórzano and Delgado Bernal (2001) provided important work in this regard. Solórzano and Delgado Bernal revisited CRT's major tenets with a focus on education, and posited five major themes "that form the basic perspectives, research methods, and pedagogy of a critical race theory in education" (2001, p. 312). These themes provide a necessary foundation for educators seeking to address and understand the role of race in education. Solórzano and Delgado Bernal posited that critical race pedagogy should address the following:

1. *The Centrality of Race and Racism and Intersectionality with Other Forms of Subordination:* The concept of intersectionality recognizes that race and racism often work in tandem with other forms of oppression and marginalization, such as gender and class oppression (p. 312).

2. *The Challenge to Dominant Ideology:* "A critical race theory in education challenges the traditional claims of the educational system to objectivity, meritocracy, color-blindness, race neutrality, and equal opportunity" (p. 313).

3. *The Commitment to Social Justice:* Solórzano and Delgado Bernal proposed that a commitment to social justice envisions the elimination of all forms of oppression and subordination, including: racism, sexism, classism, and homophobia (p. 314).

4. *The Centrality of Experiential Knowledge:* Recognizes the experiential knowledge of historically underrepresented groups, including students of color, as a strength from which knowledge may be drawn. This includes such methods as storytelling, family history, biographies, parables, and narratives, just to name a few. Solórzano and Delgado Bernal also incorporated oral history and counterstorytelling as examples of experiential knowledge and forms of resistance (p. 314).

5. *The Interdisciplinary Perspective:* Such a framework in education, according to Solórzano and Delgado Bernal, recognizes the importance of grounding analysis of race and racism within a historical and contextual context while using multidisciplinary methods (p. 314).

Educators committed to social justice may find these tenets especially useful in fostering a healthy classroom climate. For example, take Amanda Lewis's (2003) book, *Race in the Schoolyard: Negotiating the Color Line in Classrooms and Communities*. In the book, Lewis described her interview with London, a nine-year-old African American elementary school student. As London made clear, racial microaggressions are not confined to adults, or to loud, overt actions. Even at her tender age, London has learned to recognize that a person's harsh tone is layered with historical, political, and racial undertones:

Amanda: Has anybody ever been mean to you or treated you differently because of your color?
London: Yeah.
Amanda: How so?
London: People in the store.
Amanda: What happened?
London: A month ago. He accused me because he just, he just start yelling but I don't know why though.
Amanda: Do you think he was yelling at you because you were black?
London: Yes.
Amanda: How do you know?
London: I don't know, it just sounded like it (p. 138).

Unfortunately, London's experience is not an isolated incident. The pernicious nature of racism means that racial microaggressions are not confined to episodes of erratic behavior. To the contrary, they are woven into the fabric of everyday occurrences, such as a young child going to the local store, or to the school's attendance office.

I was in high school when my family underwent the process of becoming naturalized citizens. In addition to paying various legal and filing fees, we were required to obtain all sorts of documentation, medical records, proof of continuous residency, and paycheck stubs. My siblings and I were each dispatched to our schools to obtain copies of our attendance files. One day during lunch, I built up my courage and went in to see our school attendance clerk. Although my high school was mostly composed of students, faculty, and staff of Color, our attendance clerk was a White woman, Ms. Turner. She was a brunette with a flipped bob haircut, à la Mary Tyler Moore, who favored skirt ensembles. On this day, she wore a two-piece, seafoam green outfit. I arrived in the office with my best friend in tow, and handed Ms. Turner an envelope. The envelope contained a letter from our lawyer explaining that I needed a copy of my school attendance records, and the purpose behind my request. Without looking up, Ms. Turner exclaimed, "Oh no. I hope they don't send you back, you're one of the good ones." In less than a minute, Ms. Turner had not just outed me to my friend, she also provided me with one of the indelible memories that mark my youth. A memory of a racial microaggression.

As the previous examples illustrate, the automatic, preconscious, or unconscious fashion in which racial microaggressions unfold is reflective of a larger social culture that continues to embrace and normalize White, majoritarian narratives and experiences. We acknowledge that the responsibility of combating racial microaggressions is a large one. Still, we also recognize that historically that responsibility has fallen to the marginalized, with both overt and covert expectations to assimilate and acculturate into the dominant culture. However, in the face of the history of White supremacy in this country, including within educational structures and institutions, the job of combating racial microaggressions belongs to everyone, and not just to marginalized communities. To follow, we offer some suggestions about what educators can do to address issues of race and racial microaggressions in their classrooms.

So What Can Educators Do?

Talking about race and racism is never easy. Even for the most seasoned educators, such conversations are measured and deliberate (Tatum, 1992). However, experienced educators will know that silence in the face of uncomfortable conversations is never acceptable, because silence equals tacit approval. Instead, conversations on race and racism in the classroom should be reasoned and reflective.

While in graduate school I worked with a sociology professor who was conducting research on the college-going process for students of color. I was assigned to a very diverse high school within the largest school district in California. Among my tasks was to review interview audiotapes and transcripts between our researchers and student, parent, teacher, and counselor focus groups. Our focus groups aimed to investigate the college-going process for students of color, including soliciting examples of how students of color were prepared by their high schools, or not, to pursue higher education. One day, I sat down to review a parent group transcript. The group, composed of African American mothers, spoke in depth about their experiences with their local high school. One mother, Mrs. Taylor, provided an especially poignant anecdote. Mrs. Taylor spoke about a daily ritual between her and her high school–aged son. She said, "Every day he comes home from school, I greet him with a positive attitude, and we sit down to talk. I want to hear all about his day, and talk about his experiences. I know that he faces challenges; and it's my job to support him and 'de-program' him from the negativity he encounters throughout the day." Although Mrs. Taylor did not use the terminology of racial microaggressions, it was clear that this is what she was alluding to. She had seen the school take a toll on her older children, especially her sons, and understood all too well the enduring role of race and racism in the classroom. I found it powerful that Mrs. Taylor recognized the racial barriers and stereotypes her son confronted on a daily basis, and that she worked hard to bolster and support him in order to help him succeed.

Just as Mrs. Taylor took careful measures to talk with and educate her son on race and resiliency, so, too, do we recommend that educators take an intentional approach when addressing race and racism in the classroom. The history of race and racism in America casts a long shadow (Loury, 2002). As such, conversations on race need to be contextually grounded and multipronged. We recommend using insights from critical race theory to engage in these difficult dialogues. More specifically, we recommend the following three-pronged approach, informed by CRT and CRT in education, to examine and address racial microaggressions in the classroom:

1. Recognize the enduring role of race and racism in the US, including within educational settings. Conversations about race and racism should always be historically grounded. History will not only help students understand the permanence of race, but will also offer important reflections on challenging racist and deficit thinking.

2. Confirm the reality of microaggressions. This approach will help students by providing an opportunity to validate their experiences and to *name their pain*. An important auxiliary step is to provide students with the skills and/or resources necessary to interrupt such behavior. For example, students and teachers might utilize print and digital media to recognize microaggressions, and engage in classroom discussions to craft response scenarios. Such practices will help give students the knowledge and ana-

lytical skills necessary to tackle racial microaggressions outside the classroom.

3. Support students and teachers of color's resiliency and/or resistance to microaggressions. Educators can help students find examples within and about communities of color that challenge racial microaggressions. Rich sources of material include individual and family oral and pictorial histories, and artistic and cultural artifacts, which can demonstrate how people have challenged and still challenge racial microaggressions.

Ultimately, educators must be diligent about disrupting normative racist beliefs and assumptions that continue to permeate U.S. society; beliefs such as questioning when students of color are placed in advanced or honors courses, or assuming that a student of color's entry into a selective college or university is due only to affirmative action practices. It would be beneficial to challenge students and teachers that espouse such beliefs, concerning such racist attitudes. Indeed, even in mono-racial classrooms, issues of race must be problematized. To do otherwise, educators run the risk of being complicit in supporting negative and hostile learning environments that impair the educational attainment of all students, and with promoting the racial status quo.

Conclusion

Interrupting racist thoughts and practices does not happen overnight. Creating and fostering healthy classrooms for all students takes time and diligence, and no amount of multiculturalism by proxy, such as only celebrating holidays like Martin Luther King, Jr.'s birthday or *Cinco de Mayo*, is a sufficient replacement for meaningful discussions and teachings about race. Educators committed to social justice will know that their job entails modeling and teaching students how to identify and confront their own, and others', automatic and unconscious, everyday racism. One effective way of doing this is by fostering a healthy classroom climate, one where tension is real, and honest talk helps promote teachable moments. With this in mind, educators are encouraged to address race in the classroom with candor and care.

> *For two years I worked in an urban elementary school with a high enrollment of students of color. Students at Ross Elementary spoke something like 40 different languages, while the teachers at the school were mostly female and predominantly White. There were teachers with decades of experience, and others fresh from their credentialing programs. Still, it was not the experience that made the teacher. Experience helped, but I found that the most effective teachers engaged with their students in a "culture of caring" (Valenzuela, 1999). They held high expectations for all of their students, and*

they respected their students' backgrounds and experiential knowledge. I was struck at how different teachers managed their classrooms. For instance, there were two teachers that exemplified distinctly different approaches to teaching. Where some people saw chaos in Ms. Cydell's fifth-grade class, I saw the encouragement of intellectual curiosity. Ms. Cydell was new to teaching. She had earned her credentials from a small, vibrant teachers college, devoted to improving the education of all children. Ms. Cydell was liked by almost all of her students. Her class was by no means perfect, but it did allow students to have ownership of their space. As such, it was not unusual to see students linger in her room after school. Down the hall, in Ms. Jones's fourth-grade classroom, things were very different. Ms. Jones was also new to teaching. She had earned her credentials from the local state college. Unlike Ms. Cydell, Ms. Jones emphasized order and discipline. At lunch she marched her students to and from the multipurpose room/cafeteria in a single and silent file. She admonished them when they fell out of line, "we can stand out here all day until you learn to be quiet and follow directions." Sometimes followed by, "aren't you ashamed by the way you are behaving in front of 'Ms.' or 'Mr.' So and So?" As an outsider, I observed from a distance. My experience at Ross Elementary helped me understand the difficulty of being a good and effective teacher. I saw firsthand the long hours that good teachers dedicated to their students before, during, and after school. I also never forgot Ms. Jones's class. I always wondered what her students thought and felt as she drilled them to be obedient and to follow directions. Undoubtedly, discipline is an important trait, but I was also taken aback at the implied messages Ms. Jones was sending to her mostly Brown and Black students. Unwittingly or not Ms. Jones's actions contributed to a daily barrage of messages that her students likely encountered. Both inside and outside of the classroom they were reminded that theirs was a subordinate position. Nondominant students, like those in Ms. Jones's classroom, too often live in a militarized and police state, where surveillance is real and threatening. Unfortunately, Ms. Jones's hyperadherence to punishment, disguised as discipline, translated into subtle but sustained assaults, or microaggressions, on her student's dignity and hope. Their classroom offered them no respite from the outside world.

Experiences like those at Ross Elementary School are not isolated incidents. There are many teachers like Ms. Cydell and Ms. Jones across the country. Indeed, across the US, the composition of the teacher corps remains predominantly White and female, even in most majority minority schools. However, the manner in which Ms. Cydell and Ms. Jones approached their teaching and their students was radically different. Ms. Cydell, while not perfect, was taught to value and honor her students' voices and needs. And while she held her students to high expectations, she also made adjustments to meet her students' needs, a skill in any classroom, but especially in a classroom of thirty plus students. On the other hand, Ms. Jones's overreliance on discipline to control Brown and Black bodies not only reenforces historic racial divides, it also indoctrinates nondominant students into a "culture of poverty" (Ladson-Billings, 2006). As Ladson-Billings (2006) highlighted, proponents rely on a culture of poverty to "describe what they see as a pathology of poor students and hide behind child poverty [and difference] as an excuse for why they cannot be successful with some students" (p. 105). For educators committed to social justice, CRT's tenets and guiding principles dictate that educators be truthful and caring. Educators committed to social justice help validate their students' experiences with race and racism by helping them name their pain. They also equip their students with the skills and knowledge necessary to succeed inside and outside of their classrooms. One way to do this is by identifying and confronting racial microaggressions, which are often subtle and nuanced, but are always damaging.

Notes

1. As an example of the continuing power of race in shaping educational access and opportunity, we can look to the fate of African American Ohio mother, Kelly Williams-Bolar. In 2011 Ms. Williams-Bolar, the mother of three, was jailed for 10 days, and received three years probation for sending her children to a neighboring school district. Rather than use her own home address in Akron, Ms. Williams-Bolar used her father's address to register her children in a better school district. As a result, both Ms. Williams-Bolar and her father were charged with felonies, including defrauding the school system of $30,500 in tuition. See http://www.theroot.com/buzz/criminal-or-great-parent-black-mother-jailed-sending-daughters-white-school for more information
2. We can look towards the perennial debate over race-conscious affirmative action policy, which will once more find its way before the highest court in the land. Although the Supreme Court narrowly upheld the limited use of race in university admissions in the University of Michigan's 2003 law school case *Grutter v. Bollinger*, the Court rejected *Grutter*'s undergraduate companion case, *Gratz v. Bollinger* (2003). The Court's split decision in the Michigan cases, coupled with the ongoing controversies surrounding Justice Lewis Powell's single-authored opinion in *Regents of the University of California v. Bakke* (1978), and the pending outcome of the latest Supreme Court contest around affirmative action in *Fisher v. University of Texas at Austin* contributes to lingering doubts and confusion about the benefits and value of the policy.
3. The concept of critical mass is often utilized in discussions concerning affirmative action policies in higher education. Critical mass "asserts that because students of color add to the diversity of White students, universities should commit to enriching the education of students of color by ensuring that they are not isolated and marginalized, that is, by admitting, retaining, and graduating a 'critical mass' of underrepresented students" (Yosso, Parker, Solórzano, & Lynn, 2004, p. 17). Proponents of critical mass believe in the importance of moving away from the token presence of historically underrepresented students in higher education, toward the enrollment and graduation of a robust number of such students.
4. For instance, see the February 2011 case of Murray State University student Arlene Johnson. The Associated Press reported that Ms. Johnson, an African American freshman at the rural Kentucky campus, sought an apology from her White political science professor for an overtly racist incident in class. In the spring semester, Ms. Johnson arrived to find that Professor

Wattier, had begun class early; the day's assignment included viewing a movie. Johnson asked Wattier about this, including about the fact that nowhere in his syllabus did he explain that it was customary for him to begin class early when movies are shown. Wattier was unapologetic, and lamented that it was part of Johnson's heritage to be late. He added bluntly, "The slaves never showed up on time to their owners and were lashed for it. I just don't have the right to do that." See http://www.thegrio.com/news/msu-professor-suspended-after-telling-black-student-slaves-were-always-later.php

References

Allen, W. R., & Solórzano, D. G. (2001). Affirmative action, educational equity, and campus racial climate: A case study of the University of Michigan Law School. *Berkeley La Raza Law Journal, 12*(2), 237–363.

Bell, D. (1989). *And we are not saved: The elusive quest for racial justice.* New York, NY: Basic Books.

Bell, D. (1992). *Faces at the bottom of the well: The permanence of racism.* New York, NY: Basic Books.

Bell, D. (2004). *Silent covenants: Brown v. Board of Education and the unfulfilled hopes for racial reform.* New York, NY: Oxford University Press.

Bell, D. (2005a). *Brown v. Board of Education* and the interest-convergence dilemma. In R. Delgado & J. Stefancic (Eds.), *The Derrick Bell reader* (pp. 33–39). New York, NY: New York University Press.

Bell, D. (2005b). Minority admissions and the usual price of racial remedies. In R. Delgado & J. Stefancic (Eds.), *The Derrick Bell reader* (pp. 261–267). New York, NY: New York University Press.

Carroll, G. (1998). *Environmental stress and African Americans: The other side of the moon.* Westport, CT: Praeger.

Coates, R. (2008). Covert racism in the USA and globally. *Sociology Compass, 2*(1), 208–231.

Crenshaw, K., Gotanda, N., Peller, G., & Thomas, K. (Eds.), (1995). *Critical race theory: The key writings that formed the movement.* New York, NY: New Press.

Crenshaw, K. W. (2011). Twenty years of critical race theory: Looking back to move forward. *Connecticut Law Review, 43*(5), 1253–1352.

Delgado, R., & Stefancic, J. (2001). *Critical race theory: An introduction.* New York, NY: New York University Press.

D'Souza, D. (1995). *The end of racism: Principles for a multiracial society.* New York, NY: Free Press.

Fry, R., & Gonzales, F. (2008). *One-in-five and growing fast: A profile of Hispanic public school students.* Washington, DC: Pew Hispanic Center.

Gándara, P., & Contreras, F. (2009). *The Latino education crisis: The consequences of failed social policies.* Cambridge, MA: Harvard University Press.

Gratz v. Bollinger et al. 539 U.S. 244 (2003).

Grutter v. Bollinger et al. 539 U.S. 306 (2003).

Ladson-Billings, G. (1994). *The dreamkeepers: Successful teachers of African American children.* San Francisco, CA: Jossey-Bass.

Ladson-Billings, G. (2006). It's not the culture of poverty, it's the poverty of culture: The problem with teacher education. *Anthropology and Education Quarterly, 37*(2), 104–109.

Ladson-Billings, G., & Tate, W. F. (1995). Toward a critical race theory of education. *Teachers College Record, 97*(1), 47–68.

Lakoff, G. (2002). *Moral politics: How liberals and conservatives think.* Chicago, IL: University of Chicago Press.

Lakoff, G. (2006). *Thinking points: Communicating our American values and vision.* New York, NY: Farrar, Straus, and Giroux.

Lawrence, C. R. III. (1995). The word and the river: Pedagogy as scholarship, as struggle. In K. Crenshaw, N. Gotanda, G. Peller, & K. Thomas (Eds.), *Critical race theory: The key writings that formed the movement* (pp. 336–351). New York, NY: New Press.

Lewis, A. E. (2003). *Race in the schoolyard: Negotiating the color line in classrooms and communities.* New Brunswick, NJ: Rutgers University Press.

Loury, G. (2002). *The anatomy of racial inequality.* Cambridge, MA: Harvard University Press.

Matsuda, M. (1991). Voices of America: Accent, antidiscrimination law, and a jurisprudence for the last reconstruction. *Yale Law Journal, 100*(5), 1329–1407.

Oakes, J. (2005). *Keeping track: How schools structure inequality* (2nd ed.). New Haven, CT: Yale University Press.

Orfield, G. (2001). Schools more separate: Consequences of a decade of resegregation. The Civil Rights Project, Harvard University. Retrieved from http://civilrightsproject.ucla.edu/research/k-12-education/integration-and-diversity/schools-more-separate-consequences-of-a-decade-of-resegregation/?searchterm

Pierce, C. (1970). Offensive mechanisms. In F. Barbour (Ed.), *The Black seventies* (pp. 265–282). Boston, MA: Porter Sargent.

Pierce, C. (1974). Psychiatric problems of the Black minority. In S. Arieti (Ed.), *American handbook of psychiatry* (pp. 512–523). New York, NY: Basic Books.

Pierce, C. (1975). The mundane extreme environment and its effects on learning. In S. Brainard (Ed.), *Learning disabilities: Issues and recommendations for research* (pp. 1–23). Washington, DC: National Institute of Education.

Solórzano, D. G. (1997). Images and words that wound: Critical race theory, racial stereotyping and teacher education. *Teacher Education Quarterly, 24*(3), 5–19.

Solórzano, D. G. (1998). Critical race theory, race and gender microaggressions, and the experience of Chicana and Chicano scholars. *International Journal of Qualitative Studies in Education, 11*(1), 121–136.

Solórzano, D. G., Allen, W., & Carroll, G. (2002). Keeping race in place: Racial microaggressions and campus racial climate at the University of California, Berkeley. *Chicano-Latino Law Review, 23,* 15–111.

Solórzano, D. G., Ceja, M. & Yosso, T. (2000). Critical race theory, racial microaggressions, and campus racial climate: The experiences of African American college students. *Journal of Negro Education, 69*(1–2), 60–73.

Solórzano, D. G., & Delgado Bernal, D. (2001). Examining transformational resistance through a critical race and LatCrit theory framework: Chicana and Chicano students in an urban context. *Urban Education, 36*(3), 308–342.

Tate, W. (1997). Critical race theory and education: History, theory, and implications. In M. Apple (Ed.), *Review of research in education* (pp. 195–247). Washington, DC: American Educational Research Association.

Tatum, B. D. (1992). Talking about race, learning about racism: The application of racial identity development theory in the classroom. *Harvard Educational Review, 62*(1), 1–24.

Tatum, B. D. (1997) *'Why are all the Black kids sitting together in the cafeteria?': And other conversations about race.* New York, NY: Basic Books.

Valenzuela, A. (1999). *Subtractive schooling: U.S.-Mexican youth and the politics of caring.* Albany, NY: State University of New York Press.

West, C. (1993). *Race matters.* Boston, MA: Beacon Press.

Yosso, T. J., Parker, L., Solórzano, D. G., & Lynn, M. (2004). From Jim Crow to affirmative action and back again: A critical race discussion of racialized rationales and access to higher education. *Review of Research in Education, 28*(1), 1–25.

Yosso, T. J., Smith, W. A., Ceja, M., & Solórzano, D. G. (2009). Critical race theory, racial microaggressions, and campus racial climate for Latina/o undergraduates. *Harvard Educational Review, 79*(4), 659–691.

EIGHT

The Racialization of Threat

Responding to the Punishment and Purging of Black and Latina/o Youth in School

Tara M. Brown

Introduction: School Exclusion and Threat

Each year, tens of thousands of students are excluded from K–12 public schools in the United States through out-of-school suspension and expulsion. Of great concern is that they are disproportionately Black and Latina/o (and male). Many have attended schools that have not served them well, and, as a result, they have experienced significant academic difficulties and alienation from school. Under the guise of "color-blind" disciplinary policies and procedures, such as zero tolerance, schools purge themselves of these youth who are often seen as "'disciplinary problems,' rather than as learners" (Brown, 2007, p. 433).

Disciplinary exclusion often exacerbates other difficulties that children and adolescents have with school, and has devastating implications for their academic achievement and quality of life. Time spent out of regular classrooms, and delays in (re)admission to schools, following exclusion, can lead to significant gaps in learning, and difficulties in readjusting to school. Once excluded, students are often sent to alternative schools for "at risk" youth, many of which offer dismal academic instruction (Gagnon & Leone, 2005; Lange & Sletten, 2002). Further, exclusion increases the likelihood that a student will "drop out of school altogether" (Gordon, 2004, p. 173). This, in turn, exponentially increases their vulnerability to poverty; unemployment; ill health; environmental hazards such as illegal drugs, gun violence, toxic waste, and certain types of crimes; and incarceration

(Greenberg & Schneider, 1994). It is estimated that about half of Latina/os and Blacks in state prisons do not have a high school diploma or GED, as compared to about 30% of Whites (Educational Testing Service, 2006).

For many Black and Latina/o youth, exclusionary disciplinary action is a clear conduit to school failure, decreased opportunity, and diminished quality of life. But why are so many young people of color subject to punishment and exclusion in school, as compared to White youth? This can be explained, in part, by the widespread racialization of threat, which poses Black and Latina/o youth, particularly (but not exclusively) boys and young men, as "menaces to society." As such, their behaviors—even those of elementary age children—are more likely to be seen as threatening, and to be met with unduly harsh punishment (Ferguson, 2000; Nolan, 2011; Rios, 2011).

The imagined social threat of Black and Latina/o youth reflects the "atmospheric" nature of racism as veiled, elusive, omnipresent, and insidious. It is (re)produced through implicit messages that bombard the American public from multiple sectors of society, such as education, news and entertainment media, politics, and law enforcement. The language is coded—urban youth, illegals, gang bangers, hustlers, baby mamas, oppositional students—but we all know who they are talking about. No one has to explicitly tell us. The threat is in the air, permeating the collective psyche, and driving the campaign to surveil, control, and punish Black and Latina/o youth, and to purge them from public spaces.

In *The War Against the Poor*, Gans (1995) outlined several types of social threat that socioeconomically disenfranchised people are imagined to pose to society. The first is threat to safety, which is primarily associated with physical injury and violent crime. The second is moral or ethical threat, referring to behaviors seen as immoral, "socially unacceptable," or as infringing on the rights of others, such as lawbreaking and unmarried parenthood. These two types are central to how threat is communicated about Black and Latina/o youth.

This paper will examine how messages about Black and Latina/o youth as safety and moral or ethical threats are communicated, manifested, and reinforced in communities and schools, contributing to the overrepresentation of these youth in school exclusion and, subsequently, school failure. While race is rarely acknowledged, formally, in official policies, practices, and statements that shape perceptions of Black and Latina/o youth, the routine targeting of these particular young people for surveillance, control, and punishment, produces highly racialized messages of threat. I will examine this further in a discussion about the elusive and structural nature of current-day racism in the United States (Darder & Mirón, 2007), as a way to frame some recommendations for eliminating racist school disciplinary practices and their deleterious effects on Black and Latina/o youth.

Threats in the Community

As Darder and Mirón (2007) asserted, "U.S. citizens are systematically warned to be afraid of the poor and the different [non-White]" (p. 137). The deluge of media portrayals that characterize them as dangerous, serves to justify "the rampant incarceration" (p. 137) of, particularly, low-income Blacks and Latina/os. The focus on "deviance" and crime obscures the racial, ethnic, and class biases that are deeply embedded within structures of opportunity (e.g., the job market and the education system), and positions Blacks and Latina/os as threats to society.

Increased surveillance, control, and containment, legitimized through the propagation of fear, shapes everyday life in low-income communities of color. This is reflected in increased efforts to surveil and criminalize Black and Latina/o youth, increasing the likelihood that they will come into confrontation with law enforcement. For example, a growing number of cities and towns are instituting ordinances known as "sagging pants laws" which outlaw dress that exposes undergarments, under penalty of fines, community service, and possible jail time (Baxter & Marina, 2008; Hunter, 2007). While these ordinances are theoretically "color-blind," and pertain to the exposure of all undergarments (including showing bra straps, which has been popular among girls and young women of all races), the intent of these ordinances is to target the popular style of dress of, primarily, Black and Latino male youth. Based on decades-old "decency laws," such ordinances veil their true discriminatory nature, and pose young men of color as threats to ethical codes of conduct. Further, proponents of the criminalization of sagging pants often equate this style of dress with prison culture, conceptually linking youth who adopt this style to prison inmates.

The long-time fear of young people "roaming the streets . . . involved in criminal activities of all types" (Treaster, 1994) has led to crackdowns on truancy in many communities that involve law enforcement and, thus, criminalize school absenteeism. Communities targeted for these crackdowns are often low-income and predominantly Black and Latina/o. For example, school districts in California and Texas had outfitted persistently truant children with Global Positioning System (GPS) devices for tracking and apprehension by law enforcement. While such legislation is officially "raceless," Milloy (2007) pointed out that, in Maryland, it was proposed solely for Prince George's County, "the only predominantly Black county in the Washington [DC] area." Although crackdowns on truancy are often framed as educational interventions, they usually reflect and reinforce the perception that youth of color must be contained in order to minimize the threats they pose to society. Largely missing are discussions about how schools, which have historically marginalized and pushed Black and Latina/o youth out of school, are complicit in why they do not go to school (Brown & Rodríguez, 2009b; Fine & Smith, 2001; Smyth & Hattam, 2004).

"Anti-gang ordinances" have also been enacted to clear the streets of threatening youth. In many cities, police officers can disperse and arrest groups of three or more young people for "loitering and other suspicious activity" (Somerville Board of Aldermen, 2004). These ordinances target primarily Blacks and Latina/os in impoverished neighborhoods where recreational spaces for young people are in short supply. Like truancy crackdowns, they "allow police to continue legalized harassment and street sweeps of youth in Black and Latino communities" (Lipman, 2003, p. 349). Further, they reinforce the idea that young people of color are suspicious, and that when they congregate, they are likely to engage in criminal activity.

The above examples coalesce with countless other menacing images in the news and entertainment media that degrade Black and Latina/o youth. Black and Latina/o girls and young women are portrayed as unwed "baby mamas" who violate decent norms of sexual behavior, and abuse the welfare system. Boys and young men are portrayed as violent, hypersexual, and criminally inclined. Further, hip-hop music and culture, an important venue for personal and sociopolitical expression created for and by particularly, low-income, urban youth of color, has been widely demonized. For example, hip-hop music (and rap, in particular) "has been framed negatively, as a contributor to an array of social problems, crime and delinquency" (Tanner, Krahn, & Hartnagel, 2009, p. 694). The ubiquity of messages communicated about Black and Latina/o youth as threats emanates from and permeates multiple facets of these young people's everyday lives, including school.

Threats in the Schools

Perceptions of Black and Latina/o youth as threats impact how supposedly "color-blind" school disciplinary policies and procedures are applied to them. While theoretically impartial, disciplinary practices are often profoundly subjective. Many infractions commonly outlined in schools' codes of discipline are not clearly defined; nor are the types of consequences they merit. Offenses like "disruption," "disrespect," "defiance," and "threat," as well as their concomitant punishments, are largely left to the discretion of school personnel. Further, "despite the provision of hearings, school administrators [have] considerable discretional power in imposing exclusionary sanctions" (Brown, 2007, p. 440). Consequently, research shows that disciplinary policies and procedures are often interpreted and carried out in ways that result in more frequent and more severe punishment of Blacks and Latina/os.

In a study of disciplinary records in a large urban school district in the Midwest, Russell Skiba (2001) found "no evidence that African-American students [were] punished more in school because they act out more" (p. 182) than White students. Rather, he found that they are punished for "less serious, more subjective reasons" (p. 182). Further, the over-referral of Black boys to special education increases their likelihood of being punished through exclusion, as students identified as having special needs are much more likely to be suspended than those who have not been so identified (Christle, Nelson, & Jolivette, 2004). Such racialized disparities have been attributed to factors like institutional bias, school culture, and school adults' beliefs and perceptions (Dance, 2002; Gordon, 2004; Nolan, 2011).

In a seminal ethnographic study of disciplinary practices in an elementary school on the West Coast, Ann Ferguson (2000) found that beliefs among White teachers included perceptions of Black boys (and to a lesser degree, Black girls) as inherently different from and more criminally disposed than White children. As a result, she posited, "misbehavior [by Black boys] is likely to be interpreted as symptomatic of ominous criminal proclivities" (p. 89). Ferguson (2000), like Dance (2002) and others, framed racial or ethnic disparities in school discipline as, "in large part a function of macro-level problems such as the criminalization of black [and, I would add, Latino] males" (Monroe, 2005, p. 49). This is the threat in the air that seeps into the subjectivities of school adults and the idiosyncrasies of school disciplinary practices.

Racialized messages of threats also seep *out* of the educational arena. The presumed impartiality of disciplinary policies frames racial, ethnic, and class overrepresentation as evidence that low-income students and students of color are inherently more disruptive and unruly than other students. This is reinforced by media images of violence against teachers, and "Persistently Dangerous Schools" lists that negatively publicize high-poverty, high-minority schools. Further, students classified as "disruptive"—disproportionately Black and Latina/o—are characterized as moral or ethical threats to acceptable codes of behavior, and to the rights of other learners. This is used as justification to remove them from schools (National Center for Education Statistics (NCES), 2003), despite research showing that classroom misbehavior often results from boring and irrelevant curriculum, unmet learning needs, and disrespect by teachers (Brown, 2011; Brown & Rodríguez, 2009b; Kelly, 1993; Noguera, 2003; Sekayi, 2001). Exclusionary practices also serve as a means of purging schools of young people who threaten the imagined benevolence of schooling by challenging racism and unfair treatment (Fine, 1991). This often happens in conjunction with local law enforcement, which has become increasingly more involved in school matters, particularly in high-poverty, high-minority schools.

In addition to academic implications, research shows that students often experience exclusion as rejection and racialized injustice, and they feel ostracized by and resentful of being removed from mainstream classroom environments (Sekayi, 2001; Skiba & Knesting, 2001; Skiba & Noam, 2002). This fosters disengagement among students, who are often already experiencing difficulties with school. Describing the experiences of excluded students, Lange and Sletten (2002) aptly stated that, "a series of suspensions, missed classes, disciplinary actions and academic failures leave this group of students weary of the school experience and distrustful that the education system can be a tool for their success" (p. 11).

The academic and socio-emotional effects of exclusionary disciplinary practices on young people can be devastating. Although theoretically impartial, these practices are often imbued with institutional and interpersonal racism, and both reflect and cultivate racialized perceptions of threat. This is a seldom discussed but significant factor in why many Black and Latina/o youth do not succeed in school, and why approximately half of them do not graduate from high school (Rumberger, 2011). Having been purged from the school system without a high school diploma, these young people (and their future families) are extremely vulnerable to poverty and all of its hazards. Thus, the implications of racialized threat, as acted upon through school disciplinary practices, are far-reaching.

The Elusive Nature of Racism and Racialized Threat

The production and use of the racialized threats posing as disciplinary practice is simultaneously facilitated and obfuscated by what Bonilla-Silva (2007) described as "'New Racism' practices" (p. 3). Whereas social practices that disadvantage non-Whites were once codified and overt, they are now "subtle, institutional, and apparently nonracial" (p. 3). One example of this, as Massey and Denton (1993) pointed out, is how for people of color, "crime, violence, and disorder are reported at rates higher than their actual incidence in real life . . . and blacks [and Latina/os] are very disproportionately paired with these negative stimuli relative to their actual levels of involvement in the population" (p. 70). This constructs them as prone to indecent, pathological, and threatening behaviors, and communicates highly racialized images of threat to the American public. School agents draw and act upon these images in ways that target Black and Latina/o students for more frequent and severe punishment, bolstering beliefs that they are more prone to rule-breaking and misbehavior than White students. This occurs through school disciplinary policies and individuals that profess to be "color-blind."

Today, many Whites in the United States say they hold nonracist and nondiscriminatory principles. However, they often do not translate into everyday beliefs and practices (Bonilla-Silva, 2007; Massey & Denton, 1993). Many frame racism as a problem of individual prejudice: mainly other people's prejudices. K–12 schools and districts and universities usually adopt this perspective when addressing racial and ethnic disparities that result from biases and discrimination. Thus, they address these problems with professional development programs and cultural awareness and sensitivity training for, particularly, White teachers and administrators. The idea is that more positive attitudes about non-White people and cultures (and low-income people) will lead to more equitable educational outcomes.

However, Bonilla-Silva (2007) argued for a "materialist interpretation . . . [of racism, which] sees the views of actors as corresponding to their systemic location" (p. 8). In this view, Whites in the United States, as the dominant racial group, think and behave in ways that perpetuate racial and ethnic stratification, because they benefit from doing so in a society where White privilege (and others' disadvantage) is deeply, structurally embedded (Branscombe, Schmitt, & Schiffhauer, 2007; McIntosh, 1988). For this reason, racist attitudes are extremely resistant to change, even when they conflict with individuals' own professed principles, and those who benefit most from racial inequality are least likely to work to eradicate it. The materialist or structuralist perspective suggests that dominant groups adopt more egalitarian practices when the detriments of not doing so (e.g., in terms of money, status, and reputation) are more substantial than the benefits—when the price becomes too high. This is reflected in the historical effectiveness of strikes, boycotts, and legal challenges in creating more egalitarian social policies and practices.

The materialist or structural interpretation of racism frames the recommendations I propose for addressing the disproportionate punishment and purging of Black and Latina/o youth from K–12 schools. These recommendations are not aimed at trying to change individual racist and culturally biased beliefs, although this work is worthwhile. We must acknowledge that for all the training on this topic in K–12 schools and teacher preparation programs, racial and ethnic disparities continue to persist in multiple facets of schooling. And, in some cases, they have worsened over the last few decades. It is evident that novel approaches are necessary.

To effectively work against the unfair punishment of youth of color, it is important to become a political force. That is, to gain control over official knowledge and discourses about how, why, and to whom the benefits of schooling are afforded and denied, and to compel schools and districts to put an end to biased disciplinary practices. I believe that only those *already dedicated* to eradicating racial and ethnic disparities in K–12 schools—those who are *not* invested in the benefit of racial and ethnic disparities, because of their ideology and/or group affiliation—can do this work. If others' racist attitudes are transformed in the process, that is good. However, the point is to compel school and district personnel to do right by Black and Latina/o children, whether or not they change their beliefs.

Becoming a Political Force

Having addressed issues of disciplinary exclusion as a classroom teacher and a university researcher, I will describe what I have learned, through my own experiences and others', about some of the ways to become a political force in K–12 disciplinary procedures. The strategies outlined are primarily aimed at the school and district levels, although they could be scaled up to a state or national level. As described, all are strengthened through partnerships and alliances among those both inside and outside of school systems.

Research and Capacity-Building

Knowledge is power, and it is important for those who aim to transform inequitable disciplinary practices to understand the nature of racial and ethnic disparities in disciplinary action, more generally, and in the particular school or district of focus. Increasing knowledge through research is vital to identifying and understanding pertinent issues, and how they should be prioritized and addressed. Empirical research findings also lend credibility to arguments for change.

Students and community groups, in collaboration with universities and non-profit organizations, have used such research (Advancement Project et al., 2011; Cammarota & Romero, 2011) to illuminate and compel school districts to reform inequitable disciplinary practices. The goals of this research have been to:

- Develop the skills and knowledge needed to make a strong case that racial and ethnic biases and unfair treatment exist in school and district disciplinary procedures and practices, and that it must desist,
- Use this case in applying pressure on schools and districts to change their practices, and
- Develop capacity among, particularly, those most directly and negatively affected by school exclusion, so they can continue to build and to make this case.

Black and Latina/o youth and families must be actively engaged in this research, for several reasons. First, because they are most directly affected by the problem, they must have the capacity to sustain the effort for change, even after outside researchers and advocates have left (Reason & Bradbury, 2008). Second, competencies built through research—e.g., organizing, information gathering, data collection and analysis, writing, critical thinking, and presentation—can translate into marketable job skills, and can augment the poor quality education that many Black and Latina/o students receive. Third, those directly impacted by unjust school discipline practices have unique and valuable insights into the problem. When brought to the research process, this knowledge greatly enhances the viability and applicability of the research (Brown, 2010). Finally, positioning young people as engaged learners and experts works against the perception of them as threats to society. Participatory action research (PAR), a rigorous research methodology with a long and successful history in sociopolitical justice (Brown &

Rodríguez, 2009a; Cammarota & Fine, 2008; Lynn & Parker, 2006), can be an effective method for students, families, community members, and school personnel, to organize collaborative research.

Familiarity with the literature on school discipline and educational inequity provides insights into how to identify, understand, and explain racial disparities. It also provides researchers with the "official" language to which school and district officials are more likely to respond. It is also important to get pertinent data from the local school and district, such as codes of discipline, disciplinary policies, and related statistics. Public school districts are mandated to collect information on suspensions and expulsions, although the levels of detail vary. This is public information, but districts often do not make it readily available, and/or create barriers to access. An allied or sympathetic school or district official can help. For an excellent guide to requesting and securing public documents pertaining to school discipline, see *Mapping the Schoolhouse to Jailhouse Track Action Kit*, created by the Advancement Project (www.advancementproject.org), a legal advocacy organization.

It is also important to collect empirical data, particularly those which capture the experiences of disciplined and excluded students. Very often, discipline-related documents generated by schools, such as suspension and expulsion notifications, outline infractions like "threat," "insubordination," and "defiance," but the events leading up to them are not explained. When they are explained, as in the case of an incident report, it is always from the perspective of a school adult (Wright & Dusek, 1998)—very often the adult recommending disciplinary action. This makes it difficult to identify discriminatory practices. For example, I interviewed a Latina 11th grader suspended for persistent "defiance" and "classroom disruption" and "threat." Only after talking to her did I learn that the incidents leading to her suspension were precipitated by a teacher forbidding her to speak Spanish in the classroom.

Gathering students' experiences and perspectives, through questionnaires and interviews, can help to develop a fuller understanding of the nature of disciplinary practices and procedures. Schools would likely be reluctant to allow a researcher investigating racialized disciplinary practices to conduct classroom observations, and surreptitious investigations violate the ethics of research (Bogdan & Biklen, 2003). However, parents have the right to visit their children's classrooms, and their presence can discourage such practices which, if they do occur, can then be documented and reported. Parents can also provide information about how the school and district communicates with students and their families about their rights, as well as about disciplinary procedures, and how suspension and expulsion hearings, which are usually closed to the public, are conducted (Rossow & Parkinson, 1999). Again, the *Mapping the Schoolhouse to Jailhouse Track Action Kit* provides many useful tools for collecting empirical data.

Partnerships are very helpful throughout the process of research and subsequent action. Young people and their families and allied school adults can provide on-the-ground knowledge, and can lend legitimacy to the efforts of schools and communities. Community-based organizations, advocacy groups, and universities can also provide connections and legitimacy, as well as research skills and training, funding, visibility, and status.

Next, I will discuss, more explicitly, how research and advocacy can be applied to the problem of racial and ethnic disparities in school discipline.

Applied Research and Advocacy
Powerful challenges to the overrepresentation of Black and Latina/o youth in school disciplinary action have often enlisted university scholars and community-based research and advocacy groups. For example, the Advancement Project has partnered with students, families, and community members in school districts around the country, to document racial and ethnic disparities, and to apply pressure to schools and districts to change racist disciplinary practices. In some cases, this has been through legal action or threats thereof. Further, a growing number of university scholars are exploring how the 14th Amendment can be used to legally compel the education system to provide quality and equitable education for all children. They are also a potential source of information and support (Liu, 2006).

Leveraging publicity is another tactic that has been used to compel schools and districts to change inequitable disciplinary practices. Partnering organizations, like the Advancement Project, the Applied Research Center (ARC), Community Asset Development Re-defining Education (CADRE), and universities have helped to create and disseminate "official" research reports which can be presented to school boards and school, district, city, state, and federal officials and policymakers, and can be distributed to the media and the public (Advancement Project et al., 2011; Brady, Balmer, & Phenix, 2007; CADRE, 2002). The first best step is to present the information to schools and districts, and allow them the opportunity to work in partnership for change. However, if they are resistant, public awareness and scrutiny can be powerful tools in getting demands met.

Two important things (among many) to insist upon are:
1. More student and family control over, and more transparency in, disciplinary practices and procedures, and
2. Better tracking of and greater access to information related to those practices and procedures.

As mentioned, teachers and school and district officials have considerable discretionary power in school discipline and exclusion. Further, many procedural processes (e.g., the writing of incident reports, and suspension and expulsion hearings) are often hidden from the public (Rossow & Parkinson, 1999). It is vital that those who engage in discriminatory practices know that someone is paying attention. Therefore, "watching" and advocating at the school and classroom levels is also important. Advocates can assist students and families in learning and asserting their rights. They can also offer moral support and provide transportation and childcare so that parents can attend school meetings and visit classrooms, and, importantly, make their presence known to school personnel. As a study participant who had been expelled from school once told me, "If they know someone cares about you, they'll think twice about what they do to you."

Even in suspension and expulsion hearings that are closed to the public, students and their parents or guardians can usually have witnesses to the incident and a legal representative present (Bartlett & McCullagh, 1993). Some districts also allow teachers and other school personnel to serve as character witnesses, which can impact the outcome. These allies can advocate for students, and watch for evidence of unfairness in the process. Lastly, most states require that a written record be kept of hearing proceedings, and students and their families are entitled to a copy (Rossow & Parkinson, 1999). This can be used as data, and as a way to share information about these largely concealed procedures. Although it is skewed toward schools and districts, *The Law of Student Expulsions and Suspensions* (Rossow & Parkinson, 1999) is a useful source for learning about students' and families' rights regarding school exclusion.

Again, it is vital that the capacity to write, disseminate, and present official reports, to watch disciplinary practices and procedures, and to effectively advocate is developed among local actors—students and their families, and allied teachers and community members—to sustain the effort.

While some of the above recommendations may appear harsh, lacking in goodwill, or antischool, this is not the case. They are based on the idea that public education can and does significantly help disenfranchised youth to build secure and fulfilling lives, and reflect a commitment to making schools better at doing that. We should not give up hope that when school adults are presented with evidence of racist practices they will change because it is the right thing to do. Some will, and should be given the opportunity to do so before using more forceful tactics. That is one important use of the evidence produced through the research and documentation of discrimination and racial disparities in school discipline. Further, many K–12 teachers and administrators are already working against racial disparities of all kinds in schools, at great professional risk. They are an important audience for this chapter, and a vital resource in need of support.

There are also many others who are resistant to change. The institutional power and social status that teachers and administrators have over marginalized students and families helps them to obfuscate racially and ethnically biased practices. They have considerable structural advantages in leveraging disciplinary policies to work in their favor, and, thus, considerable support in resisting change.

In my experience, when marginalized students and families are not successful in redressing recommendations for school exclusion through school- and district-established channels, they usually believe they are out of options. That is why becoming a political force through the aforementioned strategies is so important. When schools and districts will not put a stop to the unjust punishment and removal of Black and Latina/o youth on their own, we must have the power to compel them to do so. This will move them forward in meeting the U.S. Department of Education's (2011) mission of "fostering educational excellence and ensuring equal access" to all children.

Conclusion

Since the Civil Rights Era, and particularly since the last presidential election, there has been a growing perception in the American public that we are now in a "postracial" era, in which racism is neither a factor in racial and ethnic disparities nor in one's chances for prosperity or adversity. In actuality, however, racism—institutional and interpersonal—has become better hidden. It is hidden in the disproportionate reporting and overstating of social problems among people of color. It is hidden in the disproportionate application of restrictive and punitive ordinances to low-income communities, and Black and Latina/o youth. It is hidden by professions of equality and fair treatment and "color-blind" policies. These are among the tactics of a new "racial ideology" (Bonilla-Silva, 2007, p. 9) in contemporary U.S. society, in which racism is subtle and covert, and discriminatory practices and those who carry them out are often elusive.

It is in this context that racialized perceptions of Black and Latina/o youth as threats to society are produced, and used to punish and purge them from schools in disproportionate numbers. This occurs under the guise of "impartial" policies and procedures. The effects of school exclusion can be devastating and far-reaching, particularly for young people who are already marginalized in schools and in the broader society. The overrepresentation of Black and Latina/o youth in school discipline is a profound educational and sociopolitical issue that must be addressed immediately and decisively.

The processes that (re)produce racial and ethnic disparities are deeply embedded in the structures of opportunity in U.S. society, including schools, and work to the benefit of the racially and socioeconomically privileged. For this reason, the racial, ethnic, and cultural biases manifest in discriminatory action, have "proved to be remarkably resilient" (Massey & Denton, 1993, p. 70). We must continue the difficult work of trying to transform the personal biases of those within the existing school system. In the meantime, however, we cannot continue to allow Black and Latina/o children to become collateral damage. Those of us who are dedicated to the eradication of racist practices within our schools must become a political force that can compel them to treat our children fairly. We can only do this if we have the power to exact a price that those who act unjustly are not willing to pay—whether or not they choose to change their beliefs.

Note

1. Native American youth also have disproportionate rates of suspension and expulsion.

References

Advancement Project, Education Law Center-PA, FairTest, The Forum for Education and Democracy, Juvenile Law Center, & NAACP Legal Defense and Education Fund,(2011). *Federal policy, ESEA reauthorization, and the school-to-prison pipeline*. Washington, DC: Authors. Retrieved from http://www.jlc.org/resources/publications/federal-policy-esea-reauthorization-and-school-prison-pipeline

Bartlett, L., & McCullagh, J. (1993). Exclusion from the educational process in the public schools: What process is now due. *Education & Law Journal*, (1), 3–58.

Baxter, V. K., & Marina, P. (2008). Cultural meaning and hip-hop fashion in the African-American male youth subculture of New Orleans. *Journal of Youth Studies*, *11*(2), 93–113.

Bogdan, R. C., & Biklen, S. K. (2003). *Qualitative research for education: An introduction to theories and methods* (4th ed.). Boston, MA: Pearson.

Bonilla-Silva, E. (2007). *Racism without racists: Color-blind racism and the persistence of racial inequality in the United States* (2nd ed.). New York, NY: Rowman & Littlefield.

Brady, K. P., Balmer, S., & Phenix, D. (2007). School-police partnership effectiveness in urban schools: An analysis of New York City's Impact Schools initiative. *Education & Urban Society*, *39*(4), 455–478.

Branscombe, N. R., Schmitt, M. T., & Schiffhauer, K. (2007). Racial attitudes in response to thoughts of White privilege. *European Journal of Social Psychology*, *37*(2), 203–215.

Brown, T. M. (2007). Lost and turned out: Academic, social, and emotional experiences of students excluded from school. *Urban Education*, *42*(5), 432–455.

Brown, T. M. (2010). ARISE to the challenge: Partnering with urban youth to improve educational research and learning. *Penn GSE Perspectives on Urban Education*, *7*(1), 4–14.

Brown, T. M. (2011). The effects of educational policy and local context on special education students' experiences of school removal and transition. *Educational Policy*. doi: 10.1177/0895904811417589

Brown, T. M., & Rodríguez, L. F. (Eds.). (2009a). New directions for youth development: Youth in participatory action research [Special issue]. San Francisco, CA: Jossey-Bass.

Brown, T. M., & Rodríguez, L. F. (2009b). School and the co-construction of dropout. *International Journal of Qualitative Studies in Education*, *22*(2), 221–242.

Cammarota, J., & Fine, M. (2008). Youth participatory action research: A pedagogy for transformational resistance. In J. Cammarota & M. Fine (Eds.), *Revolutionizing education: Youth participatory action research in motion* (pp. 1–12). New York, NY: Routledge.

Cammarota, J., & Romero, A. (2011). Participatory action research for high school students: Transforming policy, practice, and the personal with social justice education. *Educational Policy*, *25*(3), 488–506.

Christle, C., Nelson, C. M., & Jolivette, K. (2004). School characteristics related to the use of suspension. *Education & Treatment of Children*, *27*(4), 509–526.

Community Asset Development Re-defining Education (CADRE). (2002). *More education. Less suspension: A call to action to stop the pushout crisis in South Los Angeles*. Los Angeles, CA: Author.

Dance, L. J. (2002). *Tough fronts: The impact of street culture on schooling*. New York, NY: RoutledgeFalmer.

Darder, A., & Mirón, L. F. (2007). Critical pedagogy in a time of uncertainty: A call to action. In N. K. Denzin & M. D. Giardina (Eds.), *Contesting empire, globalizing dissent: Cultural studies after 9/11* (pp. 136–151). Boulder, CO: Paradigm.

Educational Testing Service (ETS). (2006). *Locked up and locked out: An educational perspective on the U.S. prison population.* Princeton, NJ: Author.

Ferguson, A. A. (2000). *Bad boys: Public schools in the making of Black masculinity.* Ann Arbor, MI: University of Michigan Press.

Fine, M. (1991). *Framing dropouts: Notes on the politics of an urban public high school.* Albany, NY: State University of New York Press.

Fine, M., & Smith, K. (2001). Zero tolerance: Reflections on a failed policy that won't die. In W. Ayers, B. Dohrn, & R. Ayers (Eds.), *Zero tolerance: Resisting the drive for punishment in our schools: A handbook for parents, students, educators, and citizens* (pp. 256–263). New York, NY: W. W. Norton.

Gagnon, J. C., & Leone, P. E. (2005). Elementary day and residential schools for children with emotional and behavioral disorders: Characteristics of educators and students. *Remedial & Special Education, 26*(3), 141–150.

Gans, H. J. (1995). *The war against the poor: The underclass and antipoverty policy.* New York, NY: Basic Books.

Gordon, J. M. (2004). *Looking at high school dropout problems from students' perspectives: Finding a solution* (Unpublished doctoral dissertation). McGill University, Montréal, Québec, Canada.

Greenberg, M., & Schneider, D. (1994). Violence in American cities: Young Black males is the answer, but what was the question? *Social Science & Medicine, 39*(2), 179–187.

Hunter, V. (2007, August 28). Louisiana puts spotlight on sagging pants. *The Times.*

Kelly, D. M. (1993). *Last chance high: How girls and boys drop in and out of alternative schools.* New Haven, CT: Yale University Press.

Lange, C. M., & Sletten, S. J. (2002). *Alternative education: A brief history and research synthesis.* Alexandria, VA: National Association of State Directors of Special Education.

Lipman, P. (2003). Chicago school policy: Regulating Black and Latino youth in the global city. *Race Ethnicity and Education, 6*(4), 331-355.

Liu, G. (2006). Education, equality, and national citizenship. *Yale Law Journal, 116*(2), 330–411.

Lynn, M., & Parker, L. (2006). Critical race studies in education: Examining a decade of research on U.S. schools. *Urban Review, 38*(4), 257–290.

Massey, D. S., & Denton, N. A. (1993). *American apartheid: Segregation and the making of the underclass.* Cambridge, MA: Harvard University Press.

McIntosh, P. (1988). *White privilege: Unpacking the invisible knapsack.* Retrieved from http://www.nymbp.org/reference/WhitePrivilege.pdf

Milloy, C. (2007, February 14). GPS tagging is for wild animals, not truants. *The Washington Post.* Retrieved from http://www.washingtonpost.com/wp-dyn/content/article/2007/02/13/AR2007021301270.html

Monroe, C. R. (2005). Why are 'bad boys' always Black? Causes of disproportionality in school discipline and recommendations for change. *The Clearing House, 79*(1), 45–50.

National Center for Education Statistics (NCES). (2003). *Overview of public elementary and secondary students, staff, schools, school districts, revenues, and expenditures: School year 2004–05 and fiscal year 2004.* Washington, DC: U.S. Department of Education. Retrieved from http://nces.ed.gov/pubs2007/overview04/

Noguera, P. A. (2003). *City schools and the American dream: Reclaiming the promise of public education.* New York, NY: Teachers College Press.

Nolan, K. (2011). *Police in the hallways: Discipline in an urban high school.* Minneapolis, MN: University of Minnesota Press.

Reason, P., & Bradbury, H. (Eds.). (2008). *The Sage handbook of action research: Participative inquiry and practice.* Los Angeles, CA: Sage.

Rios, V. M. (2011). *Punished: Policing the lives of Black and Latino boys.* New York, NY: New York University Press.

Rossow, L. F., & Parkinson, J. R. (1999). *The law of student expulsions and suspensions*. Dayton, OH: Education Law Association.
Rumberger, R. W. (2011). *Dropping out: Why students drop out of high school and what can be done about it*. Cambridge, MA: Harvard University Press.
Sekayi, N. R. (2001). Intellectual indignation: Getting at the roots of student resistance in an alternative high school program. *Education, 122*(2), 414–422.
Skiba, R. J. (2001). When is disproportionality discrimination? The overrepresentation of Black students in school suspension. In W. Ayers, B. Dohrn, & R. Ayers (Eds.), *Zero tolerance: Resisting the drive for punishment in our schools: A handbook for parents, students, educators, and citizens* (pp. 176–187). New York, NY: New Press.
Skiba, R. J., & Knesting, K. (2001). Zero tolerance, zero evidence: An analysis of school disciplinary practice. In R. J. Skiba & G. G. Noam (Eds.), *Zero tolerance: Can suspension and expulsion keep schools safe?: New directions for youth development* (pp. 17–43). San Francisco, CA: Jossey-Bass.
Skiba, R. J., & Noam, G. G. (Eds.). (2002). *Zero tolerance: Can suspension and expulsion keep schools safe?* San Francisco, CA: Jossey-Bass.
Smyth, J., & Hattam, R. (2004). *'Dropping out,' drifting off, being excluded: Becoming somebody without school*. New York, NY: Peter Lang.
Somerville Board of Aldermen. (2004). *Gang loitering ordinance*. Somerville, MA.
Tanner, J., M. Askbridge, & S. Wortley. (2009). Listening to rap: Cultures of crime, cultures of resistance. *Social Forces, 88*(2), 693-722.
Treaster, J. B. (1994, April 5). Despite reservations, police to begin rounding up truants. *The New York Times*, p. 3. Retrieved from http://www.nytimes.com/1994/04/05/nyregion/despite-reservations-police-to-begin-rounding-up-truants.html
U.S. Department of Education. (2011). Mission statement. Retrieved from http://www2.ed.gov/about/landing.jhtml
Wright, J. A., & Dusek, J. B. (1998). Compiling school base rates for disruptive behaviors from student disciplinary referral data. *School Psychology Review, 27*(1), 138–147.

NINE

Disrupting the Standard Education Storyline for Latin@ Students Across the P–20 Educational System

Sustaining the Alma (Soul) of the Latin@ Community Through a Counterstory of Access to the Culture of Power and the Power of Culture

María del Carmen Salazar

It is estimated that Latin@s[1] currently comprise approximately 16% of the total U.S. population (U.S. Census Bureau, 2011), representing the largest racial and ethnic minority group in the United States (Fry, 2011). A snapshot of the Latin@ population reveals that they are the fastest growing and youngest ethnic population in the country (Lopez & Minushkin, 2008), accounting for nearly 22% of total U.S. P–12 public school enrollment (National Center for Education Statistics [NCES], 2009c). Policymakers advise that current demographic trends merit a national focus on the achievement of Latin@ students across the P–20 educational system, hereafter referred to as the P–20 (Castellanos & Gloria, 2007; Valverde & Scribner, 2001). An increased focus on the achievement of Latin@ students is essential, given that Latin@s are severely undereducated and miseducated across the P–20 (Gándara & Contreras, 2009; Nieto, 2005). Yet, despite the fact that Latin@s experience persistent achievement gaps in comparison with other ethnic groups (Passel & Cohn, 2008; Fry, 2011), educational leaders have failed to demonstrate a sense of urgency in accelerating educational parity among Latin@ students and their White counterparts. This failure is most evident in educators' and policymakers' refusal to interrogate racialized barriers to P–20 educational achievement (Valenzuela, 2004; Villalpando, 2004).

In this chapter, I present the *standard education story* (Duncan, 2002), or the dominant narrative of educational achievement, about Latin@ students across the U.S. P–20 educational system as one of persistent achievement gaps, and I contest this story through the lenses of two theoretical frameworks—Critical Race Theory (CRT) and Latin@ Critical Race Theory (LatCrit). CRT in education is "a framework or set of basic insights, perspectives, methods and pedagogy that seeks to identify, analyze and transform those structural and cultural aspects of education that maintain subordinate and dominant racial positions inside and outside of classrooms" (Solórzano & Yosso, 2002, p. 25). Villalpando (2004) maintained that CRT requires the examination of institutional policies, programs, and practices that reinforce racial inequity, and "interfere with Latin@ students' rights and abilities to receive the best educational opportunities available" (p. 42). Moreover, LatCrit complements CRT (Villalpando, 2004), and provides "a framework that can be used to theorize and examine the ways in which race and racism explicitly and implicitly impact the educational structures, processes, and discourse affecting people of color generally and Latin@s specifically" (Solórzano & Yosso, 2002, p. 25). The focus on race and racism intersects with Latin@ multidimensionality, including, but not limited to, language, culture, national origin, and citizenship status (Trucios-Haynes, 2001).

Against the backdrop of CRT and LatCrit, I assert that the standard education story about Latin@s is propagated through (a) widespread acceptance and dissemination of the *dominant storyline* (Duncan, 2002) about Latin@ students—i.e., the belief that Latin@ "failure" results from their own deficits; and (b) assimilationist policies, programs, and practices—i.e., approaches that strip students of the resources they need to survive and thrive. Subsequently, I assert that the aforementioned factors deny Latin@ students access to both the *culture of power* (Delpit, 1988)—i.e., the beliefs, skills, and attitudes prized by the mainstream, dominant White culture—and the *power of culture* (Pang & Barba, 1995)—i.e., the "community cultural wealth" (Yosso, 2005) of Latin@s, that is inclusive of their linguistic, familial, and immigrant experience. As a result, the P–20 educational system reifies subordinate and dominant racial positions, and reinforces racialized barriers to educational attainment. I maintain that it is only by providing Latin@s with equal access to both the culture of power and the power of culture that students can be liberated from racialized oppression and inequity occurring across the P–20.

In what follows, I begin with an examination of the concepts, culture of power and power of culture. I then describe the standard education story for Latin@s, and provide an analysis of how educators' adherence to the dominant storyline, and assimilationist programs, policies, and practices, perpetuate the standard education story by denying Latin@ students access to the culture of power and the power of culture. Next, I advocate that in the service of providing Latin@ students with equal access to both the culture of power and the power of culture, educators must disrupt the standard education story for Latin@ youth through the use of *storytelling resistance* (Solórzano & Yosso, 2002) or *counterstorytelling*, a construct rooted in both CRT and LatCrit. I contend that the counterstory for Latin@ youth in U.S. schools weaves the narrative that educators can empower Latin@ students by advancing a cohesive, rigorous, and culturally relevant approach to schooling that is centered on sustaining the *alma* (soul) of the Latin@ community. I close with some practical solutions for improving the education of Latina@s across the P–20 system.

Access to the Culture of Power and the Power of Culture

In P–20 education across the United States, students of color generally, and Latin@ students specifically, often navigate what Bhabha (1994) referred to as the *hybrid space* between their distinct cultures. Students of color determine when they must abide by the mainstream norms of the dominant society, and when it is safe to express thoughts, behaviors, and attitudes rooted in their home culture. Unbeknownst to many of these students, what is really at stake in these daily dilemmas is a struggle for power; students of color must constantly decide when it is necessary to defer to the culture of power in order to achieve their goals, and when to instead rely on the power of (their) culture. By culture of power, I am referring to Delpit's (1988) notion regarding the mainstream knowledge required for students to fully participate in the dominant culture, encapsulated by Barton and Yang (2000) as follows:

> The "culture of power" represents a set of values, beliefs, ways of acting and being that for sociopolitical reasons, unfairly and unevenly elevate groups of people— mostly White, upper and middle class, male and heterosexual—to positions where they have more control over money, people, and societal values than their non-culture-of-power peers (Delpit, 1988). The separation of people through these arbitrary markers results in a tiered society where set rules and ideological standpoints result in barriers for those not part of the culture of power. (p. 873)

Furthermore, by power of culture, I am referring to Pang and Barba's (1995) notion that to best serve the needs of students of color, schools should implement culturally affirming approaches that are inclusive of students' cultural resources. In the context of Latin@ communities, Yosso (2005) described the concept of Latin@ cultural resources through her conceptualization of "community cultural wealth" that details the forms of capital— aspirational, navigational, social, linguistic, familial, and resistant—drawn from Latin@s' homes and communities that "often go unrecognized and unacknowledged" (p. 69).

In order for the U.S. educational system to fulfill its civic duty to prepare all students for postsecondary and workforce readiness, P–20 students of color must be provided with access to both the culture of power and the power of culture. Latin@ students are often denied access to the power of culture due to educators' deficit-based beliefs, behaviors, and attitudes toward the Latin@ culture, as well as assimilationist policies, programs, and practices that minimize or outright prohibit the inclusion of cultural resources in schooling. Without access to the power of culture, many Latin@ students experience understandable isolation, confusion, and frustration in U.S. schools, resulting in academic obstacles that effectively deny students access to the culture of power (Valencia, 2010).

In denying Latin@ students access to the power of their culture, these students may experience a loss in motivation and engagement, and may ultimately resist the acquisition of English and acculturation into U.S. culture (Behnke, Gonzalez, & Cox, 2010; Brown & Souto-Manning, 2008; Chamberlain, 2005; Fránquiz & Salazar, 2004, 2008; Reyes Cruz, 2008). A growing body of research demonstrates that loss of culture and native language often hinders, rather than enhances school success (Cummins, 1996; Deyhle, 1995; Nieto, 1996; Salazar, 2010). Additionally, researchers have demonstrated that the loss of linguistic and cultural resources promotes reactive behaviors by Latin@ students, including boundary-maintaining mechanisms; resistance to English language development; *huelgas* (strikes); disruptive, defiant, disdainful, and disrespectful behavior; and opting out of school (Brown & Souto-Manning, 2008; Dudley-Marling & Lucas, 2009; Salazar, 2008, 2010; Sleeter & Grant, 1999).

In essence, Latin@ students deprived of both the culture of power and the power of culture become oppressed by the very educational system that can potentially liberate them, rendering the hybrid space between their Latin@ and U.S. cultures a "disabling abyss" (Cummins, 2001, as cited in Clark & Flores, 2007). In order to rectify this injustice, the standard education story of racial disparities in educational attainment for Latin@ students across the P–20 merits a closer examination.

The Standard Education Story

In his article, "Beyond Love: A Critical Race Ethnography of the Schooling of Adolescent Black Males," Garrett Duncan (2002) presented the "standard education story" for adolescent Black males as one of persistent and troubling achievement gaps. While Duncan directed attention specifically to the plight of Black males, extant research demonstrates that Latin@ students across the P–20 experience a standard education story of persistent educational disparities, compared with their Black and White counterparts (NCES, 2009b).

The educational gap for Latin@s can be traced back to early childhood (Rumberger & Arellano, 2009). Research shows that 80% of the educational gap between Latin@ students and White students in the fourth grade is present before they even begin attending school (Schneider, Martinez, & Owens, 2006). While research continues to emerge on academic disparities for Latin@s at the preschool level, most of the extant research on Latin@ academic disparities can be found in the K–12 sphere (Brown, 2007; Gregory, 2003). The standard education story for Latin@s in K–12 public schools demonstrates persistent disparities in achievement, evidenced by high dropout rates, low graduation rates and achievement scores, and limited access to high-level curriculum (Draut, 2008; NCES, 2009b, 2009c). For example, while rates vary by Latin@ subgroup, it is estimated that in 2009, Latin@s accounted for 17.6% of 16- to 24-year-olds who did not complete high school and did not earn a high school diploma or equivalent credential, compared with 9.3% for Blacks and 5.2% for Whites (NCES, 2009c). Additionally, only 63.5 % of Latin@ ninth graders receive a high school diploma in four years, compared with 81% of Whites (NCES, 2010). The Latin@ dropout rate is nearly twice as high as that of Blacks, and over three times higher than the rate of Whites (NCES, 2009c). Furthermore, Latin@s also face significant disparities in content-specific achievement scores, and tend to have less access to high-level curriculum. By the end of twelfth grade, Latin@s' average math and reading scores are virtually the same as White eighth graders. Additionally, Latin@ students are more likely to be enrolled in lower-level language arts, math, and science courses than any other ethnic group (NCES, 2009a).

Similarly, Latin@ high school graduates witness significant disparities in higher education attainment. In 2007, 34% of Latin@ 25- to 29-year-olds had completed some college, compared with 50% of their Black peers and 66% of their White peers (Draut, 2008). While college enrollment is increasing overall for Latin@s, nearly half (46%) attend two-year colleges, unlike their Black and White peers, who primarily attend four-year colleges (Fry, 2011). As for graduate enrollment, less than 6% of graduate degrees (MA and PhD) are awarded to Latin@s, compared with 64% for Whites (NCES, 2011). In sum, the standard education story for Latin@ students describes persistent gaps in educational attainment across the P–20.

Dominant Storylines and Assimilationist Approaches

I posit that the standard education story about Latin@s is fueled by dominant storylines about Latin@ students and their families, as well as assimilationist policies, programs, and practices that prevent students from accessing the culture of power and utilizing the power of Latin@ culture. Dominant storylines, also known as *master narratives* (Montecinos, 1995), are defined as "a mindset of positions, perceived wisdoms, and shared cultural understandings brought to the discussion of race" (Delgado & Stefancic, 1993, p. 22). The sections that follow provide a synthesis of deficit-based, dominant storylines about Latin@ students' language, culture, family, and immigrant experience. Additionally, I detail the resulting assimilationist policies, programs, and practices that prevent Latin@ students' access to the culture of power and the power of culture.

Language

Villenas and Deyhle (1999) contended that "one of the most insidious forms of domination and oppression is rooted in language ideology" (p. 418). Throughout the P–20, one dominant storyline is that the heritage language of Latin@s is an obstacle, rather than an asset, for learning (Ruiz, 1984; Villenas & Deyhle, 1999). As a result of this dominant storyline, Latin@ students are often subjected to the prohibition of their heritage language in school through overt (Moschkovich, 2007) and structural means (Cobas & Feagin, 2008).

Incidents of overt prohibition of heritage languages in K–12 schooling can be found in headline news. In 2005, a Latino youth in Kansas was suspended from school for speaking Spanish with friends during lunch. When the principal was asked to clarify if this was a school policy, she responded, "No, but we are not in Mexico" (Salazar, 2008). Prohibition of heritage languages can be even more insidious when it is structural (Cobas & Feagin, 2008). In P–12 education, the national education policy known as No Child Left Behind (NCLB) is commonly referred to by bilingual education advocates as No Child Left Bilingual (Meyer, 2005). NCLB places a singular emphasis on English language development from preschool through high school, in lieu of bilingual development. As a result of federal and district policies favoring English-as-a-second-language (ESL) programming, English-only instruction dominates the experience of English language learners (ELLs) in P–12 education (Hopstock & Stephenson, 2003). In the higher education context, Bernal (2002) asserted that limited English skills are considered a liability; in contrast, Bernal suggested that universities develop innovative curricular and pedagogical approaches to promote bilingualism and biculturalism in order to build on and extend students' linguistic resources.

While few would downplay the importance of learning English in an English-speaking world, a singular focus on English language acquisition perpetuates linguistic violence (Skutnabb-Kangas, 1997). All too often, educators adopt the position that "learning English would solve all of the other difficulties faced by language minority students, including poverty, racism . . . and lack of access to excellent education" (Nieto, 2004, p. 216). As a result, these educators deny Latin@ students the power of speaking in their mother tongue; this despite the growing body of research demonstrating how students' lack of access to native language in school often hinders, rather than enhances educational achievement and access to the culture of power (Bernal, 2002; Cummins, 1996; Deyhle, 1995; Nieto, 1996; Salazar, 2010).

Anzaldúa (1999) eloquently summed up the importance of maintaining students' heritage language with four simple, yet powerful words: *I am my language*. Language prohibition is a symptom of the endemic linguicism that is deeply embedded in the U.S. educational system (Skutnabb-Kangas, 1997). Linguicism arises when "ideologies and structures are used to legitimate, effectuate, and reproduce an unequal division of power and resources between groups on the basis of language" (Skutnabb-Kangas, 1997, p. 56). Additionally, linguicism is closely linked with racism, and perpetuates asymmetries in power (Ricento, 2000).

Culture

Scholars find that the dominant storyline about Latin@s across the P–20 system reveals educators' preference for a "race-neutral" pedagogy that perpetuates deficit-based views of marginalized cultures, and reinforces a system of meritocracy privileging the dominant White culture (Villalpando, 2004). Valdés (1996) described U.S. schools as "bastions of mainstream White middle-class perspectives and value systems" (p. 422), operating to the obvious benefit of students already adhering to the dominant culture. Race-neutral approaches perpetuate color-blind approaches to the instruction of Latin@ students, and result in systematic racial discrimination and oppression (Villalpando, 2004). Color-blind approaches have also been found to result in Eurocentric curricula that either neglect or outright ignore contributions of communities of color (Ladson-Billings, 2003).

Educators who engage in color-blind practices lack consideration for students' sociocultural resources as tools for academic learning. By overlooking this significant component of Latin@ education, color-blind educators deny Latin@ students access to the power of culture on a daily basis.

On the opposite end of the spectrum, educators who engage in a savior mentality *see* color, but only as a signal for deprivation, perceiving themselves as bastions of hope for the underprivileged. These "saviors" are often corrupted by the *pobrecito syndrome* (Garcia, 1997), or have an inclination to lower educational standards for the "poor little ones" born to fail. Additionally, these saviors tend to display *false empathy*, described by Duncan (2002) as "a response to the plight of oppressed individuals or groups by privileged individuals who visualize themselves in places of members of oppressed groups and ask what they, the privileged, would want if they were oppressed" (p. 137). Duncan understood that this response may not only be at odds with how the oppressed would truly respond themselves, but that "such ill-informed policy may actually perpetuate the conditions that they intend to ameliorate" (2002, p. 137).

In P–12 schooling, specifically, one cannot dispute the fact that out of every 100 Latin@ kindergartners, only 13 will obtain a bachelor's degree (U.S. Census Bureau, 2009). If dominant storylines are to be believed, Latin@ students "fail" due to their linguistic and cultural deficits. In contrast, those Latin@ students who succeed are often characterized by their Latin@ peers as "sell outs." In a recent case study, Salazar (2010) found that Latin@ students discourage peers from adopting attitudes and practices they perceive as "acting *gringo*" or White. Salazar's research aligns with prior research of African American students who reject "acting White" (Fordham & Ogbu, 1986). Solórzano and Yosso (2002) added that "according to cultural-deficit storytelling, a successful student of color is an assimilated student of color" (p. 31). Nevertheless, some educators insist that assimilation is the key to success for marginalized communities (Villenas & Deyhle, 1999). In contrast, scholars argue that assimilationist policies, programs, and practices "fortify monolingualism and monoculturalism and uphold White privilege" (Villenas & Deyhle, 1999, p. 427) while accelerating the loss of, and preventing student access to cultural, linguistic, familial, and immigrant ties.

Assimilationist practices throughout P–12 schooling promote curricula, instruction, and assessment practices that reinforce the supremacy of the dominant culture and the inferiority of Latin@s. According to Ortiz (2004), the curricula in primary and secondary education entirely exclude the history of American Latin@s. Moreover, when Latin@s are included in the content of schooling, their contributions are often limited to a fun, food, and fiesta approach that provides a sanitized version of culture through a focus on celebrations (Salazar, 2008). Exclusionary and superficial approaches to culture result in a "colonization of the mind" (Villenas & Deyhle, 1999), a pedagogical approach where the "rich knowledge, beliefs, and worldviews of the Latin@ and Mexican/Chicano community are not validated or taught" (p. 421), resulting in historical amnesia for Latin@ students.

Latin@ students are trapped in a vortex of insidious practices that strip them of the power of their culture, and deny them access to the culture of power. While educators may perceive that they are giving students of color access to the culture of power through assimilationist approaches, researchers have found that U.S. public school pedagogy is selectively delivered to students of color (Ladson-Billings, 2003). P–12 Latin@ students are immersed in educational approaches that reinforce rote skills and test-taking to the exclusion of a rigorous curriculum that more adequately prepares them for postsecondary and workforce readiness, thus creating barriers to higher education matriculation and completion (Valenzuela, 1999, 2004; Swail, Redd, & Perna, 2003). Those Latin@ students who manage to beat the odds and successfully matriculate in higher education face abysmal remediation rates (Conley, 2007), which ultimately lead to significant barriers to postsecondary education completion.

Furthermore, there are few efforts to hold educators or institutions accountable for the dismal admission, retention, and matriculation rates of Latin@ students, despite the fact that Latin@s make up the fastest-growing college enrollment group in U.S. colleges and universities (Hispanic Association of Colleges and Universities [HACU], 2004). It is estimated that by 2020, Latin@s will constitute almost 25% of total traditional college-age population, ages 18 to 24 (HACU, 2004). In the face of these projections, few concerted efforts have been made by policymakers or institutions of higher education to incorporate the experiences of Latin@s into curricula and campus life. Thus, to echo Duncan's (2002) earlier point, empowering Latin@ students across the P–20 means that color must not only be *seen* by educators, but embraced as cultural "funds of knowledge" (Moll & Greenberg, 1990) essential for educational achievement.

Family

Across the P–20 system, the dominant storyline about Latin@ familial resources is one of liability and obstacles to achievement. Nieto (2005) asserted that Latin@s often feel forced to choose between their family and culture and educational achievement. A large body of P–12 research demonstrates that parental contributions are essential to the empowerment and educational success of Latin@ students across the P–20 (Arias & Morillo-Campbell, 2008; Ladson-Billings, 1994; Love & Kruger, 2005; Nieto, 2005; Valverde & Scribner, 2001). In higher education, specifically, Ortiz (2004) found that Latin@ families influence college choice, motivation, and integration of students into campus communities. Ortiz also found that higher education professionals that work with Latin@ students acknowledge the importance of integrating the family system into the college experience. In a study done by Zarate and Pachon (2006), the authors discovered that Latin@ students and their families are misinformed about the costs of college and the level of financial resources available to finance a higher education, which often deters Latin@s from pursuing what seems an unaffordable dream of higher education. Gándara and Contreras (2009) similarly found that "the strong loyalty to family among Latinos—an American value if there ever were one—can lead many to consider the opportunity costs of going to college too high" (p. 9).

In sum, family is essential to the educational achievement of Latin@ students across the P–20. For this reason, family must be perceived as an empowering asset, rather than an obstacle for learning. Until U.S. P–12 schools and institutions of higher education take time to redress these racial inequalities by bringing Latin@ families into the fold, Latin@ students will be limited in reaching their full academic potential.

Immigrant Experience

The dominant storyline often characterizes Latin@s as sharing a common immigrant experience as stealthy, dark-skinned invaders infiltrating U.S. lands, and bleeding the nation dry of its economic, linguistic, and cultural resources (Salazar, 2008). In fact, approximately 74% of Latin@s living in the United States are U.S. citizens, and this number continues to rise (U.S. Census Bureau, 2010). In 2008, Latin@s made up nearly half of the more than one million people who became U.S. citizens (National Association of Latino Elected and Appointed Officials

[NALEO], 2009). In reality, the Latin@ immigrant experience is hardly singular, as the dominant storyline proclaims, and varies as a result of immigration patterns, generational status, country of origin, language proficiency, previous schooling, and phenotype (Ortiz, 2004).

Additionally, anti-immigrant sentiment may fuel distrust from parents who fear negative repercussions to their presence in school, including deportation (Arias & Morillo-Campbell, 2008; Chávez-Reyes, 2010; Hiatt-Michael, 2007; Kochan & Reed, 2005; Schecter & Sherri, 2009; Souto-Manning & Swick, 2006). At times, parents may find themselves experiencing fear, confusion, and misunderstandings due to an unwelcoming school environment across the educational continuum (Arias & Morillo-Campbell, 2008; Chávez-Reyes, 2010; Hyslop, 2000). In the higher education context, researchers report increasing concerns by Latin@ students over an increase in anti-immigrant sentiment by university faculty, as a result of anti-immigrant legislation in the United States (Contreras, 2009; Villalpando, 2003). Villalpando reported that one student expressed, "It seems that lately, especially since the passage of anti-immigrant and anti-affirmative action legislation around the U.S., professors feel a certain freedom to speak more openly about their racist beliefs" (Villalpando, 2003, p. 631). Educators across the P–20 have a responsibility to consider that each Latin@ student brings a unique immigrant perspective that must not be denigrated or ignored, but rather tapped as a pedagogical resource.

In sum, the dominant storyline of Latin@ deficits results in assimilationist policies, programs, and practices that reinforce racial and linguistic discrimination in educational access to both the culture of power and the power of culture. Across the P–20, Latin@s, navigating a hybrid space, experience what could at best be described as fragmented, individualistic, and irrelevant education, and at worst, a systematic effort to marginalize, miseducate, and disenfranchise generations of Americans.

Disrupting the Standard Education Story

Deficit and assimilationist notions, policies, and practices fuel the standard education story of Latin@ achievement gaps. Fortunately, educators are capable of disrupting the standard education story for Latin@s through the use of *storytelling resistance* (Solórzano & Yosso, 2002), a construct rooted in Critical Race Theory (CRT) and Latino Critical Race Theory (LatCrit). CRT and LatCrit are increasingly adapted to K–12 and higher education systems as a means of analyzing racialized barriers to scholastic success, and challenging deficit tales about communities of color (Villalpando, 2004). Storytelling resistance, also known as *counterstorytelling*, can be used to shape a narrative of a U.S. educational system that empowers Latin@ students by advancing a cohesive, rigorous, and culturally relevant approach to sustaining the *alma* (soul) of the Latin@ community.

A Counterstory for Latin@ Educational Achievement

Delgado (1995) suggested that for generations, "oppressed groups have known instinctively that stories are essential tools to their own survival and liberation" (p. 243). Solórzano and Yosso (2002) described the counterstory as "a tool for exposing, analyzing, and challenging stories of racial privilege" (p. 32). I contend that the counterstory for Latin@s in education must invoke the *alma* of the Latin@ community. The term, *alma*, signifies *soul* in Spanish, and *nourishing* in Latin; the Latin@ *alma* is nourished when the full gamut of their life experiences are regarded as resources for the successful navigation of hybrid spaces. These life experiences include, but are not limited to, Latin@ students' language, culture, family values, ancestral ties, hybrid history, intellectual strengths, and immigrant experience.

I submit that the counterstory for Latin@s requires a holistic, collaborative, asset-oriented, and community-based approach to systemic educational reform. P–20 reform should be driven by communities of educators focused on increasing student access to the culture of power and the power of their culture, by dismantling inequitable structures, increasing student access to a rigorous education, and preparing students for the challenges of higher education, workforce readiness, and multicultural citizenship. The goal of liberating Latin@ students from systematic racial discrimination by providing equal access to the culture of power and the power of culture remains a utopian ideal, without specific practical prescriptions for change. Thus, the initiatives and recommendations that follow support the goals of crafting a holistic, collaborative, asset-oriented, and community-based approach to education across the P–20 system.

Increasing Alignment and Access Across the P–20

In order to create a counterstory for Latin@ scholastic success, educators must increase access and alignment across the educational continuum through the following initiatives: (a) provide intensive, high-quality, and culturally-relevant early education; (b) improve teacher preparation and development for meeting the needs of culturally and linguistically diverse students; and (c) create college and career pathways.

Start Early
The counterstory for Latin@s starts early. A vast body of research shows that access to intensive, high-quality early education can improve school readiness, and close the educational achievement gap (Crosnoe, 2007; Schneider, Martinez, &

Owens, 2006). It is essential to offer Latin@ students high-quality, comprehensive, and culturally and linguistically appropriate early education services and supports. Culturally appropriate early-learning services like New Jersey's Abbott Preschool Program build on the knowledge, resources, and values of the Latin@ community in order to develop a strong foundation for learning. Latin@ students require access to bilingual early education services in order to maintain and develop bilingual skills that will serve them well in an increasingly globalized economy. Bilingual education ideally begins at an early age, but Latin@ students need continued access to quality bilingual education across the P–20 system.

Improve teacher preparation and development in K–12 schooling
The counterstory for Latin@s requires access to quality teachers across the K–12 continuum. Researchers state that the single most important factor in determining students' performance is the quality of their teachers (Alliance for Excellent Education, 2008). Unsurprisingly, students of color typically have less qualified teachers and principals (Darling-Hammond, 2003). Indeed, research indicates a gap in teacher and principal quality for students of color as compared with their more affluent and White peers (Akiba, LeTendre, & Scribner, 2007). The reasons cited for the quality gap include: (a) inadequate training on issues of cultural and linguistic diversity in teacher and principal preparation programs; (b) lack of access to resources that capitalize on the strengths of the communities of color; (c) negative perceptions and low expectations of students of color and their families; and (d) low numbers of teachers of color (Grinberg, Goldfarb, & Saavedra, 2005).

Solutions for decreasing the educational gap often focus on teachers; however, this narrow focus oversimplifies a complex issue. In order to impact the quality of education offered to Latin@ students, the nation must move beyond a teacher-only focus. The focus should instead be on developing a quality community of educators, inclusive of all who contribute to the educational success of children, such as principals, paraprofessionals, and school counselors, as well as members of the larger Latin@ community. It is also vital to provide Latin@ students with access to Latin@ educators who reflect their own experiences, struggles, and opportunities, and are willing to extend themselves in the ways necessary to build trusting relationships with students and parents.

Create college and career pathways
The counterstory for Latin@s requires access and early orientation to postsecondary education and career pathways. College preparation begins in early childhood with the acquisition of knowledge and skills necessary for educational success. Additionally, orientation to college and effective career pathways in elementary school, such as the Early Academic Outreach Program (EAOP) and Mathematics, Engineering, Science Achievement (MESA) (Cooper, Cooper, Azmitia, Chavira,

& Gullatt, 2002), must accelerate in the middle grades, and intensify in high school. A college- and career-ready diploma is essential for the success of Latin@ students, ensuring that they are prepared with the skills and knowledge necessary for college, work, and global citizenship (Alliance for Excellent Education, 2008).

Upon entering the higher education system, Latin@ students often face steep odds in college completion (Gándara & Contreras, 2009). Institutions of higher education need to respond to the changing demographics of the nation by (a) engaging in curriculum reform that emphasizes inclusiveness; (b) providing professional development for faculty on supporting diverse students; (c) implementing programs of study that attract Latin@ students; and (d) increasing retention efforts and funding opportunities.

The nation is also facing a growing call for access to higher education for undocumented Latin@ students. Approximately 1.5 million of the nation's 11.9 million undocumented immigrants are under the age of 18 (Passel, 2009). Many of these children have lived in the United States since early childhood, and self-identify as Americans (Brown, 2007). Each year, U.S. high schools graduate an estimated 65,000 undocumented students, of whom only 5% ever attend college (Frum, 2007). Currently, in 40 states, undocumented students are required to pay nonresident or out-of-state tuition, which costs an average of 140% more than resident tuition. In recent years, 10 states have passed laws called the DREAM Act that permit undocumented students to pay in-state tuition rates (Frum, 2007), thereby increasing access to a higher education for millions of U.S. educated Latin@s. It is important for this trend to continue if *every* Latin@ student is to have a realistic opportunity to experience postsecondary success.

Conclusion

Current P–20 practices reinforce racialized barriers in access to educational equity (Bernal, 2002; Salazar, 2008; Swail, Redd, & Perna, 2003; Valenzuela, 2004). CRT and LatCrit scholars operate on the premise that racial discrimination is not always about race, but about power. The standard education story of "failure" for Latin@s is fueled by the deficit-based, dominant storyline about Latin@ students and their families, as well as the assimilationist policies, programs, and practices that disempower Latin@ students across the P–20. Deficit-based storylines and assimilationist approaches are particularly insidious for Latin@s because of what Trucios-Haynes (2001) described as a desire for Whiteness. This scholar stated:

> Latinos/as, more than others, are seduced by Whiteness because we are not called Black, we are not even identified as a race—at least not officially. We are seduced by whiteness because we do not see . . . the racialization of our language, our culture, our history. (p. 1)

If educators across the P–20 educational system cannot grasp the racialized barriers to educational attainment for Latin@ students, these students may be seduced by Whiteness and reject the power of their culture, and/or resist Whiteness and reject the culture of power. It is imperative that educators across the P–20 provide Latin@ students with access to both the resources prized by the culture of power, as well as the liberating and empowering resources inherent in their own culture. I provide a counterstory for the achievement of Latin@ students and their families centered on sustaining the *alma* (soul) of the Latin@ community. In this way, Latin@ students are enabled to use the power of their culture in learning, thereby enhancing their ability to master, and eventually challenge the oppressive elements of the culture of power. Generations of Americans are at stake if educational leaders do not fundamentally shift the way they conceptualize education for Latin@ students. A holistic, asset-based approach to education provides opportunities for Latin@s across the P–20 to liberate themselves from the oppression of systematic racial discrimination, contributing to a more competent, equitable, and diverse nation.

Note

1. Latin@s are often described as a monolithic group; however, they represent a vast heterogeneity in terms of national origin, language proficiency, language variety, acculturation pattern, political orientation, socioeconomic status, and more. The Latin@ category includes persons often residing in the United States who are of Mexican, Puerto Rican, Cuban, and South or Central American culture or origin, regardless of race. The Latin@ category includes residents who can trace their ancestry in the United States to the 16th century, as well as recent immigrants. The information in this chapter addresses general issues and trends impacting Latin@s; however, distinct subgroups are impacted in diverse ways.

References

Akiba, A., LeTendre, G. K., & Scribner, J. P. (2007). Teacher quality, opportunity gap, and national achievement in 46 countries. *Educational Researcher, 36*(7), 369–387.

Alliance for Excellent Education. (2008). *What keeps good teachers in the classroom? Understanding and reducing teacher turnover*. Retrieved from http://www.all4ed.org/about_the_crisis/teachers/teacher_turnover

Anzaldúa, G. (1999). *Borderlands la frontera: The new mestiza*. San Francisco, CA: Aunt Lute Books.

Arias, M. B., & Morillo-Campbell, M. (2008). *Promoting ELL parental involvement: Challenges in contested times* [PDF]. Retrieved from http://www.greatlakescenter.org/docs/Policy_Briefs/Arias_ELL.pdf

Barton, A. C., & Yang, K. (2000). The culture of power and science education: Learning from Miguel. *Journal of Research in Science Teaching, 37*(8), 871–889.

Behnke, A. O., Gonzalez, L. M., & Cox, R. B. (2010). Latino students in new arrival states: Factors and services to prevent youth from dropping out. *Hispanic Journal of Behavioral Sciences, 32*(3), 385–409.

Bernal, D. D. (2002). Critical race theory, Latino critical theory, and critical raced-gendered epistemologies: Recognizing students of color as holders and creators of knowledge. *Qualitative Inquiry, 8*(1) 105–126.

Bhabha, H. K. (1994). *The location of culture*. London, UK: Routledge.

Brown, S. E. (2007). *America's future and Latino students*. Retrieved from www.edexcelencia.org/ppt/ SC_Latin@_Students_Future.ppt (no longer accessible).

Brown, S., & Souto-Manning, M. (2008). 'Culture is the way they live here': Young Latin@s and parents navigate linguistic and cultural borderlands in U.S. schools. *Journal of Latinos and Education, 7*(1), 25–42.

Castellanos, J., & Gloria, A. (2007). Research considerations and theoretical application for best practices in higher education. *Journal of Hispanic Higher Education, 6*(4), 378–396.

Chamberlain, S. P. (2005). Recognizing and responding to cultural differences in the education of culturally and linguistically diverse learners. *Intervention in School and Clinic, 40*(4), 195–211.

Chávez-Reyes, C. (2010). 'Starting at the top': Identifying and understanding later generation Chicano students in schools. *Journal of Latinos and Education, 9*(1), 22–40.

Clark, E. R., & Flores, B. B. (2007). Cultural literacy: Negotiating language, culture, and thought. *Voices From the Middle, 15*(2), 8–14.

Cobas, J., & Feagin, J. (2008). Language oppression and resistance: The case of middle class Latinos in the United States. *Ethnic and Racial Studies, 31*(2), 390–410.

Conley, D. T. (2007). *Redefining college readiness*. Eugene, OR: Educational Policy Improvement Center.

Contreras, F. (2009). Sin papeles y rompiendo barreras: Latino students and the challenges of persisting in college. *Harvard Educational Review, 79*(4), 610–632.

Cooper, C. R., Cooper, R. G., Azmitia, M., Chavira, G., & Gullatt, Y. (2002). Bridging multiple worlds: How African American and Latino youth in academic outreach programs navigate math pathways to college. *Applied Developmental Science, 6*(2), 73–87.

Crosnoe, R. (2007). Early child care and the school readiness of children from Mexican immigrant families. *International Migration Review, 41*(1), 152–181.

Cummins, J. (1996). *Negotiating identities: Education for empowerment in a diverse society*. Ontario, CA: California Association for Bilingual Education.

Cummins, J. (2001). *Negotiating identities: Education for empowerment in a diverse society* (2nd ed.). Los Angeles, CA: California Association for Bilingual Education.

Darling-Hammond, L. (2003). Keeping good teachers: Why it matters, what leaders can do. *Educational Leadership, 60*(8), 6–13.

Delgado, R. (Ed.). (1995). *Critical race theory: The cutting edge*. Philadelphia, PA: Temple University Press.

Delgado, R., & Stefancic, J. (1993). Critical race theory: An annotated bibliography. *Virginia Law Review, 79*(2), 461–516.

Delpit, L. D. (1988). The silenced dialogue: Power and pedagogy in educating other people's children. *Harvard Educational Review, 58*(3), 280–298.

Deyhle, D. (1995). Navajo youth and Anglo racism: Cultural integrity and resistance. *Harvard Educational Review, 65*(3), 403–444.

Draut, T. (2008). *Economic state of young America* [PDF]. Retrieved from www.demos.org/pubs/esya_5_7_08.pdf

Dudley-Marling, C., & Lucas, K. (2009). Pathologizing the language and culture of poor children. *Language Arts, 86*(5), 362–370.

Duncan, G. A. (2002). Beyond love: A critical race ethnography of the schooling of adolescent Black males. *Equity & Excellence in Education, 35*(2), 131–143.

Fordham, S., & Ogbu, J. U. (1986). Black students' school success: Coping with "the burden of 'acting White.'" *Urban Review, 18*(3), 176–206.

Fránquiz, M. E., & Salazar, M. d. C. (2004). The transformative potential of humanizing pedagogy: Addressing the diverse needs of Chicano/Mexicano students. *High School Journal, 87*(4), 36–53.

Fránquiz, M. E., & Salazar, M. d. C. (2008). The transformation of Ms. Corazon: Creating humanizing spaces for Mexican immigrant students in secondary ESL classrooms. *Multicultural Perspectives, 10*(4), 185–191.

Frum, J. (2007). Postsecondary educational access for undocumented students: Opportunities and constraints. *American Academic, 3*(1), 81–108.

Fry, R. (2011, August 25). Hispanic college enrollment spikes, narrowing gaps with other groups. *Pew Hispanic Center analysis of the October 2010 current population survey and U.S. Census Bureau: Current population survey, 1993 to 2009*. Pew Hispanic Center. Retrieved from http://www.pewhispanic.org/2011/08/25/appendix-tables/ and http://www.pewhispanic.org/2011/08/25/hispanic-college-enrollment-spikes-narrowing-gaps-with-other-groups/

Gándara, P., & Contreras, F. (2009). *The Latino education crisis: The consequences of failed social policies*. Cambridge, MA: Harvard University Press.

Garcia, E. (1997). Effective instruction for language minority students: The teacher. In A. Darder, R. D. Torres, & H. Gutierrez (Eds.), *Latinos and education: A critical reader* (pp. 362–372). New York, NY: Routledge.

Gregory, S. T. (2003). Planning for the increasing number of Latino students. *Planning for Higher Education, 31*(4), 13–19.

Grinberg, J., Goldfarb, K., & Saavedra, E. (2005). Con pasión y con coraje: The schooling of Latino/a students and their teachers' education. In P. Pedraza & M. Rivera (Eds.), *Latino education: An agenda for community action research* (pp. 227–254). Mahwah, NJ: Lawrence Erlbaum.

Hiatt-Michael, D. B. (2007). Engaging English language learner families as partners. In D. Hiatt-Michael (Ed.), *Promising practices for teachers to engage families of English language learners* (pp. 1–10). Charlotte, NC: Information Age.

Hispanic Association of Colleges and Universities [HACU]. (2004, February 3). Hispanic higher education budget crisis worsens. Retrieved from http://www.hacu.net/hacu/NewsBot.asp?MODE=VIEW&ID=159

Hopstock, P. J., & Stephenson, T. G. (2003). *Descriptive study of services to LEP children and LEP children with disabilities: Native languages of LEP children* (Special Topic Report #1) [PDF]. Arlington, VA: Development Associates. Retrieved from http:www.ncela.gwu.edu/resabout/research/descriptivestudyfiles/native_langauges1 (no longer accessible).

Hyslop, N. (2000). *Hispanic parental involvement in home literacy*. Bloomington, IN: ERIC Clearinghouse on Reading, English, and Communication. (ERIC Document Reproduction Service No. 446340)

Kochan, F. K., & Reed, C. J. (2005). Collaborative leadership, community building, and democracy in public education. In F. W. English (Ed.), *The SAGE handbook of educational leadership: Advances in theory, research, and practice* (pp. 68–84). Thousand Oaks, CA: SAGE.

Ladson-Billings, G. (1994). *The dreamkeepers: Successful teachers of African American children*. San Francisco, CA: Jossey-Bass.

Ladson-Billings, G. (2003). New directions in multicultural education: Complexities, boundaries, and critical race theory. In J. A. Banks & C. A. McGee Banks (Eds.), *Handbook of research on multicultural education,* (2nd ed., pp. 50–65). San Francisco, CA: Jossey-Bass.

Lopez, M. H., & Minushkin, S. (2008). *2008 national survey of Latinos: Hispanic voter attitudes*. Pew Hispanic Center. Retrieved from http://pewhispanic.org/reports/report.php?ReportID=90

Love, A., & Kruger, A. C. (2005). Teacher beliefs and student achievement in urban schools serving African American students. *Journal of Educational Research 99*(2), 87–98.

Meyer, L. (2005). *No child left bilingual? An analysis of U.S. educational policy and its impacts on English language learners and their school programs, parents and communities*. Portsmouth, NH: Heinemann Press.

Moll, L., & Greenberg, J. B. (1990). Creating zones of possibilities: Combining social contexts for instruction. In L. Moll (Ed.), *Vygotsky and education: Instructional implications and applications of sociohistorical psychology* (pp. 319–348). Cambridge, UK: Cambridge University Press.

Montecinos, C. (1995). Culture as an ongoing dialog: Implications for multicultural teacher education. In C. Sleeter & P. McLaren (Eds.), *Multicultural education, critical pedagogy, and the politics of difference* (pp. 291–308). Albany, NY: State University of New York Press.

Moschkovich, J. (2007). Using two languages while learning mathematics. *Educational Studies in Mathematics, 64*(2), 121–144.

National Association of Latino Elected and Appointed Officials [NALEO]. (2009, April 6). *Latinos pursuing dream of U.S. citizenship help set naturalization record in 2008*. Retrieved from http://www.naleo.org/pr/pr04-06-09.html

National Center for Education Statistics [NCES]. (2009a). Average reading scale scores and selected achievement gaps of 4th-, 8th-, and 12th-grade students, by sex and race/ethncitiy: Selected years, 1992–2009 [Data file]. Retrieved from http://nces.ed.gov/programs/coe/tables/table-rgp-1.asp

National Center for Education Statistics [NCES]. (2009b). *The condition of education* [Data file]. Retrieved from http://nces.ed.gov/programs/coe/figures/figure-1er-1.asp

National Center for Education Statistics [NCES]. (2009c). *Drop out rates in the United States* [Data file]. Retrieved from http://nces.ed.gov/programs/coe/figures/figure-sd1.asp (no longer accessible).

National Center for Education Statistics [NCES]. (2010). Public school graduates and dropouts from the common core of data: School year 2007–08 [PDF]. Retrieved from http://nces.ed.gov/pubs2010/2010341.pdf

National Center for Education Statistics [NCES]. (2011). *The condition of education 2011* (NCES 2011-033). Retrieved from http://nces.ed.gov/fastfacts/display.asp?id=72

Nieto, S. (1996). *Affirming diversity: The sociopolitical context of multicultural education* (2nd ed.). New York, NY: Longman.

Nieto, S. (2004). *Affirming diversity: The sociopolitical context of multicultural education* (4th ed.). Boston, MA: Pearson.

Nieto, S. (2005). A project of hope: Defining a new agenda for Latino/a education in the 21st century. In P. Pedraza & M. Rivera (Eds.), *Latino education: An agenda for community action research* (pp. 463–470). Mahwah, NJ: Lawrence Erlbaum.

Ortiz, A. M. (2004). Promoting the success of Latino students: A call to action. *New Directions for Student Services, 2004*(105), 89–97.

Pang, V. O., & Barba, R. H. (1995). The power of culture: Building culturally affirming instruction. In C. A. Grant (Ed.), *Educating for diversity: An anthology of multicultural voices* (pp. 341–358). Boston, MA: Allyn & Bacon.

Passel, J. S. (2009). *A portrait of unauthorized immigrants in the United States*. Retrieved from http://pewresearch.org/pubs/1190/portrait-unauthorizedimmigrants-states

Passel J. S., & Cohn, D. (2008). *U.S. population projections: 2005–2050*. Retrieved from http://pewhispanic.org/reports/report.php?ReportID=85

Reyes Cruz, M. (2008). Mexican immigrant parents advocating for school reform. New York, NY: LFB Scholarly.

Ricento, T. (2000). Historical and theoretical perspectives in language policy and planning. *Journal of Sociolinguistics, 4*(2), 196–213.

Ruiz, R. (1984). Orientations in language planning. *NABE: Journal for the National Association for Bilingual Education, 8*(2), 15–34.

Rumberger, R. W., & Arellano, B. D. (2009). Understanding and addressing the California Latino achievement gap in early elementary school. In R. A. Gutiérrez & P. Zavella (Eds.), *Mexicans in California: Transformations and challenges* (pp. 61–76). Champaign, IL: University of Illinois Press.

Salazar, M. (2008). English or nothing: The impact of rigid language policies on the inclusion of humanizing practices in a high school ESL program. *Equity & Excellence in Education, 41*(3), 341–356.

Salazar, M. (2010). Pedagogical stances of high school ESL teachers: Huelgas in high school ESL classrooms. *Bilingual Research Journal, 33*(1), 111–124.

Schecter, S. R., & Sherri, D. L. (2009). Value added?: Teachers' investments in and orientations toward parent involvement in involvement. *Urban Education, 44*(1), 59–87.

Schneider, B., Martinez, S., & Owens, A. (2006). Barriers to educational opportunities for Hispanics in the United States. In M. Tienda, & F. Mitchell (Eds.), *Hispanics and the future of America* (pp. 179–227). Washington, DC: National Academies Press.

Skutnabb-Kangas, T. (1997). Human rights and language policy in education. In R. Wodak & Corson. D. (Eds.), *Encyclopedia of language and education: Vol I, Language policy and political issues in education* (pp. 55–66). Dordrecht, the Netherlands: Kluwer.

Sleeter, C. E., & Grant, C. A. (1999). *Making choices for multicultural education: Five approaches to race, class, and gender* (3rd ed.). Upper Saddle River, NJ: Merrill.

Solórzano, D. G., & Yosso, T. J. (2002). Critical race methodology: Counter-storytelling as an analytical framework for education research. *Qualitative Inquiry, 8*(1), 23–44.

Souto-Manning, M., & Swick, K. J. (2006). Teachers' beliefs about parent and family involvement: Rethinking our family involvement paradigm. *Early Childhood Education Journal, 34*(2), 187–193.

Swail, W. S., Redd, K. E., & Perna, L. W. (2003). *Retaining minority students in higher education: A framework for success*. San Francisco, CA: Wiley.

Trucios-Haynes, E. (2001). Why 'race matters': LatCrit theory and Latina/o racial identity. *La Raza Law Journal, 12*(1), 1–42. Retrieved http://homepage.smc.edu/preciado_christina/Current/Sociology%2031/Readings/Why%20Race%20Matters%20LatCrit.pdf

U.S. Census Bureau. (2009). *Profile America facts for features: Hispanic heritage month 2010*. Retrieved from http://www.census.gov/newsroom/releases/archives/facts_for_features_special_editions/cb10-ff17.html

U.S. Census Bureau. (2010). Statistical portrait of Hispanics in the United States, 2010: Hispanic population, by nativity: 2000 and 2010 [Data file]. Retrieved from http://www.pewhispanic.org/files/2012/02/phc-2010-hispanic-statistical-portrait-04.png

U.S. Census Bureau. (2011, March). *Overview of race and Hispanic origin: 2010* [PDF]. Retrieved from http://www.census.gov/prod/cen2010/briefs/c2010br-02.pdf

Valdés, G. (1996). *Con respeto: Bridging the distance between culturally diverse families and schools*. New York, NY: Teachers College Press.

Valencia, R. R. (2010). *Dismantling contemporary deficit thinking: Educational thought and practice*. New York, NY: Routledge.

Valenzuela, A. (1999). *Subtractive schooling: U.S.-Mexican youth and the politics of caring*. Albany, NY: State Universtiy of New York Press.

Valenzuela, A. (2004). *Leaving children behind: How 'Texas-style' accountability fails Latino youth*. Albany, NY: State University of New York Press.

Valverde, L. A., & Scribner, K. P. (2001). Latino students: Organizing schools for greater achievement. *NASSP Bulletin, 85*(624), 22–31.

Villalpando, O. (2003). Self-segregation or self-preservation? A critical race theory and Latina/o critical theory analysis of a study of Chicana/o college students. *International Journal of Qualitative Studies in Education, 16*(5), 619–646.

Villalpando, O. (2004). Practical considerations of critical race theory and Latino critical theory for Latino college students. *New Directions for Student Services, 2004*(105), 41–50.

Villenas, S., & Deyhle, D. (1999). Critical race theory and ethnographies challenging the stereotypes: Latino families, schooling, resilience, and resistance. *Curriculum Inquiry, 29*(4), 413–445.

Yosso, T. (2005). Whose culture has capital? A critical race theory discussion of community cultural wealth. *Race, Ethnicity and Education, 8*(1), 69–91.

Zarate, M. E., & Pachon, H. P. (2006). Perceptions of college financial aid among California Latino youth. Los Angeles, CA: Tomás Rivera Policy Institute (TRPI). Retrieved from http://www.trpi.org/PDFs/Financial_Aid_Surveyfinal6302006.pdf

TEN

African American Politics and Education

An Analysis of Electoral Structures, African American Representation, and Educational Outcomes

Bettie Ray Butler and Chance W. Lewis

The social construction of race and the ideals of education have been a perennially salient policy issue (Meier, Stewart, & England, 1989) since 1954, with the seminal Supreme Court ruling in *Brown v. Board of Education of Topeka, Kansas*.[1] This case serves as the benchmark for most studies that analyze educational disparities among students of color. The *Brown* decision—as it is often termed—overruled the separate-but-equal doctrine,[2] and unanimously declared that all dual education systems must be dismantled. Such systems were considered a direct violation of the equal protection clause of the United States Constitution, and hence, they were deemed unconstitutional.

Over 50 years have passed since the initial ruling, and educational inequities continue to permeate American schools. The disparities that were present then, exist today—but in more subtle forms of segregation. Paradoxically, African American students find themselves attending schools that are, in reality, just as segregated and unequal as they were decades ago (Ladson-Billings, 1994). From this it is plausible to conclude that race, though contentious by nature, remains a significant facet of the nation's landscape. It serves as a powerful social, economic, and political force. Despite the growing popularity of the idea of racial neutrality, race—when used as an explanatory variable—has consistently proven to be a strong predictor of educational success. Findings such as these have been used to explain why students of color, compared to their Anglo peers, perform at lower levels on standardized testing.

This study sought to assess the dynamics of race and standardized testing by looking at the influence of politics. In essence, the interest is in determining whether the appointment, or election, of key educational officials has the potential to thwart the negative relationship between a student's racial identification and their performance on high-stakes tests. The very idea that increases in African American student performance can somehow be indirectly contingent upon African American representation further debunks the myth of a postracial era.

To better grapple with this idea, this chapter has been divided into four sections. Section one will review the representative bureaucracy literature that links elected and nonelected officials to student performance, and presents a causal story to further clarify the relationship between electoral structures, African American representation, and educational outcomes. Section two outlines the assumptions by which this analysis is guided; assumptions which are necessary in tracing each causal link. Section three tests the implications from the causal story, and offers a discussion of the findings. Last, section four provides recommendations for educators and policymakers regarding more innovative strategies to improve academic performance on standardized exams.

Representative Bureaucracy and Educational Outcomes

Kenneth J. Meier and his colleagues can be credited for offering extensive investigations into the importance of a theory of representative bureaucracy (i.e., as the bureaucracy becomes more demographically representative of the public it serves, it is most likely to make policy decisions that are more responsive to that constituency) to explain educational outcomes—a relationship which focuses on whether representation among teachers of color translates into benefits for students of color (Meier & England, 1984; Meier & Stewart, 1991; Meier & Stewart, 2003; Meier et al., 1989; Meier, Wrinkle, & Polinard, 1999; Stewart, England, & Meier, 1989).[3] One of their earlier studies recognized the value of African American street-level bureaucrats (i.e., teachers), and suggested that these teachers are the single most effective force in narrowing racial disparities among African American students (Meier et al., 1989). Another study conducted by Meier and his team of researchers further asserted that African American teachers not only depress disparities, but they can also be linked to increased levels of student performance (Meier & Stewart, 1992; Meier et al., 1999).

Culturally Relevant Pedagogy

Meier's work, though significant in its own right, is but a small contribution to an even larger body of scholarship concerning cultural pedagogy, and the relevance of teacher-student relationships. The ongoing debate within this literature questions whether teachers' descriptive characteristics (e.g., race, culture, etc.) somehow impact, directly or indirectly, their students' ability to effectively engage in the learning process (Ehrenberg & Brewer, 1995; Ehrenberg, Goldhaler, & Brewer, 1995). Interestingly enough, the general consensus among this particular community of scholars is particularly favorable toward the idea of *cultural synchronization* as a mode of maximizing student learning. Here, cultural synchronization refers to the interpersonal context that exists between the student and teacher, which is oftentimes aligned by cultural and/or racial congruence (Irvine, 1990).

The model of *culturally relevant pedagogy* is of paramount importance here, because it serves as a bridge between cultural synchronization and student achievement. This model was intended to address academic performance, by way of prompting teachers to encourage students to accept and affirm their cultural identity while adopting critical perspectives that help them challenge the perpetuation of inequities that are often found in P–12 institutions (Ladson-Billings, 1995). Yet, for this model to be effective, teachers must first acknowledge that such inequities are prevalent, and then seek to understand why they persist. Only then can they garner the attention of their pupils, and have a lasting impact on student achievement.

The use of culturally relevant pedagogy in some sense is natural for African American teachers who instruct African American learners. Aside from some of the most logical explanations, the basis for this rationale is embedded within the literature. Three reasons why African American instructors are more adept at influencing African American student performance have been consistently reiterated:

1. They are successful in empowering and engaging these students for the purpose of instruction;
2. On occasion, many serve as positive role models, and some transform their teacher-student relationships into mentor-protégé relationships; and
3. They effectively negate the negative consequences that stem from institutional inequities (Alexander & Miller, 1989; Buxton, 2000; Clewell & Villegas, 1998; Dee, 2004a; Foster, 1990; King, 1993; Kram, 1983, 1985; Ladson-Billings & Henry, 1990; Meier et al., 1999).

Because of these explanations—and similar ones—African American teachers are perceived to be responsible for upward trends in student achievement, and have been statistically associated with academic improvement among racially similar pupils (Dee, 2004a, 2004b; Ferguson, 1998; Viadero, 2001).

Contribution
As is evident, African American teachers make pertinent contributions with respect to academic performance among African American students. Insofar as rep-

resentative bureaucracy is concerned, how far up the hierarchy does one need to go in order to maintain similar effects? That is, does the appointment, or election, of key African American education officials have any influence on achievement? To the degree that is warranted, to date, these questions have only been partially addressed.

This study goes beyond the previous work in that it attempts to formally connect the top-down approach to outcomes. While other studies simply assess the link between electoral structures, political representation, and bureaucratic appointments (Meier & Smith, 1994; Meier et al., 1989), this paper extends the assessment by demonstrating whether the benefits of bureaucratic representation spill over into educational outcomes.

Admittedly, prior studies have explored the relationship between representation and educational outcomes; but either they only examine how street-level bureaucratic representation—contingent upon political representation—influences outcomes (Meier et al., 1999; see Figure 10.1, Arrow A), or simply how electoral structures impact bureaucratic representation (Meier, Gonzalez Juenke, Wrinkle, & Polinard, 2005; see Figure 1, Arrow B). However, no study has investigated—using a top-down approach—the link between electoral structures, political representation, bureaucratic appointments, and outcomes, altogether (see Figure 1, Arrow C).[4]

Figure 10.1 A Hierarchical Representation of How the Aim of This Study Is a Mere Extension of Previous Literary Contributions.

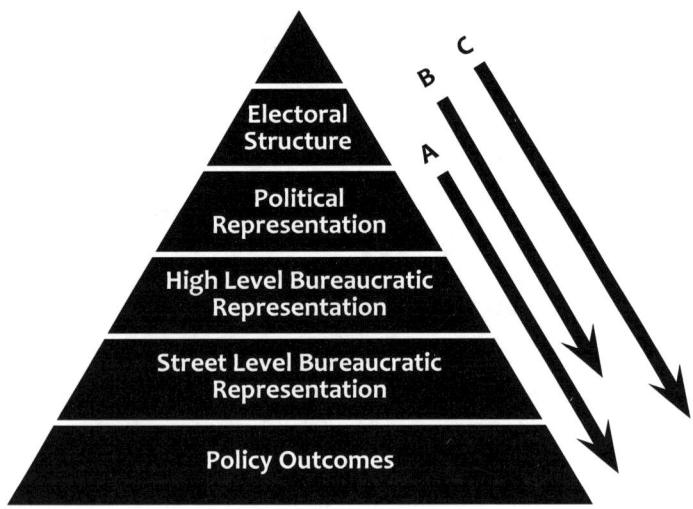

The aim of this paper is to provide an interrelated causal story that depicts this relationship (i.e., Arrow C) by showing how different methods of selection for school board elections generate opportunities for African American candidates to secure political positions. This enables them to appoint a larger number of administrators who share descriptive similarities, and is likely to also then facilitate the hiring of more African American teachers, who are presumably effective at improving student performance among African American students (Meier et al., 1999).

Assumptions
In order for the hypothesized causal story to be substantiated there are several assumptions that must be satisfied. Assumption one—and by far the most important—suggests that *African American teachers want to maximize their students' individual potential, and make them more receptive to instruction and academically productive*. Assumption two suggests that *the quality of African American representation matters, and is largely dependent upon the officials' ability to secure administrative and instructional positions for African Americans*. Assumption three suggests that *the type of electoral structure determines the percentage of quality African American school board members elected to office*.

It is these three assumptions that guide the present analysis, and allow for the clear articulation of a set of testable hypotheses. The hypotheses are as follows:

H_1 African American school board members elected in ward-based systems will form a representative bureaucracy that positively influences African American student performance.

H_2 African American school board members elected in at-large systems will be less apt to form a representative bureaucracy, and will have minimum influences on African American student performance.

The idea behind supporting ward systems is fairly straightforward; when compared to at-large systems, the literature links this particular method of selection to greater African American political representation—which is of extreme necessity when forming the type of representative bureaucracy needed to impact educational outcomes (Meier & Stewart, 2003). With this, it is plausible to expect ward systems to be more closely associated with education benefits for African American students, in comparison to at-large systems.

Data and Analysis
The primary data source for this analysis comes from the Texas School District Data Set, which contains information collected on 1,040+ school districts between the years 1993 to 2001. This data set includes structural and representational measures, in addition to multiple performance indicators. The present analysis excludes districts that utilized the appointive system as a method of selection, since the focus of this study is a comparative assessment between ward and at-large systems.

A series of ordinary least squares (OLS) models are estimated to test whether the politics of education—the election and appointment of key education officials—is indirectly linked to educational outcomes. Though the primary interest is in how the structure of representative bureaucracy affects high-stakes testing, other measures of student performance are considered in an effort to provide the strongest explanatory power, and to clarify the usefulness of the hypothesized causal story.

Dependent Variables

This study examines 13 educational outcome indicators, which, in this analysis, can be measured using performance variables. Of these variables, the most relevant measure is the African American pass rate. This measure captures the percentage of African American students who passed the TAAS[5]—the Texas state-mandated standardized exam. This test is administered to students enrolled in several different grade levels; however, for the purpose of this study the authors will specifically pay attention to those students in the 9th grade or higher. At the secondary level, passing this exam is critical to the student, because it is one of the many graduation requirements that they must fulfill in order to receive a high school diploma.

Other measures of African American student performance include: student attendance rates, dropout rates, percentage taking advanced classes,[6] percentage taking AP classes, percentage passing AP classes, percentage taking either the SAT or ACT, SAT average, ACT average, ratio of students scoring above 1110 on the SAT, percentage in gifted classes, percentage in special education, and the percentage in vocational education. Of these variables above, one in particular warrants further explanation.[7] The ratio of students scoring above an 1110 on the SAT is significant, because this score represents those students that are believed to be college-ready.

In sum, there are four quantitative or numerical measures (e.g., standardized exam pass rates, SAT average, ACT average, and above 1110 on the SAT), three academic measures (e.g., taking advanced classes, taking AP classes, and passing AP classes), two standard measures (e.g., attendance and dropout rates), and three tracking measures (e.g., percentage in gifted, special education, and vocational classes).

Independent Variables

One set of the independent variables identified within this study consists of two distinct structure types—ward and at-large electoral methods of selection. The structure variable was dichotomized, allowing each system to be coded using a dummy variable. At-large systems were coded 0, and ward systems were coded

1. This structure variable ultimately tests for differences in student performance between each system.

The second set of the independent variables consists of three separate representation measures; the first at the school board level, the second at the administrative level, and the third at the teacher level. All of the representational measures constitute the percentage of African Americans either appointed or elected to each position. These representation variables are needed to link electoral structures to student performance—as outlined by the hypothesized causal story.

Interactive Variable
An interactive variable was created to capture the effects of both structure and political representation, simultaneously. This interaction term multiplies structure effects by the overall percentage of African American school board representation. This variable is of significant interest, in that it helps to link—though indirectly—structure to representation, and then representation to performance. Inclusion of this interaction allows for a statistical interpretation of the significance of the hypothesized causal link. This interaction, though slightly altered, is highly recommended by scholars who conduct studies with similar contexts (Meier & Ray, 2005; Engstrom & McDonald, 1981).

Control Variables
A set of control variables is also included within this analysis. These controls are as follows: the percentage of Black students, percentage of low-income students, Anglo performance indicators, state aid, average teacher salary, and average teacher experience. Several of these controls have been frequently used in similar analyses, and hence are used here to ensure that the causal link is modeled accurately.

To prevent serial correlation, duration effects were absorbed. In doing this, one is able to control for most of the variance attributed to yearly fluctuations. Controlling for the specified time intervals, in the long run, makes it possible to avoid potential misinterpretations of statistical significance.

Results
Using the method of OLS, four regression equations were estimated at the three different stages of a representative bureaucracy. Table 1 reports the findings for the effects of electoral structures and African American school board representation on African American student performance. Table 2 reports the findings for the effects of electoral structure, African American school board representation, and African American administrative representation on African American student performance. Table 3 simply adds African American teacher representation to the list of effects from Table 2, and reports its overall effect on student performance among African Americans.

Table 1 illustrates that the interaction between structure and African American school board representation is significant and positive for three out of the thirteen performance measures. These include TAAS pass rates (0.09), SAT average (0.62), and percentage in gifted classes (0.05). The effects of this interaction suggest that ward electoral structures and African American school board representation work together to positively influence African American performance on the Texas state mandated standardized exams. Simply put, for each additional African American board member, pass rates, SAT averages, and the percentage of students enrolled in gifted classes all increase when the board member is elected in a ward, rather than at-large district.

When examining ward electoral systems and African American school board representation, independently, it is worth mentioning that there is a negative correlation between structure and political representation with respect to the percentage of African American students in special education. These small, yet important coefficients are perceived to be a positive result because this performance measure is associated with academic tracking—which is a sign of institutional inequity. Hence, this finding can be interpreted to suggest that ward electoral structures and greater African American school board representation both have the potential to decrease the percentage of African Americans enrolled in special education and lower-level courses across the curriculum. In other words, the percentage of African American students assigned to special education and lower-level curriculum tracks are expected to decline in direct response to greater African American presence on school boards, and increased number of ward districts. A possible explanation for this relationship may, in part, deal with the understanding that African American school board members are generally more sensitive to inequitable instructional practices that seemingly target African American students. As a result, they may, therefore, tend to monitor special education referrals and tracking assignments more cautiously, as a function of cultural likeness; which potentially allows them to be more attuned to the needs of this specific group of students, in comparison to a board member that might not be as familiar with the history and culture of African American students.

Table 2 adds African American administrative representation to the former model illustrated in Table 1. When assessing this variable alone, one can see that a positive and significant relationship exists between the percentage of African American administrators in a district and the percentage of African American students who pass their state mandated standardized exams (0.06). However, the previous structure and political representation effects on this performance variable disappear in this table. Altogether, the results in this table can be interpreted to suggest that for every one unit increase in African American administrative representation, exam pass rates for African American students will increase by 0.06.

Table 10.1 Effects of Structure and African American Political Representation on Educational Outcomes Specific to African American Students

AA Performance Measures	Structure		AA Sch Bd Rep		Structure* AA Sch Bd Rep		R square	N
TAAS Pass Rates	-4.22	***	-0.04		0.09	**	0.64	5164
Attendance	3.01	***	-0.03		-0.22	***	0.24	6189
Drop Out	0.19		-0.01		0.002		0.08	4431
Taking Advanced Classes	-1.45	***	0.06	***	-0.02		0.30	4826
Taking AP Classes	-1.89	***	-0.001		0.05		0.37	1637
Passing AP Classes	-4.80		0.01		-0.07		0.53	272
Taking SAT/ACT	-2.67		0.12	**	-0.09		0.19	1720
SAT Average	-2.68		-0.30		0.62	**	0.53	1328
ACT Average	-0.11		-0.001	***	0.01		0.25	1479
Above 1110 SAT/ACT	0.47		-0.01		-0.01		0.79	2188
% In Gifted Classes	-0.72	**	0.01		0.05	**	0.62	1623
% In Special Edu.	-1.34	***	-0.03	***	-0.003		0.87	4561
% In Vocational Edu.	0.06		-0.01		0.02		0.93	4424

Note. These coefficients were found when controlling for percentage of Black students, percentage of low income, Anglo performance indicators, state aid, average teacher salary, and teacher experience.
**p < .05
***p < .01

Table 10.2 Effects of Structure and African American High Level Representation on Educational Outcomes Specific to African American Students

AA Performance Measures	Structure		AA Sch Bd Rep		Structure* AA Sch Bd Rep		AA Admin Rep		R square	N
TAAS Pass Rates	-4.27	***	-0.05	**	0.08		0.06	**	0.64	5164
Attendance	3.07	***	-0.03		-0.20	***	-0.08	**	0.24	6189
Drop Out	0.20		-0.01		0.003		-0.003		0.08	4431
Taking Advanced Classes	-1.45	***	0.06	***	-0.02		0.01		0.30	4826
Taking AP Classes	-1.88	***	1.8E-04		0.06		-0.01		0.37	1637
Passing AP Classes	-4.72		0.01		-0.07		-0.03		0.53	272
Taking SAT/ACT	-2.91		0.11	**	-0.10		0.13	**	0.19	1720
SAT Average	-2.50		-0.30		0.64	**	-0.12		0.53	1328
ACT Average	-0.10		-0.01	***	0.01		-0.01	**	0.25	1479
Above 1110 SAT/ACT	0.48	**	-0.01		-0.004		-0.01		0.79	2188
% In Gifted Classes	-0.83	***	-2.3E-04		0.04	**	0.07	***	0.62	1623
% In Special Edu.	-1.22	***	-0.02	**	0.02		-0.14	***	0.88	4561
% In Vocational Edu.	0.05		-0.01		0.02		0.01		0.93	4424

Note. These coefficients were found when controlling for percentage of Black students, percentage of low income, Anglo performance indicators, state aid, average teacher salary, and teacher experience.

**p < .05
***p < .01

Table 10.3 Effects of Structure and African American High/Low Level Representation on Educational Outcomes Specific to African American Students

AA Performance Measures	Structure		AA Sch Bd Rep		Structure* AA Sch Bd Rep		AA Admin Rep		AA Teacher Rep		R square	N
TAAS Pass Rates	-4.30	***	-0.05	**	0.08		0.04		0.12	**	0.64	5164
Attendance	3.15	***	-0.02		-0.20	***	-0.04		-0.23	***	0.24	6189
Drop Out	0.19		-0.01		0.003		-0.004		0.01		0.08	4431
Taking Advanced Classes	-1.49	***	0.05	***	-0.02		-0.02		0.13	***	0.31	4826
Taking AP Classes	-1.88	***	-9.2E-05		0.05		-0.01		0.01		0.37	1637
Passing AP Classes	-4.94		0.01		-0.06		0.04		-0.12		0.53	272
Taking SAT/ACT	-2.89		0.10	**	-0.10		0.08		0.24	**	0.20	1720
SAT Average	-2.14		-0.28		0.64	**	0.13		-0.89	**	0.53	1328
ACT Average	-0.10		-0.01	***	0.01		-0.01		-0.004		0.25	1479
Above 1110 SAT/ACT	0.48	***	-0.01		-0.003		-0.01		-0.01		0.79	2188
% In Gifted Classes	-0.86	***	-0.004		0.04	**	-0.03	**	0.44	***	0.70	1623
% In Special Edu.	-1.20	***	-0.02		0.03		-0.11	***	-0.17	***	0.88	4561
% In Vocational Edu.	0.04		-0.01	**	0.01		-0.002		0.09	***	0.93	4424

Note. These coefficients were found when controlling for percentage of Black students, percentage of low income, Anglo performance indicators, state aid, average teacher salary, and teacher experience.
**p < .05
***p < .01

Similar to the prior table, Table 2 detects a significant negative relationship between African American administrative representation and the percentage of African American students in special education (-0.14). The findings, here, suggest that higher-level bureaucratic representation—like political representation—has the potential to minimize the percentage of African Americans in special education classes, and is likely to do so for the same reasons mentioned earlier.

Table 3 takes the theory of representative bureaucracy one step further by adding African American teacher representation into the model. It appears that this explanatory variable is also positively associated with state mandated standardized exams. From the table, it is plausible to conclude that as African American teacher representation increases, one will likely see small, however significant, increases in the African American exam pass rate (0.12).

This table provides further evidence in regards to the effects of African American teacher representation on the percentage of African American students in special education. Table 3 depicts a statistically significant relationship between these two variables. Like the previous findings, decreases in the percentage of African American students assigned to special education classes can be tied to this increased presence of African American teachers.

Discussion

We began this research with three basic assumptions:

1. African American teachers want to maximize their students' individual potential, and make them more receptive to instruction and academically productive;

2. The quality of African American representation matters, and is largely dependent upon the officials' ability to secure administrative and instructional positions for African Americans; and

3. The type of electoral structure determines the percentage of quality African American school board members elected to office.

This is the notion that scholars (Meier et al., 1989) refer to as representative bureaucracy. It addresses the fact that if more school board members, educational administrators, and teachers reflect the representation of the student body—namely, African Americans for this study—this leads to increased levels of student performance for this population. Also, this representative bureaucracy allows for increased opportunities for cultural synchronization and culturally relevant pedagogy at the classroom level. However, we suggest in this paper that the representation of African Americans has to increase at higher levels (i.e., school administrators and classroom teachers) if the full potential of African American students is to be realized.

To support this notion of the impact of representative bureaucracy, our findings highlighted three important points:
1. Ward electoral systems, when combined with school board representation, positively influences African American students' passing scores on state mandated standardized exams, African American SAT average, and the percentage of African American students in gifted classes;
2. The percentage of African American administrators positively influences the percentage of African American students who pass their state mandated standardized exams; and
3. The higher the percentage of African American teachers the lower the percentage of African American students in special education.

Based on the significance of these findings for increasing the achievement levels, the following recommendations should be considered by the constituents listed below.

Recommendations for School Board Members

Based on the findings of this study, the following recommendations are warranted for school board members:

- Allocate a permanent line item in the annual budget for strategic diversity recruitment initiatives at the administrative levels.
- These findings should be utilized to recruit new African American administrators from outside of the district, and develop and mentor new African American administrators from outside of the school districts, and develop and/or mentor new African American administrators from within the school district.
- Provide funding for innovative design of teacher recruitment initiatives specific for the demographics of the respective school districts, to attract more African American teachers.
- These innovative recruitment strategies would include loan forgiveness on student loans in exchange for a certain number of years of teaching in the respective school districts, closing costs on homes purchased in a certain mileage radius of the school, and merit pay based on increases in student achievement.

Recommendations for School Administrators

The findings in this study form the foundation of the following recommendations for school administrators:

- Collaborate with the Human Resources Department to visit job fairs at Historically Black Colleges and Universities (HBCUs) and other community agencies that produce a high number of prospective teaching candidates.
- Provide tailored professional development opportunities for teachers to effectively learn how to implement culturally relevant pedagogy into their classrooms in a way that is most practical for students.
- Design a school-wide initiative that is aimed specifically at significantly reducing the number of African American students that are recommended for special education.
- All classroom teachers should receive training on classroom management, which can greatly reduce the number of African American students recommended for special education.
- Design classroom procedures that must occur before teachers can recommend a student for special education.

Recommendations for Teachers

Based on the findings of this study, the following recommendations are warranted:
- Utilize culturally relevant pedagogy in presenting all lessons to students. This provides a cultural context for students to see their lives inside of the academic curriculum.
- Incorporate successful standardized test taking strategies into all classroom activities.
- This will allow all students, particularly African American students, to understand these valuable strategies, so that they can perform at a high level on the standardized tests.
- Design a process for recommending more African American students for gifted education.
- As teachers provide more engaging, culturally based lessons, this can assist in more African American students demonstrating those unique characteristics that could potentially qualify them to be tested for gifted education.

Conclusion

This study sought to develop a more interrelated causal story about the effects of a representative bureaucracy—inclusive of African American elected officials, administrators, and teachers—on student performance. Using data from several hundred Texas school districts, the results reveal that the politics of education—the election and appointment of key African American education officials—is indirectly linked to both performance on high-stakes testing and special education referrals. From these findings, recommendations were made to school board members, administrators, and teachers with regard to using their position to create more innovative strategies for improving academic performance; and hence, generate educational benefits for African American students.

Notes

1. *Brown v. Board of Education of Topeka* 347 U.S. 483 (1954).
2. *Plessy v. Ferguson* 163 U.S. 537 (1896) upheld that a state could provide separate but equal facilities for Blacks.
3. A term coined initially by Donald Kingsley (1944). See also Selden (1997), and the works of David Levitan, Norton Long, Paul Van Riper, Hanna Pitkin, Samuel Krislov, and Fredrick Mosher for a foundational review of the representative bureaucracy literature.
4. To the knowledge of the authors, no published study has been conducted that addresses this phenomenon.
5. This particular high-stakes test, at the time of the investigation, was referred to as the TAAS (the Texas Assessment of Academic Skills) test. Today, however, it is most often known as the STAAR (the State of Texas Assessment of Academic Readiness) test.
6. According to the Texas Education Agency, the term, *advanced classes*, refers to honors and pre-AP courses in the subject areas of English language arts, mathematics, science, social studies, economics, and languages other than English.
7. The other dependent variables' meanings, and their incorporation in this study, for the most part, can be easily interpreted.

References

Alexander, L., & Miller, J. W. (1989). The recruitment, incentive and retention programs for minority preservice teachers. In A. M. Garibaldi (Ed.), *Teacher recruitment and retention with a special focus on minority teachers* (pp. 45–51). Washington, DC: National Education Association.

Buxton, M. R. (2000). The African-American teacher: The missing link. *The Black Collegian, 30*(2), 116–120.

Clewell, B. C., & Villegas, A. M. (1998). Introduction. *Education and Urban Society, 31*(1), 3–17. doi:10.1177/0013124598031001001

Dee, T. (2004a). The race connection: Are teachers more effective with students who share their ethnicity? *Education Next, 4*(2), 52–59.

Dee, T. (2004b). Teachers, race, and student achievement in a randomized experiment. *Review of Economics and Statistics, 86*(1), 195–210.

Ehrenberg, R. G., & Brewer, D. J. (1995). Did teachers' verbal ability and race matter in the 1960s? Coleman revisited. *Economics of Education Review, 14*(1), 1–21.

Ehrenberg, R. G., Goldhaber, D. D., & Brewer, D. J. (1995). Do teachers' race, gender, and ethnicity matter? Evidence from National Educational Longitudinal Study of 1988. *Industrial and Labor Relations Review, 48*(3), 547-561.

Engstrom, R., & McDonald, M. (1981). The election of Blacks to city councils: Clarifying the impact of electoral arrangements on the seats/population relationship. *American Political Science Review, 75*(2), 344–354.

Ferguson, R. F. (1998). Teachers' perceptions and expectations and the Black-White test score gap. In C. Jencks & M. Phillips (Eds.), *The Black-White test score gap* (pp. 273–317). Washington, DC: Brookings Institution.

Foster, M. (1990). The politics of race: Through the eyes of African-American teachers. *Journal of Education, 172*(3), 123–141.
Irvine, J. J. (1990). *Black students and school failure: Policies, practices and prescriptions.* New York: Basic Books.
King, S. H. (1993). The limited presence of African-American teachers. *Review of Educational Research, 63*(2), 115–149.
Kingsley, J. D. (1944). *Representative bureaucracy: An interpretation of the British civil service.* Yellow Springs, OH: Antioch Press.
Kram, K. E. (1983). Phases of the mentor relationship. *Academy of Management Journal, 26*(4), 608–625.
Kram, K. E. (1985). *Mentoring at work: Developmental relationships in organizational life.* Glenview, IL: Scott, Foresman.
Ladson-Billings, G. (1994). *The dreamkeepers: Successful teachers of African American children.* San Francisco, CA: Jossey-Bass.
Ladson-Billings, G. (1995). Toward a theory of culturally relevant pedagogy. *American Educational Research Journal, 32*(3), 465–491.
Ladson-Billings, G., & Henry, A. (1990). Blurring the borders: Voices of African liberatory pedagogy in the United States and Canada. *Journal of Education, 172*(2), 72–88.
Meier, K., & England, R. (1984). Black representation and educational policy: Are they related? *American Political Science Review, 78*(2), 392–403.
Meier, K., Gonzalez Juenke, E., Wrinkle, R., & Polinard, J. (2005). Structural choices and representational biases: The post-election color of representation. *American Journal of Political Science, 49*(4), 758–768.
Meier, K., & Ray, B. (2005, April). *Race, politics, and electoral bias: The quality of African American representation.* Paper presented at the meeting of the Midwest Political Science Association, Chicago, IL.
Meier, K., & Smith, K. (1994). Representative democracy and representative bureaucracy: Examining the top-down and bottom-up linkages. *Social Science Quarterly, 75*(4), 790–803.
Meier, K., & Stewart, J. (1991). *The politics of Hispanic education: Un paso pa'lante y dos pa'tras.* Albany, NY: State University of New York Press.
Meier, K., & Stewart, J. (1992). The impact of representative bureaucracies: Educational systems and public policies. *American Review of Public Administration, 22*(3), 157–171.
Meier, K., & Stewart, J. (2003). The impact of representative bureaucracies: Educational systems and public policies. In J. A. Dolan & D. H. Rosenbloom (Eds.), *Representative bureaucracy: Classic readings and continuing controversies* (pp. 125–133). Armonk, NY: M. E. Sharpe.
Meier, K., Stewart, S., & England, R. (1989). *Race, class, and education: The politics of second-generation discrimination.* Madison, WI: University of Wisconsin Press.
Meier, K., Wrinkle, R., & Polinard, J. (1999). Representative bureaucracy and distributional equity: Addressing the hard question. *Journal of Politics, 61*(4), 1025–1039.
Selden, S. (1997). *The promise of representative bureaucracy: Diversity and responsiveness in a government agency.* New York, NY: M. E. Sharpe.
Stewart, J., England, R., & Meier, K. (1989). Black representation in urban school districts: From school board to office to classroom. *Political Research Quarterly, 42*(2), 287–305.
Viadero, D. (2001). Teachers' race linked to students' scores. *Education Week, 21*(3), 8.1.

Afterword

Walter R. Allen

It was the best of times, it was the worst of times, it was the age of wisdom, it was the age of foolishness. Charles Dickens, *A Tale of Two Cities* (1859)

This important, timely volume asks how do we change the U.S. educational system, which promises equal opportunity, yet continues to practice grotesque forms of racism, racial discrimination, and racial inequality? It is easy to draw parallels with the extreme social inequality—if not widespread social upheaval— Charles Dickens's classic novel depicts about England and France during 1775. The United States is currently experiencing unprecedented levels of disparity between rich and poor. For those at the top, it is indeed the best of times, as wealth continues to flow and concentrate in their hands. However, for those at the bottom—and increasingly in the middle—it is the worst of times, as hard-fought economic gains are lost, and dreams slip away. Who knew the glorious experiment that was America, rising from the ashes of rebellion in the American Colonies and in France, would flounder on the shoals of the very demons the age of Enlightenment presumably defeated? Now, like then, the poor, destitute, and disenfranchised who have no bread are cynically told to eat cake. Black and Brown people are told since racism is dead and the playing field is now level, they have only themselves to blame for failure in a rigged game.

Educational inequality is inextricably tied to social inequality in the United States (while racial inequality is tied to both). The American Dream explicitly promises hope for a better future to all who develop their talents, work hard, and follow the rules. In particular, universal public education promised to prepare all for opportunities and employment as a means toward upward mobility. However, race, racial discrimination, and racial inequality have always been glaring contradictions in the American story of dreams, opportunities, and new beginnings. America originated as a racial democracy (e.g., rights for Whites, but not for people of color), where founding documents and philosophies accommodated human slavery; thereby crippling any sincere efforts to embrace Enlightenment ideas which celebrated human freedom, self-determination, and dignity. America's free market Capitalism has also fuelled racial disparity, as Black and Brown people were systematically exploited and denied opportunities for employment and the accumulation of wealth. Indeed, the property rights of slaveholders trumped the human rights of Blacks in the U.S. Constitution. The seeds of Black and Brown educational underdevelopment and underachievement were planted in the nation's earliest days (e.g., slaves were killed and maimed for learning to read); and these seeds have been liberally watered and replenished over the ensuing years (e.g., Jim Crow segregation in schools). The historical roots of Black and Brown racial subordination are seen today in underresourced and underachieving K–12 schools with non-White, poor student majorities.

This volume systematically lays bare the myth of postracialism in U.S. education, revealing it to be no more than a cynical admonishment for Black and Brown children and communities, who have been denied the bread of equal educational opportunities, to instead eat the cake of accountability and high-stakes testing. These are, indeed, the best of times for African Americans. The President of the United States is a brilliant Black man, his wife—a sister—is intelligent and beautiful, and their daughters embody all the promise of great futures. We have more accomplished Black and Brown people in high places than ever before; we are lawyers, doctors, corporate executives, college presidents, entertainment stars, and ranking political officials. However, they are among the fortunate few who successfully navigated the treacherous waters of environmental racism and racial discrimination, which all people of color must swim from cradle to grave in America. Sadly, for the majority of Black and Brown people, these are the worst of times; we are disproportionately represented among the nation's most vulnerable, afflicted, and deprived. On virtually every measure of well-being, viability, and quality of life, Black and Brown individuals lag behind (e.g., unemployment, homicide, wealth, drugs, prison, and health). We have been demoralized and downtrodden by a society that communicates, in ways writ large and small, that we really do not matter.

This volume courageously rejects the new orthodoxy which declares race no longer matters in the United States. For as Supreme Court Justice, Harry Blackmun, sagely counseled in *Regents of the University of California v. Bakke* (438 U.S. 265, 1978), "In order to get beyond racism, we must first take account of race. There is no other way." Those who argue a postracial America follow time-honored traditions in the United States of denying the reality of and responsibility for systemic racism (e.g., justifications for slavery argued the innate, biological inferiority of Blacks as cause, rather than rapacious Capitalism). Postracialism endeavors to assign discussion of race to the dustbin of history, leaving no space to debate the continuing significance and pernicious effects of race. We are told, in no uncertain terms, that whether Black and Brown people rise or fall in schools—or in society—is solely of their own making. This volume challenges such views by systematically and empirically detailing how environmental racism and racial discrimination set massive, persistent stumbling blocks before Black and Brown people, who seek better educational opportunities in pursuit of their American Dreams. The contributing authors show how academic learning and achievement are racialized, with devastating effects for Black and Brown youth. The authors powerfully demonstrate that it is not the people, but the places; failure factories produce low academic achievement, while schools rich with opportunities to learn produce academic success. The authors renew our hope by detailing the fundamental changes necessary in educational practice, policy, and funding to deliver educational equity for America's Black, Brown, poor, and disenfranchised youth. This country must face squarely our history (and present) of racial inequality, and live up to our founding ideals, so the American Dream becomes real for all.

> America never was America to me, And yet I swear this oath—America will be!
> Langston Hughes, "Let America Be America Again" (1938)

List of Contributors

Walter R. Allen is Allan Murray Cartter Professor of Higher Education in the Graduate School of Education and Information Studies, Distinguished Professor of Education and Sociology, and Faculty Associate for the Ralph Bunche Center for African American Studies at the University of California, Los Angeles. He was on faculty at the University of Michigan, the University of North Carolina, Howard University, Duke University, University of Zimbabwe and St. Petersburg State University (Russia). His teaching and over 100 scholarly publications focus on race/ethnicity, educational equity, higher education, social inequality and family. Dr. Allen is also a frequent consultant to industry, government and the courts on issues related to race, education and equity.

Dorinda J. Carter Andrews is an associate professor of teacher education at Michigan State University. She is also a core faculty member of the African American and African Studies Program. Her research is broadly focused on race and educational equity. She studies Black student achievement in suburban and urban schools, urban teacher preparation, and critical race praxis with K-12 educators. She is a former industrial engineer, high school math teacher, and kindergarten teacher and has teaching experience in suburban, urban, charter, and independent schools in metropolitan Atlanta, Nashville, and Boston. As an educational consultant, she partners with urban and suburban school districts with varying student demographics to address student achievement inequities and build culturally inclusive environments. Carter Andrews is also an editor of and contributing author to the book *Legacies of Brown: Multiracial Equity in American Education*.

Tara M. Brown is an assistant professor of education at the University of Maryland, College Park. She holds a doctorate degree in education from Harvard University and is the recipient of a Spencer Research Fellowship and a Jacobs Foundation Dissertation Fellowship. Tara is a former alternative education, classroom teacher. Tara's research focuses on urban and secondary education, specifically disciplinary exclusion and dropout, using qualitative, mixed methods, and participatory and action research methodologies. Her most recent community-based participatory study focuses on the social, educational, and economic causes and implications of school dropout among young adults living in post-industrial cities in the Northeast.

Bettie Ray Butler is an assistant professor of Urban Education in the Department of Middle, Secondary, and K-12 Education (MDSK) at the University of North Carolina at Charlotte. Her research interest focuses on issues of equity, representation, and achievement among K-12 students in urban settings.

Erin L. Castro is a visiting faculty member in the department of Educational Leadership and Policy at the University of Utah. Her research focuses on issues of equity in education, specifically around college and career readiness policy, community colleges, and qualitative methodologies. She examines the experiences of chronically underserved students in their transition from secondary to postsecondary education as well as the social science employed to understand their experiences and improve policy.

Floyd Cobb is a curriculum director for a public school district and an adjunct professor with the Morgridge College of Education at the University of Denver. His research interest focuses on the intersection of organizational culture as it relates to racial equity and access in the P-20 continuum.

Bridgette Coble is the Director of Career Services at Metropolitan State University of Denver. While her career spans the realm of private industry and higher education, it has always involved elements of diversity, career advising, organizational development and education/training. Her research interests include strategies for achieving inclusive excellence in higher education, mentoring programs for students of color and African American college student experiences. Critical Race Theory and racial identity theories have become key frameworks that guide her work.

Kristin Deal is currently a doctoral student in higher education at the Morgridge College of Education, University of Denver. Her research interests include critical race studies in education, graduate student socialization, critical Whiteness studies, social justice education, and student affairs curriculum development.

John Diamond is an associate professor of education at Harvard University. He is a sociologist of education who studies the relationship between social inequality and educational opportunity. More specifically, he examines how educational leadership, policies, and practices shape students' educational opportunities and outcomes. His current research includes a case study of school leadership and organizational change in a small urban high school and a study of race and educational opportunity in multiracial suburbs. He is currently writing a new book, *Despite the Best Intentions: How Racial Inequality Persists in Good Schools* (with Amanda Lewis). Diamond holds a B.A. in Sociology and Political Science from the University of Michigan and a Ph.D. in Sociology from Northwestern University.

Judson Laughter earned his PhD from Peabody College of Vanderbilt University in Language, Literacy, and Culture. He is now an assistant professor of English Education at the University of Tennessee, Knoxville. His research interests include multicultural teacher education, critical race theory, and action research. He enjoys crossword puzzles, cycling, and traveling.

María C. Ledesma is an assistant professor in Educational Leadership & Policy at the University of Utah's College of Education. Her research interests include critical policy analysis, including the analysis of race-conscious affirmative action policy at public selective institutions. Dr. Ledesma earned her doctorate from UCLA's Graduate School of Education & Information Studies, where she was also Student Regent for the University of California's Board of Regents, the first Latina to hold this post.

Chance W. Lewis is the Carol Grotnes Belk Distinguished Professor and Endowed Chair of Urban Education in the College of Education at the University of North Carolina at Charlotte. Additionally, he is the Director of *The Urban Education Collaborative* which is publishing a new generation of research of works in urban schools. Dr. Lewis' primary research interests are focused on the improvement of African American male academic success in K-12 schools and the recruitment/retention of African American male teachers.

Pedro Noguera is the Peter L. Agnew Professor of Education at New York University. He holds tenured faculty appointments in the departments of Teaching and Learning and Humanities and Social Sciences at the Steinhardt

School of Culture, Education and Development at NYU. He is also the Executive Director of the Metropolitan Center for Urban Education and the co-Director of the Institute for the Study of Globalization and Education in Metropolitan Settings (IGEMS). Dr. Noguera is the author of seven books and over 150 articles and monographs. His most recent books are "Creating the Opportunity to Learn" with A. Wade Boykin (ASCD, 2011) and "Invisible No More: Understanding and Responding to the Disenfranchisement of Latino Males" with A. Hurtado and E. Fergus (Routledge, 2011). Dr. Noguera appears as a regular commentator on educational issues on CNN, National Public Radio, and other national news outlets. He serves on the boards of numerous national and local organizations including the Economic Policy Institute and The Nation Magazine. In 2009 he was appointed by the Governor of New York to serve as a Trustee for the State University of New York (SUNY).

Laurence Parker is a professor in the Department of Educational Leadership & Policy at the University of Utah. His main research interests are critical race theory and educational policy and leadership issues in K-12 and higher education.

Tuesda Roberts is a doctoral student in the Curriculum, Instruction and Teacher Education program in the department of teacher education at Michigan State University, where she is also pursuing certification in Urban Education and Chicano/Latino Studies. Ms. Roberts is a former high school teacher and university lecturer whose scholarly interests involve critical studies in race and education and culture and equity in education. Her research interests are two-fold and include the socializing effects of schools in the lives of students of color and the educational praxes of teachers in urban schools. Ms. Roberts earned her B.A. in Spanish from The University of North Carolina at Asheville and a dual M.A. degree in Foreign Language Education/Teaching English to Speakers of Other Languages from New York University.

Louie F. Rodríguez is an associate professor and Co-Director of the Doctorate in Educational Leadership at California State University, San Bernardino (CSUSB). His current work focuses on issues of equity and access, specifically around the dropout crisis facing the Latino community. He is the principal investigator of the *PRAXIS Project, a* school/community-based project aimed at understanding and advocating for educational excellence by directly engaging youth, educators, and community-stakeholders in the process of empirical research to positively impact educational policy and practice at the local and regional levels. Dr. Rodriguez completed his doctorate in education from Harvard University.

María del Carmen Salazar is an assistant professor at the University of Denver Morgridge College of Education in the areas of curriculum and instruction and teacher education. Her doctorate is in bilingual and multicultural foundations of education. Her research and teaching fields include teacher education, linguistically diverse education, and college readiness for English Language Learners.

Daniel Solorzano is a Professor of Social Science and Comparative Education in the Graduate School of Education and Information Studies at the University of California, Los Angeles (UCLA). His teaching and research interests include critical race theory in education; critical race pedagogy; racial microaggressions in education; and the postsecondary access, persistence, and graduation of Students of Color in the United States. Dr. Solorzano has authored over seventy research articles and book chapters on issues of educational access and equity for underrepresented student populations in the United States. Solorzano received his B.A. in Sociology and Chicano Studies and a M.Ed. in Urban Education from Loyola University of Los Angeles and went on to obtain his M.A. and Ph.D. in the Sociology of Education from the Claremont Graduate School. In 2006, Professor Solorzano received the *UCLA Education Department Distinguished Teacher Award*. In 2007 he was awarded the *UCLA-wide Distinguished Teacher Award*. In 2010, Solorzano received the *UCLA Ronald McNair Scholars Program Mentor of the Year Award*. In 2011, Solorzano was given the American Education Research Association (AERA) *Multicultural/Multiethnic Education Special Interest Group's Carlos J. Vallejo Memorial Award for Lifetime Scholarship*. In 2012, Solorzano received the *AERA Social Justice in Education Award* and gave the *Social Justice in Education Lecture*. Also in 2012, Solorzano was awarded the Critical Race Studies in Education Association (CRSEA) *Derrick A. Bell Legacy Award*.

Frank Tuitt is the Associate Provost for Inclusive Excellence and Associate Professor of Higher Education at the Morgridge College of Education at the University of Denver. Dr. Tuitt is a scholar devoted to the examination and exploration of topics related to access and equity in higher education; teaching and learning in racially diverse college classrooms; and diversity and organizational transformation. His research critically examines issues of race, inclusive excellence, and diversity in and outside the classroom from the purview of faculty and students. Dr. Tuitt is a co-editor of and contributing author to the book *Race and Higher Education: Rethinking Pedagogy in Diverse College Classrooms*.

ROCHELLE BROCK &
RICHARD GREGGORY JOHNSON III,
Executive Editors

Black Studies and Critical Thinking is an interdisciplinary series which examines the intellectual traditions of and cultural contributions made by people of African descent throughout the world. Whether it is in literature, art, music, science, or academics, these contributions are vast and far-reaching. As we work to stretch the boundaries of knowledge and understanding of issues critical to the Black experience, this series offers a unique opportunity to study the social, economic, and political forces that have shaped the historic experience of Black America, and that continue to determine our future. Black Studies and Critical Thinking is positioned at the forefront of research on the Black experience, and is the source for dynamic, innovative, and creative exploration of the most vital issues facing African Americans. The series invites contributions from all disciplines but is specially suited for cultural studies, anthropology, history, sociology, literature, art, and music.

Subjects of interest include (but are not limited to):

- EDUCATION
- SOCIOLOGY
- HISTORY
- MEDIA/COMMUNICATION
- RELIGION/THEOLOGY
- WOMEN'S STUDIES
- POLICY STUDIES
- ADVERTISING
- AFRICAN AMERICAN STUDIES
- POLITICAL SCIENCE
- LGBT STUDIES

For additional information about this series or for the submission of manuscripts, please contact Dr. Brock (Indiana University Northwest) at brock2@iun.edu or Dr. Johnson (University of San Francisco) at rgjohnsoniii@usfca.edu.

To order other books in this series, please contact our Customer Service Department:

(800) 770-LANG (within the U.S.)
(212) 647-7706 (outside the U.S.)
(212) 647-7707 FAX

Or browse online by series at www.peterlang.com.